Musical Statics: An Attempt To Show The Bearing Of The Facts Of Acoustics On Chords, Discords, Transitions, Modulations, And Tuning, As Used By Modern Musicians...

John Curwen

MUSICAL STATICS.

MUSICAL STATICS:

AN ATTEMPT TO SHOW THE BEARING OF THE FACTS
OF ACOUSTICS ON CHORDS, DISCORDS, TRANSITIONS, MODULATIONS,
AND TUNING, AS USED BY MODERN MUSICIANS.

BY

JOHN CURWEN.

NEW EDITION,

REVISED BY

T. F. HARRIS, B.Sc.,

Author of "Handbook of Acoustics."

LONDON:
J. CURWEN & SONS, LTD., 8 & 9 WARWICK LANE, E.C.
PRICE THREE SHILLINGS AND SIXPENCE.

PREFACE.

———◆———

Natural philosophers define Statics as "the study of the forces acting upon bodies at rest," but it is only in a figurative sense that we can use these words in reference to music, for, scientifically speaking, the whole of music is motion, or vibration, not rest. But the term will answer our purpose for describing whatever relates to music *physically*, and apart from mental processes and emotional feelings. We take it to mean music "as it stands" in scales and chords rather than "as it moves" in progressions and compositions.

We could study music without the aid of science, as most do. But if science has any light to throw upon the subject why should we reject it? Dr. Stainer ("Theory of Harmony," p. xii) says he has found "after many years of thoughtful and careful study, that the real bearing of the science of acoustics on the art of composition is exceedingly slight." Perhaps Dr. Stainer expected too much from it, or it may be that he had not seen the discoveries of the great musician-philosopher of the present day, Professor Helmholtz, or perceived their bearing on the habits of practical musicians For my part, I do not set up science as the first teacher of art. Art begins tentatively and then science comes in to help. I take for granted that whatever music-habits are commonly practised by musicians and commonly accepted by men of taste are right, and that if science has not discovered the reason, undoubtedly some day it will. I agree with Dr. Stainer that "the history of music shows how plainly the art has always successfully stretched forward, while lagging lawgivers have from time to time varied their tenets as they learnt bit by bit to appreciate its new beauties." We are very glad if mathematics confirm good taste, but away with mathematics from the region of our musical studies if they do not do so. I readily accept Dr. Stainer's assertion that "that which is pleasing is right; that which is unpleasant is wrong" But this recent and able writer on music has evidently been so disappointed in his acoustical studies that he goes to the opposite extreme when he says "I feel certain that the true theory of Harmony (whenever or by whomsoever it is discovered) must be learnt from musical literature, *not* from experimental philosophy—in the concert, *not* in the lecture room." My certainty is that while musical taste will have the *most* to do in the matter, no true "Theory of Harmony" can be developed without the aid of musical science, in its early steps. The truth is that the temperament of musicians—the artistic temperament generally—is unfriendly to that patience which philosophical investigation requires, while the philosopher is often tempted to forget that "there are more things in heaven and earth than are dreamt of in his philosophy." Especially is this true in musical studies, for the philosophy of the mind has quite as much to do with the questions which arise, as physics or mathematics.

Lord Bacon says that science is nothing but the humble "interpreter of Nature." Now the Nature to be interpreted in this case, is, not imagined inversions of the scale of partial tones, or the doubling or three-folding of supposititious roots, not even the beautiful relations of number, but the actual accepted music of all nations and times. That which the human ear is known to approve, in musical performances, is the proper object of musical science. Musicians have tried and tried again various melodies, chords, progressions, &c., rejecting some and adopting others, until they have satisfied their own and the common ear. They have thus adopted certain habits and fallen into certain practices. These habits and practices science has to study. The use of science is to discover the underlying reasons which have led to the adoption of these habits and practices. When these reasons are discovered three advantages immediately arise. First, the knowledge is no longer tentative and empirical ; it is certain and well defined.   Second, erroneous preconceptions are corrected, and new tentative processes are suggested, thus opening the paths of fresh discovery.   Third, a better classification is often obtained for purposes of study and of memory.   For example, the pianoforte makers had found out by experiment that they obtained a purer tone when the hammer struck the string somewhere about one-ninth of its length from the end ; but it was a long time before science had discovered that that was the best place to knock out the harsh harmonics.   As soon, however, as this "underlying reason" was discovered, the pianoforte maker became more certain.   Guesswork and experiment were gone.   He could fix the stroke of the hammer with precision, so as to prevent the string vibrating in sevenths, ninths, elevenths, thirteenths, &c.   This clear knowledge would also suggest to him where the dampers (as well as the hammers) should or should not be placed, and help his understanding and memory in all his dealings with the instrument.   Another example is in the case of the musical scale.   This, Dr. Stainer says, is "arbitrary."   It has, he says, "but just settled into its present form, and all our congratulations on its beauty will not prevent it from undergoing change if artists should, in time, deem it advisable to remould it."   But if philosophy shows us that this accepted scale is in agreement with scientific principles of acoustics, then we gain confidence in upholding it against all the various temperaments which have been invented, and we feel a ground of certainty which helps us in all our studies.   Again, musicians have formed the habit of using certain chords, and certain positions of chords, as well as certain discords and resolutions, more than others.   If we find that science confirms the musical instinct in this matter we shall lay down the rules for pupils with the greater confidence, and perhaps be enabled to discover others.   And yet again, musicians have given great prominence to the interval of a fifth in music.   We find it in the structure of the scale, in the progression of chords, in the changes of keys, and in the quality of musical sounds.   If philosophy can show us the "underlying reason" of this, young students will not suppose that it is mere red tape which binds them in their observation of fifths ; their knowledge will be better defined, and they will more easily grasp the great relations of music.

Thus, useful as Statics may be made in the study of music, we must not forget that Æsthetics, or the laws of taste and feeling, are yet more important.   What is good when taken "as it stands" may be very unsuitable when taken in relation to the things around it ; and what is somewhat bad in Musical Statics may, by some over-ruling law of Musical Æsthetics, be felt as both suitable and good. This distinction between Musical Statics and Musical Æsthetics should be clearly borne in mind.   Musical Statics teach those truths in music which arise from the great laws of nature, which are unchangeable and indubitable.   Æsthetics teach principles which are founded on our own susceptibilities, and are more or less subject to variation.   On the one hand Statics must not pretend to authority which it does not possess, and try to impose hard and impracticable rules on art ; and on the other hand Æsthetics must not give to the laws of taste and theory the authority which can belong only to unchangeable Statics.

The discoveries of Professor Helmholtz are but recent, and those few musicians who are also philosophers have not had time to apply his principles to all the acknowledged habits of ancient and modern music.   My own contributions to this study will be but meagre and imperfect.   I hope that they will prove suggestive, and that other more successful cultivators will soon strike their plough into this field of interesting study.

JOHN CURWEN

PLAISTOW, LONDON, E.
14th November, 1874.

PREFACE TO THE NEW EDITION.

In revising this work, and bringing it up to date, I have endeavoured to make only such alterations as the progress of acoustical science absolutely required.   Thus, no further experimental details, proofs, descriptions, or figures have been introduced than were in the original edition. Students who require such will find them in my "Handbook of Acoustics."

October, 1897.

T. F. HARRIS.

Musical Statics.

CONTENTS.

CHAPTER V.

STATICS AND ÆSTHETICS: THE BORDER LAND.

Musical Statics.

CHAPTER VI.

TRUE INTONATION VERSUS TEMPERAMENT.

MUSICAL STATICS.

CHAPTER I.

SOUND-IMPULSES AND WHAT THEY TEACH.

Noise, Inflection, and Tone.— Sonorous pulses of the air which strike the ear in a very irregular and unsteady manner produce a *Noise*. Sonorous pulses which are regular, but steadily increase or steadily decrease in their rate of speed, produce an *Inflection* like those of the speech-voice. A *Tone* is distinguished from Noise by its regularity, and from Inflection by its Continuity at one definite pitch.

"Sounds are either *musical* or *non-musical*. The vast majority of those ordinarily heard—the roaring of the wind, the din of traffic in a crowded thoroughfare–belong to the second class. Musical sounds are, for the most part, to be heard only from instruments constructed to produce them. The difference between the sensations caused in our ears by these two classes of sounds is extremely well marked, and its nature admits of easy analysis. Let a note be struck and held down on the harmonium, or on any instrument capable of producing a sustained tone. However attentively we may listen, we perceive no change or variation in the sound heard. A perfectly continuous and uniform sensation is experienced as long as the note is held down. If, instead of the harmonium, we employ the pianoforte, where the sound is loudest directly after the moment of percussion, and then gradually dies away, diminution of loudness is the only change which occurs.

"In the case of non-musical sounds, variations of a different kind can be easily detected. In the howling of the wind the sound rises to a considerable degree of shrillness, then falls, then rises again, and so on. On parts of the coast, where a shingly beach of considerable extent slopes down to the sea, a sound is heard in stormy weather which varies from the deep thundering roar of the great breakers, to the shrill tearing scream of the shingle dragged along by the retreating surf. Similar variations may be noticed in sounds of small intensity, such as the rustling of leaves, the chirping of insects, and the like. The difference, then, between musical and non-musical sounds seems to lie in this, that the former are constant, while the latter are continually varying. The human voice can produce sounds of both classes. In singing a sustained note it remains quite steady, neither rising nor falling. Its conversational tone, on the other hand, is perpetually varying in height even within a single syllable; directly it ceases so to vary, its non-musical character disappears, and it becomes what is commonly called 'sing-song.'

"We may, then, define a musical sound as a *steady* sound, a non-musical sound as an *unsteady* sound. It is true we may often be puzzled to say whether a particular sound is musical or not: this arises, how-ever, from no defect in our definition, but from the fact that such sounds consist of two elements, musical and non-musical, of which the latter may be the more powerful, and therefore absorb our attention, until it is specially directed to the former. For instance, a beginner on the violin often produces a sound in which the irregular scratching of the bow predominates over the regular tone of the string. In bad flute playing, an unsteady hissing sound accompanies the naturally sweet tone of the instrument, and may easily surpass it in intensity. In the tones of the more imperfect musical instruments, such as drums and cymbals, the non-musical element is very prominent, while in such sounds as the hammering of metals, or the roar of a waterfall, we may be able to recognise only a *trace* of the musical element, all but extinguished by its boisterous companion."—"*Sound and Music,*" Second Ed., by Sedley Taylor, pp. 47-49.

Origin of Tone.— A musical tone is produced by waves or pulses of the air striking the ear in regular order and rapid succession. "No matter," says Dr. Tyndall, "how the impulses are obtained; if they only follow each other quickly enough, and in perfectly equal intervals of time, a musical tone is the result. If the ticks of a clock, for example, could follow each other with sufficient rapidity they would link themselves together to form a continuous musical tone. A quick succession of taps produces a musical tone. A quick succession of puffs does the same." A stroke on a bell or tuning-fork sets it in vibration; these vibrations move the air in pulses which pass along in all directions; and a succession of these impulses reaching the ear with sufficient rapidity and regularity, produces in the mind a musical tone. The harmonium reed of a certain size and length will allow only a certain number of puffs in a second to pass through the hole it guards; these separate pulses spread through the air in every direction, and, reaching the ear, are felt as a musical tone. A violin string is set in vibration by the resined bow, or a pianoforte string is knocked into vibration by the sharp blow of its hammer; these vibrating strings set pulses of the air in motion, which, spreading on all sides, touch the ear and become a sound. A delicate puff of air blown into a flute or organ pipe sets the air within into quick and regular pulsatory movements. These pulses spread through the air, and, reaching a human ear, are heard as a tone.

Propagation of Tone.

The impulses which give rise to sound are not shot like an arrow from their origin to the ear, but they are *passed on* through the air, or other medium, until the ear is reached. Each impulse creates another, and then rebounds, that creating another again, and again rebounding. So that nothing really passes from the origin of sound to the ear except a certain system of vibrations which is set up between the two. It is not easy to form a clear conception of this mode of propagation, because our words mislead us. If we use the word *wave* and show how waves are propagated on a still pond when a stone is dropped in, we can indeed prove, by a cork floating on its surface, that, while the wave is "passed on," the water itself does not move forward; but we are liable to have the imagination misled, first because the water-waves consist of up and down vibrations of their particles, while the sound-waves consist of to and fro vibrations; and second, because the wave-action of water is formed by alternate rising and falling, whereas the sound wave is made by alternate thickening, or condensation, and thinning, or rarefaction. If we use the word "pulse" we get from it, indeed, the idea of alternate thickening and thinning, but we are liable to be misled, first because in the real pulse there is a substance which actually passes forward, whereas the impulse of sound is only a communicated form of disturbance; and second, because the pulse moves only in one direction, while the impulses which give rise to sound oscillate to and fro. Fig. 2, p. 4, shows the process. It is an attempted picture of two impulses—each impulse being reckoned to contain a thickening and thinning, a condensation and a rarefaction. As the prong of the tuning-fork moves forward to the tube, it crowds up or condenses the particles of air near it, and these, being driven forward against the still elastic air beyond, are made to rebound again; but, in doing so, they have given their motion to another impulse, which again creates a third, and so on. As the prong of the fork moves backward from the tube it thins or rarefies the air near it with corresponding results. And so the air, during a certain length, is in constant oscillation from thick to thin. In thinking of the voice, we must imagine such impulses as these to extend from the mouth upward, downward, forward, sideward, and in all directions—forming spheres of impulses.

In books of science the word "wave" is commonly used to represent the sound impulse. If we employ it for this purpose we should be careful to think of what we may call a *compressed* wave. That which in a wave is represented by height, in a sound impulse is represented by the crowding together of the particles of which it is formed. Helmholtz ("Popular Lectures on Scientific Subjects," p. 73) says:—

"To return from waves of water to waves of sound. Imagine an elastic fluid like air to replace the water, and the waves of this replaced water to be compressed by an inflexible plate laid on their surface, the fluid being prevented from escaping laterally from the pressure. Then on the waves being thus flattened out, the ridges where the fluid had been heaped up will produce much greater density than the hollows from which the fluid had been removed to form the ridges. Hence the ridges are replaced by condensed strata of air, and the hollows by rarefied strata."

But the figure of the wave is convenient, because it can represent very exactly (though symbolically) the *degree* in which the particles are crowded together at various points of the wave length. This could not be so perfectly represented by shading as by the form of the wave. Thus, the lower part of fig. 2 shows the same thickening and thinning as was shown in the last, but shows it symbolically by the wave form. I must refer to the works of Professor Helmholtz, to Mr. Sedley Taylor's "Sound and Music," and to Dr. Tyndall, "On Sound," for more minute descriptions of wave motion. The following quotations will help the imagination:—

"Applying a flame to a small collodion balloon, which contains a mixture of oxygen and hydrogen, the gases explode, and every ear in this room is conscious of a shock, which we name a sound. How was this shock transmitted from the balloon to our organs of hearing? Have the exploding gases shot the air particles against the auditory nerve as a gun shoots a ball against a target? No doubt, in the neighbourhood of the balloon, there is to some extent a propulsion of particles; but no particle of air from the vicinity of the balloon reached the ear of any person here present. The process was this:— When the flame touched the mixed gases they combined chemically, and their union was accompanied by the development of intense heat. The heated air expanded suddenly, forcing the surrounding air violently away on all sides. This motion of the air close to the balloon was rapidly imparted to that a little further off, the air first set in motion coming at the same time to rest. The air, at a little distance, passed its motion on to the air at a greater distance, and came also in its turn to rest. Thus each shell of air, if I may use the term, surrounding the balloon, took up the motion of the shell next preceding, and transmitted it to the next succeeding shell, the motion being thus propagated as a *pulse* or *wave* through the air.

"The motion of the pulse must not be confounded with the motion of the particles which at any moment constitute the pulse. For while the wave moves forward through considerable distances, each particular particle of air makes only a small excursion to and fro.

"The process may be rudely represented by the propagation of motion through a row of glass balls, such as are employed in the game of *solitaire*. Placing the balls along a groove, thus (fig. 1), each of them

Fig. 1.

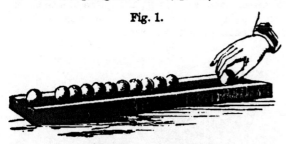

touching its neighbour, and urging one of them against the end of the row; the motion thus imparted to the first ball is delivered up to the second, the motion of the second is delivered up to the third, the motion of the third is imparted to the fourth; each ball, after having given up its motion, returning itself to rest. The last ball only of the row flies away. In a similar way is sound conveyed from layer to layer through the air. The air which fills the external cavity of the ear is finally driven against the *tympanic membrane*, which is stretched across the passage leading from the external air towards the brain. The vibrations of the membrane, which closes outwardly the 'drum' of the ear, are transmitted through a series of bones to another membrane, which closes the drum inwardly, thence through water to the ends of the auditory nerve, and afterwards along that nerve to the brain. Here the physical becomes psychical, mechanical vibrations giving birth to the consciousness of sound.

"Scientific education ought to teach us to see the invisible as well as the visible in nature; to picture with the vision of the mind those operations which entirely elude bodily vision. With regard to the point now under consideration, we must endeavour to form a definite image of a wave of sound. We must be able to see mentally the air particles when urged outwards by the explosion of our balloon crowding closely together; the particles immediately behind this condensation being separated more widely apart. We must, in short, be able to seize the conception that a sonorous wave consists of two portions, in the one of which the air is more dense, and in the other of which it is less dense than usual. A condensation and a rarefaction, then, are the two constituents of a wave of sound."—*Lectures on "Sound,"* by *Professor Tyndall, Fourth Ed., pp. 2-6.*

"Finally, I would direct your attention to an instructive spectacle, which I have never been able to view without a certain degree of physico-scientific delight, because it displays to the bodily eye, on the surface of water, what otherwise could only be recognised by the mind's eye of the mathematical thinker in a mass of air traversed in all directions by waves of sound. I allude to the composition of many different systems of waves, as they pass over one another, each undisturbedly pursuing its own path. We can watch it from the parapet of any bridge spanning a river, but it is most complete and sublime when viewed from a cliff beside the sea. It is then rare not to see innumerable systems of waves, of various length, pro-

pagated in various directions. The longest come from the deep sea and dash against the shore. Where the boiling breakers burst, shorter waves arise, and run back again towards the sea. Perhaps a bird of prey darting after a fish gives rise to a system of circular waves, which, rocking over the undulating surface, are propagated with the same regularity as on the mirror of an inland lake. And thus, from the distant horizon, where white lines of foam on the steel-blue surface betray the coming trains of wave, down to the sand beneath our feet, where the impression of their arcs remains, there is unfolded before our eyes a sublime image of immeasurable power and unceasing variety, which, as the eye at once recognises its pervading order and law, enchains and exalts without confusing the mind.

"Now, just in the same way you must conceive the air of a concert-hall or ball-room traversed in every direction, and not merely on the surface, by a variegated crowd of intersecting wave-systems. From the mouths of the male singers proceed waves of six to twelve feet in length; from the lips of the songstresses dart shorter waves, from eighteen to thirty-six inches long. The rustling of silken skirts excites little curls in the air, each instrument in the orchestra emits its peculiar waves, and all these systems expand spherically from their respective centres, dart through each other, are reflected from the walls of the room, and thus rush backwards and forwards, until they succumb to the greater force of newly generated tones. Although this spectacle is veiled from the material eye, we have another bodily organ, the ear, especially adapted to reveal it to us. This analyses the interdigitation of the waves, which in such cases would be far more confused than the intersection of the water undulations, separates the several tones which compose it, and distinguishes the voices of men and women—nay, even of individuals—the peculiar qualities of tone given out by each instrument, the rustling of the dresses, the footfalls of the walkers, and so on."—*"Popular Scientific Lectures," by Professor Helmholtz. pp.* 78, 79.

Vibration, Wave, and Tone.—

We have thus placed before us two motions—first, the vibrating particles of air; second, the wave or impulse to which they give rise. There are three elements to consider in the Vibration of a particle. First, the time it takes to perform its vibration; second, the extent of its vibration; and third, the manner in which it performs this vibration—that is, its varying velocity at different points in its journey. There are three corresponding elements of a Wave. First, its *length*; second, its *degree* of condensation and rarefaction (called, when we are using the symbol of a water wave, its *amplitude*); and third, the manner, or *form*, of its condensation or rarefaction. These corresponding elements of a Particle Vibration, and of a Sound Wave are intimately connected with and dependent on one another. First, the more rapidly the particles vibrate, the shorter the length of the corresponding wave; the more slowly they vibrate, the longer the wave. Second, the greater the extent of particle vibration, the greater the degree of condensation and rarefaction of the wave; or, in other words, the greater its amplitude. Third, according to the manner of particle vibration will be the form of condensation and rarefaction of the sound wave. There are also three elements in a musical Tone. First, pitch; second, loudness or intensity; third, quality or timbre; and these are connected with the elements of Vibration and Wave in the following manner. First, the pitch depends on the rapidity of the particle vibration and its corresponding length of wave.

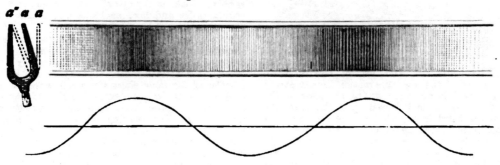

Fig. 2.   *Two Sound Impulses.*

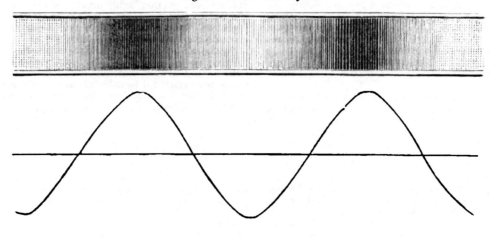

Fig. 3.   *Louder than Fig. 2.*

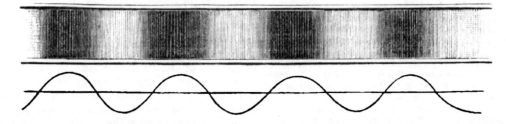

Fig. 4.   *Twice as high in pitch as Fig. 2.*

Second, the loudness of a tone arises from the wide vibration of particles and the corresponding thick condensations and thin rarefactions of the wave which they occasion. Third, the quality of a tone arises as we shall afterwards show more fully, from the manner of the vibrations and the form of wave which results. The following quotations will further enforce these points.

"During the time required by each of those sonorous waves to pass entirely over a particle of air, that particle accomplishes one complete vibration. It is at one moment pushed forward into the condensation, while at the next moment it is urged back into the rarefaction. The time required by the particle to execute a complete oscillation is, therefore, that required by the sonorous wave *to move through a distance equal to its own length.* Supposing the length of the wave to be 8 feet, and the velocity of sound in air of our present temperature to be 1,120 feet a second, the wave in question will pass over its own length of air in $\frac{1}{140}$th of a second, and this is the time required by every air-particle which the wave passes in its course to complete an oscillation. In air of a definite density and elasticity, a certain length of wave always corresponds to the same pitch. But supposing the density or elasticity not to be uniform; supposing, for example, the sonorous waves from one of our tuning-forks to pass from cold to hot air, an instant augmentation of the wave-length would occur, without any change of pitch, for we should have no change in the rapidity with which the waves would reach the ear. Conversely, with the same length of wave the pitch would be higher in hot air than in cold, for the succession of the waves would be quicker. In an atmosphere of hydrogen, waves of a certain length would produce a note nearly two octaves higher than waves of the same length in air, for, in consequence of the greater rapidity of propagation, the number of impulses received in a given time in the one case would be four times the number received in the other."—*Lectures on "Sound," by Professor Tyndall, pp.* 67, 68.

"When two notes from two distinct sources are of the same pitch, their rates of vibration are the same. If, for example, a string yield the same note as a tuning-fork, it is because they vibrate with the same rapidity; and if a fork yield the same note as the pipe of an organ or the tongue of a concertina, it is because the vibrations of the fork in the one case are executed in precisely the same time as the vibrations of the column of air, or of the tongue, in the other. The same holds good for the human voice. If a string and a voice yield the same note, it is because the vocal cords of the singer vibrate in the same time as the string vibrates. Is there any way of determining the actual number of vibrations corresponding to a musical note? Can we infer from the pitch of a string, of an organ-pipe, of a tuning-fork, or of the human voice, the number of waves which it sends forth in a second? This very beautiful problem is capable of the most complete solution."—*Lectures on "Sound," by Professor Tyndall, pp.* 60, 61.

"Having determined the rapidity of vibration, the length of the corresponding sonorous wave is found with the utmost facility. Imagine a tuning-fork vibrating 384 times per second in free air. At the end of a second from the time it commenced its vibrations, the foremost wave would have reached a distance of 1,090 feet in air of the freezing temperature. In the air of a room, which has a temperature of about 15° C., it would reach a distance of 1,120 feet in a second. In this distance, therefore, are embraced 384 sonorous waves. Dividing 1,120 by 384, we find the length of each wave to be nearly 3 feet. Determining with the syren the rates of vibration of the four tuning-forks now before you, we find them to be 256, 320, 384, and 512; these numbers corresponding to wave-lengths of 4ft. 4in., 3ft. 6in., 2ft. 11in., and 2ft. 2in. respectively. The waves generated by a man's voice in common conversation are from 8 to 12 feet, those of a woman's voice are from 2 to 4 feet in length. Hence a woman's ordinary pitch in the lower sounds of conversation is more than an octave above a man's; in the higher sounds it is two octaves. And here it is important to note that by the term vibrations are meant *complete ones;* and by the term sonorous wave are meant a condensation and its associated rarefaction. By a vibration an excursion *to and fro* of the vibrating body is to be understood. Every wave generated by such vibrations bends the tympanic membrane once in and once out. These are the definitions of a vibration and of a sonorous wave employed in England and Germany. In France, however, a vibration consists of an excursion of the vibrating body *in one direction,* whether to or fro. The French vibrations, therefore, are only the halves of ours, and we therefore call them semi-vibrations."— *Lectures on "Sound," by Professor Tyndall, pp.* 66, 67.

"The loudness of a musical sound depends entirely, as we shall easily see, on the extent of vibratory movement performed by individual particles composing the conveying medium. A sound-producing instrument can be readily observed to be in a state of rapid tremor. The vibrations of a tuning-fork are recognisable to the eye in the fuzzy, half-transparent rim which surrounds its prongs after it has been struck; and by the touch, if we place a finger gently against one of the prongs. The harder we hit the fork the louder is its sound, and the larger, estimated by both the above modes of observation, are its vibrations. The experiment may be tried equally well on any pianoforte whose construction allows the wires to be uncovered. It is natural to infer that a vibration on the part of a sound-producing instrument communicates to the particles of the air in contact with it a corresponding movement. Thus a sound of given loudness is conveyed by vibrations of given extent, and, if the sound increases or diminishes in intensity, the extent of the vibrations which carry it must increase or diminish correspondingly.

"We conclude, then, that the loudness of a musical sound depends solely on the extent of excursion of the particles which constitute the conveying medium *in the neighbourhood of our ears.* This limitation is clearly essential, since a sound grows more and more feeble, the greater our distance from the point where it is produced. This diminution of intensity as the distance from the origin of sound increases is a direct consequence of the connection between loudness and extent of vibration. We have seen that the further an air particle is from the point where a sound is produced, the smaller will be the extent of the vibration into which it is thrown by the sonorous wave. Hence, as the sound advances, it will necessarily become feebler, provided always that the waves are permitted to spread out in all directions. If they are confined, say, in a tube, the intensity of the sound will, for considerable distances remain practically constant. We have here the theory of message-pipes, which are used in large establishments to enable a conversation to be carried on between distant parts of a building. A whisper, inaudible to a person close to the speaker, may, by their means, be perfectly well heard by a listener at the other end of the tube."—*"Sound and Music," by Sedley Taylor, M.A., pp.* 52-54.

"The musical pitch of a tone depends entirely on the number of vibrations of the air in a second, and not at all upon the mode in which they are produced.

It is quite indifferent whether they are generated by the vibrating strings of a piano or violin, the vocal cords of the human larynx, the metal tongues of the harmonium, the reeds of the clarionet, oboe, and bassoon, the trembling lips of the trumpeter, or the air cut by a sharp edge in organ pipes and flutes. A tone of the same number of vibrations has always the same pitch, by whichever one of these instruments it is produced. That which distinguishes the note A of a piano, for example, from the equally high A of the violin, flute, clarionet, or trumpet, is called the *quality of the tone*."—"*Popular Scientific Lectures*," by *Professor Helmholtz*, pp. 65, 66.

"The length of a wave of water, measured from crest to crest, is extremely different. A falling drop, or a breath of air, gently curls the surface of the water. The waves in the wake of a steamboat toss the swimmer or skiff severely. But the waves of a stormy ocean can find room in their hollows for the keel of a ship of the line, and their ridges can scarcely be overlooked from the mast-head. The waves of sound present similar differences. The little curls of water with short lengths of wave correspond to high tones, the giant ocean billows to deep tones. Thus the contrabass C has a wave thirty-five feet long, its higher octave a wave of half the length, while the highest tones of a piano have waves of only three inches in length.

"You perceive that the pitch of the tone corresponds to the length of the wave. To this we should add that the height of the ridges, or, transferred to air, the degree of alternate condensation and rarefaction, corresponds to the loudness and intensity of the tone. But waves of the same height may have different forms. The crest of the ridge, for example, may be rounded off or pointed. Corresponding varieties also occur in waves of sound of the same pitch and loudness. The so-called *timbre* or quality of tone is what corresponds to the *form* of the waves of water. The conception of form is transferred from waves of water to waves of sound. Supposing waves of water of *different* forms to be pressed flat as before, the surface, having been levelled, will of course display no differences of form, but, in the interior of the mass of water, we shall have different distributions of pressure, and hence of density, which exactly correspond to the differences of form in the still uncompressed surface. In this sense, then, we can continue to speak of the form of the waves of sound, and can represent it geometrically. We make the curve rise where the pressure, and hence density, increases, and fall where it diminishes—just as if we had a compressed fluid beneath the curve, which would expand to the height of the curve in order to regain its natural density."—"*Popular Scientific Lectures*," by *Professor Helmholtz*, pp. 73, 74.

The Scale of Absolute Pitch.—

When *sixteen* impulses reach the ear in a second, they form the slowest succession of sonorous impressions that can be recognised as a continuous musical tone. When 5,000 such impulses reach the ear in a second, they produce about the highest musical tone the common human ear can appreciate.

Any number of vibrations and fractions of a vibration per second may create a new and distinct musical tone. The number of musical tones thus made possible is beyond calculation. No ear could distinguish so many. No memory could retain them. No notation could name them. Musicians and philosophers are obliged to select. They take a certain tone which lies midway between the two extremes of high and low, as the standard of pitch. It is called "Middle C." Unfortunately musicians have not exactly agreed upon what this "Middle C" should represent. According to the French standard (diapason normal), it is produced by 261 complete vibrations per second. The Tonic Sol-fa standard is slightly lower than this— about 258 or 259. At concert pitch, it rises as high as 270. See Helmholtz's "Sensations of Tone," 2nd ed., p. 493, *et seq.*

Having selected this one tone out of the boundless possibilities of musical sound, further selection is greatly aided by the phenomenon of the "Octave." The very first noticeable thing in reference to pitch is the fact that when the number of vibrations producing one tone is double that producing another, the two tones will blend so perfectly and are so much like each other, that they are, for convenience, called by the same name, and are said to be "octaves" one of the other.

How the tones which lie between one octave and another are yet further selected will be shown presently. Meantime, let us survey this great region of sounds, which we have now the power of naming. The C-four (C_4), of 16 complete vibrations a second, which stands a fourth octave lower than "Middle C," is producible by an open organ-pipe 32 feet in length, and gives a sound so slow in its musical impulses that one can "hear the silences" between them. Its only use is to fill up and strengthen the accompanying tones of higher octaves. C-three (C_3), of 32 vibrations a second, producible by a 16-foot organ-pipe, commences the octave of sounds into which the Double-bass and Pianoforte among stringed instruments, and the Ophecleide, Bombardon, and Harmonium among wind instruments, introduce their lowest tones. Before the next octave the Bassoon and the Bass Trombone commence their sounds. C-two (C_2) (on the second ledger line below the bass staff in the staff notation) is produced by 64 vibrations, and an eight-foot organ-pipe. At this point the Violoncello, the Horns, and the Harp enter. Before the completion of the octave, the Bass Voices come in. C-one (C_1), in the second space of the bass staff, gives us 128 vibrations in a second, and is produced by a four-foot organ-pipe. In this octave commence the Viola, the Violin, the Tenor Trombone, the Cornet, the Trumpet, the Tenor and Contralto Voices; and before the

THE REGION OF MUSICAL SOUNDS.

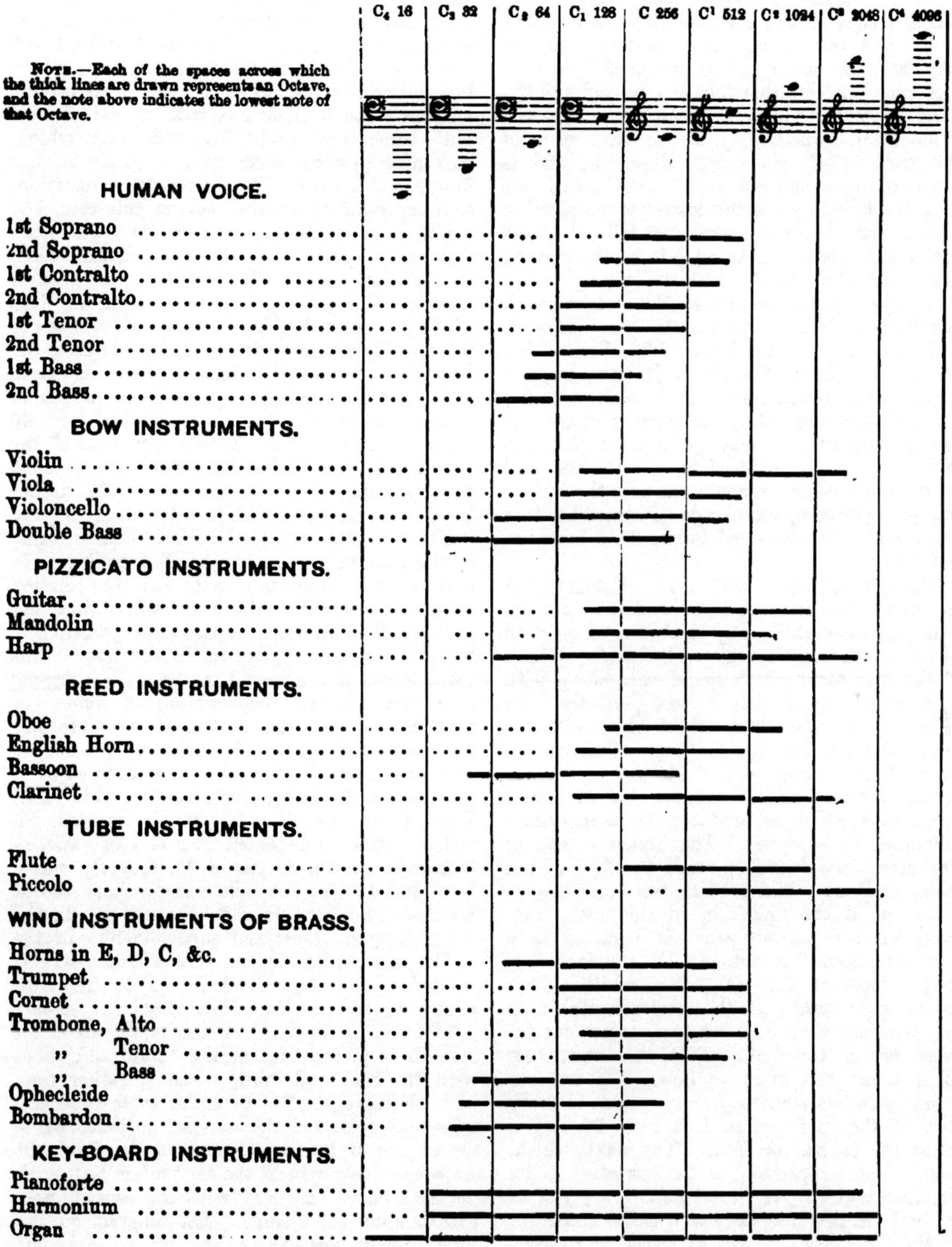

	C_4 16	C_3 32	C_2 64	C_1 128	C 256	C^1 512	C^2 1024	C^3 2048	C^4 4096

NOTE.—Each of the spaces across which the thick lines are drawn represents an Octave, and the note above indicates the lowest note of that Octave.

HUMAN VOICE.

1st Soprano

2nd Soprano

1st Contralto

2nd Contralto

1st Tenor

2nd Tenor

1st Bass

2nd Bass

BOW INSTRUMENTS.

Violin

Viola

Violoncello

Double Bass

PIZZICATO INSTRUMENTS.

Guitar

Mandolin

Harp

REED INSTRUMENTS.

Oboe

English Horn

Bassoon

Clarinet

TUBE INSTRUMENTS.

Flute

Piccolo

WIND INSTRUMENTS OF BRASS.

Horns in E, D, C, &c.

Trumpet

Cornet

Trombone, Alto

   ,,   Tenor

   ,,   Bass

Ophecleide

Bombardon

KEY-BOARD INSTRUMENTS.

Pianoforte

Harmonium

Organ

octave is finished, the Alto Trombone, the Clarinet, the English Horn, the Mandolin, the Guitar, and the Oboe have come in. The unmarked C, commonly called the "middle C," which stands in the staff notation between the treble and bass clefs, gives us 256 complete impulses in a second, and is produced by a two-foot pipe. About this tone the Second and the First Soprano in human voices, as well as the Flute enter. One-C (C^1), in the third space of the treble staff, gives 512 vibrations, and is produced by a one-foot pipe. Just above this tone the Piccolo gives the lowest of its piercing sounds, and the other instruments fall out of the ranks until there is nothing left in the musical array but the Piccolo with its piping tones, occupying the greater part of the octaves which commence with C^2 (1,024 vibrations in a second), and C^3 (2,048 vibrations). The Violin, the Piccolo, the Harp, the Piano, Harmonium, and Organ alone remain with their highest tones, in this last octave. Only the chirping of crickets can go higher. It may be noticed that the middle C can be produced by every voice, and all the principal instruments, and that the further one goes either upward or downward from that tone, the fewer voices and instruments there are to follow.

Proportions of the Common Scale.

—The common scale consists of a given tone (any tone which may be chosen or given to us out of the whole region of absolute pitch), of the *four* tones which sound best along with it, or which blend with it most perfectly, and of *two* other tones which do not blend with the principal tone, but are the best which can be found for blending well with the four tones already chosen. Let us suppose that we have a given tone which is produced by seventy-two vibrations in a second. The higher octave of this given tone (which we call the first of the scale, or DOH) would require *two* vibrations to every *one* of the first; or, in this case, 144. This, we have already seen, is regarded as a mere "replicate," or octave. Of the four consonant tones of the scale, that which blends the most *perfectly* (not the most sweetly) with the principal tone requires *three* vibrations for every *two* of the first; or, in this case, 108. It is called the fifth, or SOH. The next in blending quality requires *four* vibrations to every *three* of the first; or, in this case, 96. It is called the fourth, or FAH. The next which, though not so perfect, is far sweeter in its blending, requires *five* vibrations to every *four* of the first; in this case, 90. It is called the third, or ME. The last, nearly as sweet in its consonance as the third, requires *five* vibrations to

every *three* of the first; in this case, 120. It is called the sixth, or LAH. Up to this point only the simplest ratios have been used. If we had taken the lower octave of LAH (60) the order of simplicity of proportion would have remained unbroken; thus, 2 to 1—3 to 2—4 to 3—5 to 4 —6 to 5. Of the two dissonances, one, which lies close below the principal tone, or its octave, making a sharp dissonance with it, agrees well with three tones (RAY, ME, and SOH), which, reckoning upward, make to it a minor third, a fourth, and a sixth. It requires *fifteen* vibrations to every *eight* of the first—or, in this case, 135 —and is called the seventh, or TE. The other dissonance, lying close above the principal tone, is *a variable tone.* When it is required, as it most commonly is, to harmonise with the fifth (SOH) and seventh (TE) it gives *nine* vibrations to every *eight* of the first; or, in this case, 81. But when required to harmonise with the fourth (FAH) and sixth (LAH) it gives *ten* vibrations to every *nine* of the first; or, in this case 80 vibrations in a second. This second tone of the scale is commonly called RAY, but when we wish to distinguish its two forms we call the higher RAY, and the lower RAH. To make a pure "fifth" with LAH, the vibrational relations must be the same as the *model fifth*, DOH to SOH. To make a pure minor third with FAH, the relation must be the same as the *model minor third*, ME to SOH. The ear requires the same principle to be applied in tuning RAY to TE and SOH. This variableness of the second in the scale is argued from the absolute impossibility of voices or stringed instruments, controlled by naturally good ears, *not* seeking for true tune, taken in connection with the fact that true tune requires the variation. Experiments confirm this view. They show that RAH is chiefly wanted, in melody, after an accented FAH or LAH; and, in harmony, on the chords of R, properly called RAH, and L. In the minor mode these chords are more important than in the major. In the minor they are tonic and subdominant; in the major only supertonic and submediant. RAY is wanted in the major dominant (S) to tune with s and t, and in the minor dominant *seventh* (^{7}*M*) to tune with t. In the major dominant seventh it is the fifth of the chord, and tunes with the root and third, s and t, rather than with the seventh, f. In major tonic cadences, where the second of the scale is continued while the chords of the supertonic and the dominant are successively struck, the ear prefers RAH with the first chord and RAY with the second, notwithstanding the change. The diagram on the opposite page will enable the pupil to make his own calculations.

THE COMMON SCALE.

The number 72 here given to represent the vibrations of Doh is simply a convenient assumed number from which to reckon the other tones.

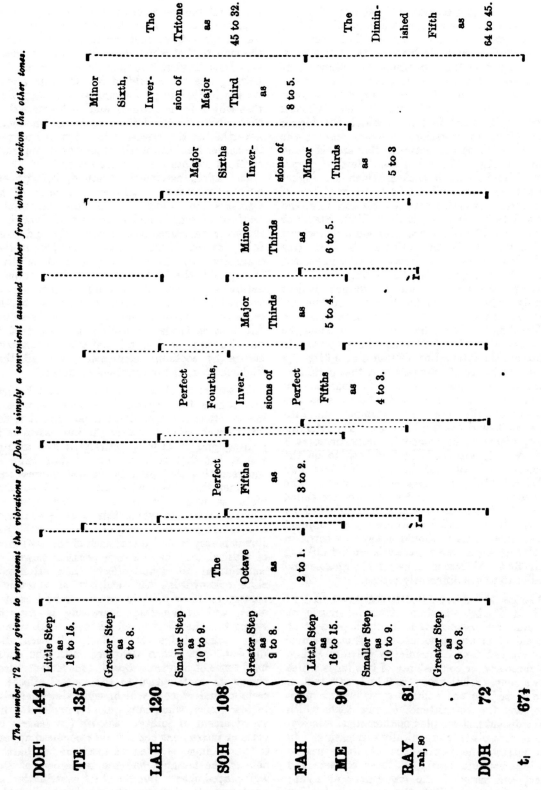

DOH¹	144	
		Little Step as 16 to 15.
TE	135	
		Greater Step as 9 to 8.
LAH	120	
		Smaller Step as 10 to 9.
SOH	108	
		Greater Step as 9 to 8.
FAH	96	
		Little Step as 16 to 15.
ME	90	
		Smaller Step as 10 to 9.
RAY rah, 80	81	
		Greater Step as 9 to 8.
DOH	72	
t₁	67½	

The Octave as 2 to 1.

Perfect Fifths as 3 to 2.

Perfect Fourths, Inversions of Perfect Fifths as 4 to 3.

Major Thirds as 5 to 4.

Minor Thirds as 6 to 5.

Major Sixths Inversions of Minor Thirds as 5 to 3.

Minor Sixth, Inversion of Major Third as 8 to 5.

The Tritone as 45 to 32.

The Diminished Fifth as 64 to 45.

The Intervals of Adjacent Tones in this common scale can be easily calculated from the diagram. It will be seen that there are three sorts of intervals between the tones sung. The largest is that in which the higher tone gives *nine* vibrations to every *eight* of the lower. This occurs between Doh and Ray, Fah and Soh, and Lah and Te. We call it the "Greater Step." The next is that in which the higher tone gives *ten* vibrations to every *nine* of the lower. This occurs between Ray and Me, and Soh and Lah. We call it the "Smaller Step." The third interval is that in which the higher tone gives *sixteen* vibrations to every *fifteen* of the lower. It occurs between Me and Fah, and Te and Doh. We call it the "Little Step," or semitone. The difference between a "greater" and a "smaller"—the difference between Ray and Rah—is called a *komma*, a very important interval in music. In calculating from this diagram, the pupil should be warned against simply adding and subtracting to find the intervals. Thus, he must not suppose that by subtracting 72 vibrations from 108 vibrations, he will get a number (36) which he may take to represent the interval or difference of a fifth; for while the figure 36 may represent that particular fifth, it represents no other. As long as you count vibrations, each particular fifth has its own number of difference. For example, the fifth between 96 and 144 would be 48. The intervals must, therefore, be named by proportions, as 3 to 2, &c. It will easily be seen how, to aid the memory, the scale has been divided into two "Tetrachords," or strings of four tones. The sequences d r m f followed by s l t d¹ are called disjunct tetrachords, and s₁ l₁ t₁ d followed by d r m f (being united in d) are called conjunct tetrachords. But it should always be borne in mind that these two tetrachords are not alike in their first and second steps; their greater and smaller steps are differently placed.

Organic Impressions and Mental Effects.—Certain effects of music on the mind are *organic*—that is, not dependent on the aid of mental associations. Thus, a single pure musical tone is organically pleasure-giving, the succession or co-existence of two tones which bear a simple relationship (as 2 to 1, or 3 to 2, or 4 to 3, &c.), to one another gives organic pleasure, and the co-existence of two tones which bear a distant and complex mathematical relationship to each other is organically displeasing. In this respect the impressions of the sense of hearing resemble nearly all those of taste and touch, and many of the impressions of sight: they are organic. But the sense of hearing excels all the senses in the readiness with which it passes over its impressions from the organic to the mental—from that which does not elevate the man to that which does. "Musical sounds," says Isaac Taylor, "so take hold of the mind as nothing else takes hold of it. On this ground we are invited to go forward step by step, from that which is mechanical and mathematical, to that which, in the loftiest sense, is emotional; nevertheless, the precise point at which we pass the border from the world of Matter to the world of Mind escapes our keenest search." * * * "The mind, percipient of sound, is, with exquisite exactness, cognisant not only of all *differences* of sound, but of the mensurable *relations* of sound; and in respect of these it is intensely sensitive, both pleasurably and painfully, towards them as *true* or *not true* mathematically; and then, beyond this, it is alive, throughout the wide circuit of its emotional nature—up from the gentlest sentiments or sympathies, to the stormiest passions—to the *suggestive meaning* of melody and of harmony. All that is tender in feeling, and all that is tumultuous in passion, all that attempers human nature by soothing excitements, and all that maddens it, is at the command of music."

If we try to place ourselves near that border-line where the organic impression becomes a mental effect, we can, at least, see that it is not left to each mind to *receive* the impression as it pleases, and to fashion entirely *its own* mental result, but that all minds obey certain laws in the reception they give to musical impressions. To trace these laws with any attempt at completeness would be to forsake the study of musical statics, to which this tract is confined, and to enter on the region of musical æsthetics. But it is easy to notice that each of the *differentia* of musical tone has its own peculiar power of contributing to mental effect; thus, all minds alike acknowledge the tendency of a musical passage rising *in pitch* to produce mental excitement, and of a passage increasing *in force* to strengthen the effect of all its tones. All minds alike acknowledge the effect of particular *rhythms*, even when delivered with the dull, hard tones of a drum. *Speed* of movement, also, brings its contribution to the mental effect; a certain kind of tune which, sung slowly, melts to tears, may, when sung quickly, excite to the abandonment of jollity. *Quality* (or *timbre*) of voice or instrument has also its recognised appeal to the feelings, as when we speak of the harshness of the trumpet and the tenderness of the well-played oboe. But the chief contribution to mental effect comes from the relationships of the scale, whether its tones succeed one another in melody or co-exist in harmony. It is difficult to separate this from the other elements of organic, passing over into mental impressions. Wherever there is scale relation, there also are speed, force, rhythm, quality. But Callcott was depending on scale-relation alone, when he used the *sixth* of the scale so effectively to express "the tributary *tear;*" Handel trusted only to scale-relation, when he set the *seventh* of the scale to express that final urgent plea with the angels, "Take, O *take* me to your care;" and Mendelssohn used, with other contrivances of transition and of rhythm, the *third* of the scale to express, as only that scale-relation can express, the living peace of "*rest* in the Lord." In classic songs, as well as in national ballads, the instances are innumerable, in which the composer relies for his effect almost exclusively on a single tone, *bearing a certain scale-relation*, put in an effective position. All minds agree in acknowledging these mental effects of tones in scale. In the "Tonic Sol-fa Method," advantage is taken of the easy recognition of the mental effects of "the seven tones" in slow music, to assist the learner in his first efforts to produce these tones, and with great success. *Harmony* complicates or heightens these personal characters of the scale tones. Every tone produces its proper mental effect best in its own chord; that is, when used as a root. *The modes* of using this great common scale in harmony—the major mode leading the mind to its own set of beautifully varied and satisfactory closes or cadences; and the modern minor mode, leading the mind to a weird and mystic imitation of them—the "mode" brings also its great contribution to mental effect. But this subject, as well as those of transition, of chromatic effect, of discords, of imitations, of musical forms, all of which contribute to the mighty union of organic and mental forces which music wields, belongs so plainly to the æsthetics rather than to the statics of our art, that we cannot further pursue it here. We must also guard ourselves against expecting too much from the expressive power of music. It is always general, not specific. There cannot *literally* be any "Songs without Words." It was a beautiful poetical idea of Mendelssohn's to give such a name to certain melodies for the pianoforte. They certainly express sentiments in a *general* and indefinite way. Only one *class* of feelings can be uttered by each song, but within that class each heart must give its own interpretation to Mendelssohn's "Songs without Words."

Just Intonation.—As far as the fifth chapter of this tract I deal only with Just Intonation or true tune, because this is what the world is coming to, even in its musical instruments, and what, for its finest musical effects, the world has already attained. It is readily acknowledged that nothing exceeds in harmonic beauty a trio or quartet by well-trained singers or by players on stringed instruments; and this effect is produced by each one tuning with the others as perfectly as possible. At the sixth chapter are shown some of the defects of what is called "Temperament."

CHAPTER II.

Partials, and What they Teach.

There are no physical facts which throw more light on the Art of Music, than those which relate to the Compound Nature of nearly all musical tones.

On careful examination of any ordinary musical sound, it will be found to be made up of two, three, four, or more tones of different pitch. If, for example, any key on the lower half of the keyboard of a pianoforte be smartly struck and held down, not only will the tone corresponding to that note be heard, but also a tone an octave above, another a fifth above that, and others still higher. These separate constituent parts of the whole mass of tone we may call, after Helmholtz, Partials or Partial Tones, and the whole mass of tone, a Compound Tone; or following Tyndall, we may style the lowest, the Primary or Fundamental, and all those above, Overtones.

There is a tendency both in vibrating strings and in vibrating columns of air, to divide and subdivide themselves into a number of vibrating parts, at the same time that they are vibrating as wholes. They thus produce these spontaneous Partials or Overtones. These latter are often termed Harmonics, but it is better to reserve this latter term for the tones intentionally, or, as it were, artificially produced in a vibrating string or column of air. Thus, if we blow gently into an open organ-pipe we get a fundamental and several overtones; if we then blow more forcibly, the fundamental disappears, the pitch seems to rise an octave, and we get what is commonly, and correctly, termed the first Harmonic; blow more strongly still, and this disappears, the pitch rises a fifth, and we obtain the second Harmonic.

The *first* constituent part of a compound tone, that is, the *first* partial, is the primary or fundamental itself; it is produced by the string or air column vibrating as a whole: let us call it d_1. The second partial results from the simultaneous vibration of the string or air column in *two* parts, or the multiplication of the vibrations of a primary by *two*; this will give, in relation to the fundamental, d. The *third* partial arises from division of lengths or multiplication of vibrations by *three*, producing s; the *fourth* partial by *four*—d¹; the *fifth* by *five*—m¹; the *sixth* by *six*—s¹; and so on. The ear requires some training to observe the partials. The uneven partials (III, V, VII, &c.), are usually easier to distinguish than the even partials (II, IV, VI, VIII, &c.), because the latter are either octaves of the primary or some previous secondary, and, therefore, *blend* too perfectly to be easily distinguished. See the diagram. The third partial is generally the easiest to distinguish, and then the fifth; the seventh is usually very weak. The piano, harmonium, and concertina are best adapted for observation because their partials are strong. Professor Helmholtz suggests that the sound of the expected partial should be produced softly on the instrument, *before* sounding the primary, so that the ear may be led to the tone it has to observe. Thus, strike G_1 gently on the piano, and, after letting the damper sink, strike C_2 loudly, keeping the attention fixed on the sound of G_1, which will then be heard as the third partial of C_2. Mr. Sedley Taylor says:—

"In applying the direct analysis to the sounds of a musical instrument, it is best first to produce gently the note corresponding in pitch to the tone which it is wished to isolate, and then to develop the compound sound containing it as a constituent. If the observer has succeeded in keeping his attention unswervingly fixed on the note for which he is listening, he will hear it come out clearly from the mass of tones included in the composite sound. If the pianoforte note, [♩] be thus examined, the octave, [♩], and twelfth, [♩], can generally be recognised with considerable ease: the second octave, [♩], with a little trouble; the next three tones of the series with increasing difficulty, and those which succeed them not at all. The reader approaching this phenomenon for the first time must not be disappointed if, on trying this experiment, he fail to hear the tones he is told to expect. He should vary its conditions by changing the note struck, in such a way that his attention will not be liable to be diverted by the presence of tones more acute than that of which he is in search. Thus, a note near [♩] may be advantageously chosen to observe the first octave, [♩]; one near [♩] to observe the twelfth, [♩]; one near [♩] to observe the second octave, [♩]. He may, however, altogether fail in performing the analysis with the unassisted ear. This by no means indicates any aural defect, as he may at first be inclined to imagine. It rather shows that the life-long habit of regarding the notes of individual sound-producing instruments as single tones cannot be unlearned all at once."—"*Sound and Music,*" pp. 88, 89, 90.

Partials are best perceived by ordinary observers in watching a tone *die off*. If, after striking a low tone on the piano very forcibly, we make such a one listen, and raise our own hand as one after another of the *lower* partials dies away (so that the pitch seems to rise to the octave, the octave fifth, the double octave, the double octave third, &c.), the effect of partials may be very easily caught by him. But he must remember that we do not hear simple separate partials in any case. We hear first the full klang,

```
      I   II  III  IV   V   VI, &c.,
next      II  III  IV   V   VI, &c.,
next          III  IV   V   VI, &c.; and so on.
```

As the generation of partials springs from one primary tone without reference to any other tones, we need not be surprised to find that what may for the moment be called the *scale* of partials differs from the "common scale" of melody and harmony. The common scale, from whatever point of view it is regarded, is a set of seven tones related to *one another* as well as to their "principal tone:" the scale of partials is related only to its one primary tone. The common scale is built according to various ratios: the scale of partials on successive multiplications.

PARTIALS AND HARMONICS.

```
I  II  III  IV  V  VI  VII VIII IX  X  XI  XII XIII XIV XV XVI XVII XVIII XIX XX
```

On the diagram (p. 14), the left-hand column shows the vibrations of the common scale, commencing with a tone which is supposed to vibrate *seventy-two* times in a second, and the right-hand column shows the generation of partials from the same tone, taken as a "primary." The asterisks show the points at which these two scales differ. The VIIth partial corresponds very nearly with the "flat seventh" of the common scale, ta—the tone which, in transition, would make "the fourth" in the "first flat key." The VIIth partial, in the instance before us, gives 504 vibrations in a second, while the ta near it gives four-thirds of f (which is its d), or 512. The XIVth partial gives 1,008 vibrations, while its corresponding ta gives 1,024. The XIth, XIIIth, XVIIth, and XIXth partials also fall out of the order of tones which is required for the purposes of the common scale. It will be noticed that if the first six partials could be all sounded together with an equal degree of loudness, they would form a consonant chord; even the VIIth and VIIIth might be added without much sense of discord. But, from this point, all appearance of a chord vanishes, and if the higher partials were sounded together with the others, and in an equal degree of loudness, they would form the most horrible discord conceivable. But, happily, the partials are very far from sounding with an equal degree of loudness.

Loudness of Partials.—In the tones of different instruments, different partials predominate, and with different degrees of intensity, By means of ingenious and careful experiments. Professor Helmholtz was able to measure the vibrational "excursions" and intensities of the partials. He found that the model of all beautiful tone—the tone of a well-bowed violin—contained the first eight partials, and that the intensities of those partials decreased approximately in the following progressive ratios:—

PARTIALS..	I	II	III	IV	V	VI	VII	VIII	IX	X
INTENSITIES	1	$\frac{1}{4}$	$\frac{1}{9}$	$\frac{1}{16}$	$\frac{1}{25}$	$\frac{1}{36}$	$\frac{1}{49}$	$\frac{1}{64}$	$\frac{1}{81}$	$\frac{1}{100}$

We may, therefore, conclude that, on the average, the loudness even of the *second* partial is only 25 per cent. of that given by its primary; that the intensity of the *sixth* is about 3 per cent.; and that when we reach the *tenth* it can only be heard while the primary is dying away, for it has only one per cent. of loudness. This decrease in intensity shows the subordination of the partials, and their natural use and intention as merely constituent *parts* of tones. To make this important fact more clear, the diagram on p. 15 represents degrees of loudness by lengths of lines. The intensity of the primary partial is supposed to be a full thick line across the page: the lines above show the comparative intensities of the other partials. There is a *natural* diminution of loudness as the tones go up (for the railway whistle warns us how little we could endure *loud high tones*), but this diminution is not nearly so rapid as that of the partials. The rate of diminution varies in different voices

THE PARTIAL SERIES.

THE COMMON SCALE.		PARTIALS OF DOH$_2$.	
m^2	1440	1440	XX
		1368	XIX•
r^2	1296	1296	XVIII
		1224	XVII•
d^2	1152	1152	XVI
t^1	1080	1080	XV
ta^1	1024		
l^1	960	1008	XIV•
se^1	900	936	XIII•
s^1	864	864	XII
fe^1	810		
f^1	768	792	XI•
m^1	720	720	X
r^1	648	648	IX
d^1	576	576	VIII
ta	512		
		504	VII•
s	432	432	VI
m	360	360	V
d	288	288	IV
s$_1$	216	216	III
d$_1$	144	144	II
d$_2$	72	72	I

and instruments. Thus, to take two instruments for example, the loudness of an organ-pipe depends, the force of wind being equal, on its diameter, and the loudness of a harmonium vibrator on its width. If these be measured for the tones corresponding to the scale of partials, they will give very nearly the result shown by the thin lines for the harmonium and the dotted lines for the organ. It will be noticed that the harmonium reeds I measured (although by the best maker) were not very carefully graded as to intensity. See diagram on the following page. On the other hand, in the pianoforte, the second, third, and fourth partials are often louder than the fundamental, especially in the tones of the lower half of the scale. The relative intensities of the partials on this instrument chiefly depend upon the hardness of the hammer, and the sharpness of the blow with which it strikes the strings.

ART AND SCIENCE.—*First Idea of Cadence.* Perhaps this fact, that the ear naturally and habitually prefers to have the lower tones louder, will help to solve the problem stated by Professor Airy, in the following extract. He thus gives the primary idea of cadence—that is, rest in some central sounds—and the difficulty which arises :—

" Perhaps we may well begin by considering the effect of the ordinary ring of eight bells ; the notes of which, as usually employed for the indications of joy or triumph, are a complete octave from C^1 to C (or notes at the same proportional intervals), rung in the descending order. And upon analysing our sensations, they will appear to be of this kind. From the repeated close, time after time, upon the lower C, our attention is strongly drawn to that note. In the ring of the successive bells, we perceive without effort that, bell after bell, every sound has a good relation to that lower C. (Possibly the less perfect relations of B and D to C really sharpen our perception of the better relations of the other notes to C.) But the relation of each note to that which follows it, although perceptible as harmonious, is not very harmonious. Hence the ear is impressed with a certain degree of present harmony, and with the expectation of a much better harmony, which will be produced when there occurs the stroke of the bell which unites itself in strong concord with every one of the notes past. And, on hearing that bell, the ear is satisfied, and sinks into a state of rest. It appears to us that these phenomena are correctly described by the poet Moore (himself no mean musician), in the following lines :—

' When Memory links the tone that is gone
With the blissful tone that is still in the ear,
And Hope from a heavenly note draws on
To a note more heavenly still that is near.'
The Light of the Harem.

If the reader will change the last two lines to the following, he will completely reproduce the reasoning of the text :—

' And Hope from a harmony sweet draws on
To a harmony still more sweet that is near.'

THE SCALE OF LOUDNESS IN NATURAL TONES AND IN PARTIALS.

NOTE.—This diagram shows the loudness of simple Partials in contrast with the loudness of Principal tones, which are generally also compound. It proves that the higher Partials are not loud enough to be regarded as models for a chord of co-equal tones. Only the lower Partials can have any suggestiveness in relation to a chord.

Tone	Harm.	Organ	Partial
VIII $= C^3$	$\frac{6}{10}$	$\frac{3}{16}$	$\frac{1}{64}$
VII $= B\flat^1$	$\frac{6}{10}$	$\frac{3\frac{1}{4}}{16}$	$\frac{1}{49}$
VI $= G^1$	$\frac{6\frac{1}{4}}{10}$	$\frac{4}{16}$	$\frac{1}{36}$
V $= E^1$	$\frac{7}{10}$	$\frac{4\frac{1}{2}}{16}$	$\frac{1}{25}$
IV $= C^1$	$\frac{7}{10}$	$\frac{5\frac{1}{2}}{16}$	$\frac{1}{16}$
III $= G$	$\frac{7}{10}$	$\frac{7}{16}$	$\frac{1}{9}$
II $= C$	$\frac{9}{10}$	$\frac{9}{16}$	$\frac{1}{4}$
I $= C_1$	Harm.	Organ	Partial

This is the Cadence. After this, there is a rise of an entire octave, which is always exciting; and the descent is then repeated with the same effect.

"There is, however, a circumstance which we are unable to explain. It would seem possible that, if we rang the bells upwards, from the lowest to the highest, inasmuch as each of the notes has good concord with the highest, we should derive from that series a pleasurable sensation. This, however, does not take place; the effect is unpleasant; and so strongly that (within our knowledge) the ring of the bells in ascending series is used as the alarm-signal of fire or other danger.

'The castle-bells, with backward clang,
Sent forth th' alarum peal.'
The Lay of the Last Minstrel.

The difference of effects appears to depend on some unknown physiological cause."—*Airy* "*On Sound and Atmospheric Vibrations,*" pp. 217, 218.

The mind prefers to have its region of sounds like a pyramid, broader and broader towards the base. And, other things being equal, the mind rests better on a full sound than on a weak one. Aristotle, in one of his problems, asks, "Why is it more tuneful to go from above downwards, than from below upwards?" As one solution, he asks again, "Is it that the low tones sound more noble after the high?" This is one reason why the downward scale forms a better cadence than the upward; another is, that the two *dissonances* with the tonic (the 7th and the 2nd of the scale) are better managed in one case than the other. In descending, the first dissonance (the seventh) is of light intensity, and is quickly lost in the heavier tone (the sixth) which follows, and the full-sounding dissonance (the second) is immediately resolved on the yet fuller sound of the tonic. But, in ascending, we come immediately on the louder of the two dissonances, and it does *not* (as in descending) satisfy the ear by resolving humbly downward and on a tone louder and more important than itself; it seems unresolved. This is especially the case if the accent, in ascending, is thrown on the second and fourth of the scale; that is, first on the loud dissonance and next on the "unmeaning" consonance. In descending, the accent is commonly thrown on the weak dissonance and on the strong commanding consonance of the fifth. Professor Airy's assertion that ascent of the scale means *excitement*, and descent of the scale means *rest*, is generally felt to be true, whatever may be the cause. With this corresponds the fact that dissonances nearly always resolve *downwards*.

Qualities of Tones.

It was the great discovery of Professor Helmholtz, that the quality, or *timbre*, of tones arises from the relative intensities of their partials. He discovered that some instruments give only the first partial, or the primary. The tones thus produced he called "simple tones." They are those of a tuning-fork with an appropriate resonance tube, and of a wide stopped organ-pipe, softly blown. These sounds will be found to be very soft and pleasant, with no trace of roughness, but somewhat dull, and, when low, obscure. Flutes give very nearly simple tones, the overtones being both few and weak. Tuning-forks without resonance tubes have, though slightly, the twang of the higher partials with them. Other instruments possess some of these partials, but not others, and some louder, some weaker, in the most diverse proportions. The difference of quality among instruments is entirely due to this difference in the number, the order, and the intensities of the partials. So true is this, that Professor Helmholtz was able, by combining a series of simple tones, and imitating the partials in various ways, to reproduce the quality or *timbre* of any instrument he pleased. He did this by maintaining a series of ten tuning-forks, tuned to the relative pitch of the first ten partials, in continual vibration, by means of electro-magnets. Each of these was furnished with an appropriate resonating chamber, the aperture to which could be opened or closed at pleasure. The closing of this aperture renders the sound of the corresponding fork very nearly inaudible, but on opening it, the sound swells out. Thus any desired combination of simple tones could be obtained at will, and, by regulating the distance of the forks from their resonators, with any degree of intensity. The following is a brief abstract of some of Professor Helmholtz's observations:—"Those compound tones, which contain the partials from the first to the sixth, are richer and fuller than the simple tones, but are perfectly smooth as long as the higher partials are imperceptible. Such are the tones of the pianoforte, of open organ-pipes, and the *softer* tones of the human voice and of the horn. The horn, strongly blown, produces some of the higher partials, and a coarser quality of tone. When the upper partials—that is, those above the sixth or seventh—are very distinct, the sound is cutting, or rough, on account of the beats which they make with each other. The clarinet, stopped organ-pipes, and pianoforte strings when struck or pulled at their middle point, have only the odd partials, viz, I, III, V, VII, &c. Their tone is peculiar, and often more or less nasal. The degree of roughness produced by the upper partials differs in different instruments. When the higher partials are moderate in intensity, they do not interfere with the musical value of the tone; on the contrary, they add to its character and expression. The most important instances of this are in the tones of bowed instruments—such as the violin and the violoncello; and of most reed instruments, such as the oboe, bassoon, the softly-played harmonium, and the human voice. The rough braying sound of brass instruments is extremely penetrating, and hence gives a greater *impression* of power (though not of quiet pervading influence) than sounds of a softer quality. They are consequently little used, except in a full band. When the loudness of the primary predominates, the tone is full. Thus the sound of wide open organ-pipes is fuller and *more pervading* than that of narrow ones; the sound of strings is fuller when struck by the hammers of a pianoforte or pulled by the fingers, than when struck by a piece of stick; and the sound of reed pipes with proper resonance tubes is fuller than the sound of reeds without resonance tubes." We thus see that the principal object for which partials exist is to create quality, or *timbre*, in the tones of different instruments. In the harmonium, the octave and double-octave "stops;" and in the organ, the additional octave-fifth and sesquialtera are used to render the quality of the tone more piercing. At present, they are but a coarse imitation of the real partials. Now that the subject of "quality" is better understood, makers will, doubtless, adapt these stops more delicately to their purpose. Organ builders, however, say that for purposes of accompaniment, and to sustain the pitch of congregational singing, it is necessary thus to exaggerate the partials.

ART AND SCIENCE.—*Clatter.* "In the human voice," says Helmholtz, "from six to eight overtones generally accompany the primary partial. Even in the higher tones this is the case, for partials in the region from C^2 to G^3 can be well distinguished by the ear. In a strong bass voice, partials as high as XVI may sometimes be heard." This prevalence of upper partials in the human voice is very much increased by loud strained singing with great force of breath from the chest. The voice is then like a violently overblown trumpet—unendurable. These higher partials, lying all close together, result, when strongly produced, in a harsh dissonance. I have often heard this metallic clatter from ill-trained singing classes, when they try (in vain) to sing a real *fortissimo*. I have also heard it in single voices when they were forcing a lower register into the place of the higher. Mr. Sedley Taylor describes the same effect thus :—

"When a body of voices are singing *fortissimo* without any instrumental accompaniment, a peculiar shrill tremulous sound is heard which is obviously far above the pitch of any note professedly being sung. This sound is, to my ear, so intensely shrill and piercing, as to be often quite painful I have also observed it when listening to the lower notes of a powerful contralto voice."—"*Sound and Music*," p. 136.

A true *forte* can only be produced from vocal ligaments made strong by practice. A heavy breath forcing weak vocal ligaments will only produce this miserable "clatter."

Sympathy of Tones. — Vibrations produced by one instrument have the power of awakening the vibrations of another instrument which is tuned to the same or nearly the same tone. Thus, if a sounding tuning-fork is held close to the opening of a tube of the proper length for producing its tone, the column of air in that tube will immediately begin to vibrate in sympathy with the fork, producing, if the tube is wide enough, even a louder tone than that of the fork itself. In the same way the human voice can "light up" the sound of a stretched string, or of a glass, or tube by singing the proper tone belonging to it. It may be frequently noticed that the glass shade of an ornament or of a chandelier will *resound* whenever its own tone is struck. More than this, there is power even in the partials of a strong compound tone to excite the sympathy of any adjacent strings or tubes which are attuned to answer them. Lift the damper from the strings of a piano by pressing the "loud pedal"; sound, with great force, one of the lowest tones of the instrument, and almost immediately stop with the fingers the vibrations of its string. When the sound of the primary string is thus suddenly cut off, there will still be heard vibrating a number of other strings. These, upon examination, will prove to be the octave, the octave-fifth, the double octave, the double octave-third, the double octave-fifth, &c. &c. The very strings which correspond, as nearly as piano temperament will allow, with the partials of the string just silenced. The loud compound tone had lived just long enough to light up the sympathy of these upper strings, and then to leave them sounding. Professor Helmholtz took advantage of this principle, and of the fact that vibrations of wider excursion—producing louder tones—can be set in motion by those of lesser excursion, to test the existence and intensity of partials. He had a number of globular resounders made, with an opening to fit into the ear, and a wider opening on the outer side. Each resounder would answer, by sympathy, to a tone or to tones lying within a komma of it. Knowing the pitch of the compound tone which was sounding, he also knew which of the resounders would answer to such a one or to such another of its partials, and, by this means, he could detect the presence and measure the intensity of any partial he enquired for. The following experiment will illustrate the use of resounders or resonators :— Procure a C^1 tuning-fork and a common two-ounce phial, into the bottom of which about half-an-inch of water has been poured. Strike the fork, and hold it over the mouth of the phial. By properly adjusting the height of the water, the sound of the note may be singularly augmented, but its character of tone entirely changes. It loses its metallic ring, and becomes fluty. This is a simple tone, the real simple tone of C¹. Take another phial, and fill about three-quarters full of water. Hold the same fork. By properly adjusting the water (and striking the fork sharply), another simple tone will be produced, fainter than the first, but quite distinct, and an octave higher in sound.

The length of an *open* resonance tube, which is cylindrical and not too wide, is found by dividing 1124—the number of feet per second at which sound travels (for temperature of 62°, to be diminished by 1·14 for every lower degree of temperature) by twice the *pitch* of the tone. The length of a *closed* cylindrical resonance tube is found by dividing the same number (at the same temperature) by four times the pitch. Hence, for the annexed tones we have the annexed lengths:

64	128	256	512	1024	- PITCH.
8·75	4·38	2·17	1·08	0·54	- FEET. *Open.*
4·38	2·17	1·08	0·54	0·27	- FEET.
52½	26¼	13	6½	3¼	- INCHES NEARLY } *Closed.*

The same closed tube may be made to resound to lower tones by diminishing its aperture.

The following is a translation of the directions given by Helmholtz for making resonance tubes of pasteboard:—

"The extremities were closed with tin plates, one entire, the other with a circular opening. These resonance tubes had, therefore, only one opening. Such tubes can be made flatter in pitch by diminishing their apertures. To sharpen them, when necessary, I throw in some beeswax, and place them with their closed end upon the hob till the wax is melted, and spreads itself uniformly over the bottom. The tube is then removed from the hob, and allowed to cool in the vertical position. To see whether the tube is too sharp or too flat, partly cover the aperture while the tuning-fork vibrates before it. If the covering increases the resonance, the tube is too *sharp*. But if the resonance sensibly diminishes for any covering of the aperture, the tube is generally too *flat*."

The following are the dimensions of the resonance tubes used for Helmholtz's ten tuning-forks reduced to English inches and hundredths of an inch:—

	1	2	3	4	5	6	7	8	9	10
ACTUAL PITCH ..	117½	234½	352	469½	586½	604	821½	938⅓	1173½	1208
LENGTH........	16·73	8·27	5·00	3·46	2·28	2·09	1·97	1·58	1·34	1·02 } *In Inches.*
WIDTH	5·83	3·19	2·56	2·17	2·17	1·73	1·54	1·54	1·20	1·02
DO. OF APERTURE	1·24	0·93	0·63	0·56	0·55	0·49	0·44	0·45	0·41	0·33 }

The pitch as used by Helmholtz assumes C to be 264 vibrations, instead of 256. This will be a guide for relative length, width, and opening. The tops with the aperture had best be made movable, and the whole tubes of tin. They would then pack one within another, and not break so easily. On each top should be written the name and pitch of the tone to which the tube resounds.

Show that the C fork will give C with the C box, C¹ with the C¹ box, and nothing with the C² box. But the C harmonium vibrator will give a tone with the C, C¹, G¹, C², E², G², C³ boxes, which may probably be audible as high as this.

Tones can thus be analysed by resonance tubes even without placing oneself very near the sounding body. In the following quotations, Mr. Sedley Taylor shows how resonance is due to the "cumulative effect" of vibrations, and Helmholtz describes how the strings of a horizontal piano *sympathise* with any tone struck or sung close to them, and then refers to one of the most remarkable discoveries of modern times, building upon it a bold and interesting conjecture of his own.

"Let us examine the mechanical causes to which it is due. Suppose a heavy weight to be suspended from a fixed support by a flexible string, so as to form a pendulum of the simplest kind. In order to cause it to perform oscillations of considerable extent by the application of a number of small impulses, we proceed as follows. As soon as, by the first impulse, the weight has been set vibrating through a small distance, we take care that every succeeding impulse is impressed *in the direction in which the weight is moving at the time.* Each impulse, thus applied, will cause the pendulum to oscillate through a larger angle than before, and, the effects of many impulses being in this way added together, an extensive swing of the pendulum is the result. . . It will be clear, from what has been said above that the maximum effect will be produced on the motion of the pendulum, by applying a forward and a backward impulse respectively during each alternate half second, or, which is the same thing, administering *a pair of to and fro impulses during each complete oscillation of the pendulum.* We have a simple instance of such a proceeding in the way in which two boys set a heavily laden swing in violent motion. They stand facing each other, and each boy, when the swing is moving away from him, helps it along with a vigorous push. The above considerations enable us to explain how a sounding fork can set another fork, in unison with itself, into vibration through the action of the intervening air. . . The large number of impulses make up for the feebleness of each separate impulse. Accordingly, resonance is produced more slowly between unison-forks of low, than between those of high, pitch. I find that, with two forks making 256 vibrations per second, about one second is requisite to bring out an audible resonance; while with another pair, making 1920 vibrations per second, I can with difficulty damp the first fork sufficiently soon after striking it to prevent the other from making itself heard. A column of air is easily set in resonant vibration by a note of suitable pitch. The roughest experiment suffices to establish this fact. We have only to roll up a piece of paper, so as to make a little cylinder twelve inches long and an inch or two in diameter, with both ends open, strike a common C¹ tuning-fork and hold close to one of the apertures. As soon as the fork reaches this position, its tone will unmistakably swell out. In order to estimate the increase of intensity produced, it is a good plan to move the fork rapidly to and fro a few times, close to the aperture and away from it. In the first case we have the full effect of resonance, in the second only the unassisted tone of the fork, and the contrast is very marked. We may shorten or lengthen our cylinder, within certain limits, and still obtain the phenomena of resonance, but the greatest reinforcement of tone we can attain with the fork selected will be produced by an air-column about twelve inches long. If we close one end of the paper cylinder, by placing it, for instance, on a table, and repeat our experiment at the open end, only a very weak resonance is produced; but we obtain a powerful resonance by operating with a fork (C) making *half as many vibrations per second* as that before employed. In this case, then, a column of air contained in a cylinder, of which one end was closed, resounded powerfully to a note an octave below that which elicited its most vigorous resonance when contained in a cylinder open at both ends. By operating in this fashion, with forks of different pitch, on air columns of different lengths, we arrive at the following laws, which are universally true:—1. For every single musical note there exists a corresponding air-column of definite length which resounds the most powerfully to that note. 2. The maximum

resonance of air in a closed pipe is produced by a note one octave below that to which an open pipe of the same length resounds the most powerfully."—" *Sound and Music,*" by *Sedley Taylor*, pp. 73-79.

" The process which actually goes on in our ear is probably very like that just described. Deep in the petrous bone out of which the internal ear is hollowed, lies a peculiar organ, the cochlea or snail-shell—a cavity filled with water, and so called from its resemblance to the shell of a common garden snail. This spiral passage is divided throughout its length into three sections, upper, middle, and lower, by two membranes stretched in the middle of its height. The Marchese Corti discovered some very remarkable formations in the middle section. They consist of innumerable plates, microscopically small, and arranged orderly side by side, like the keys of a piano. They are connected at one end with the fibres of the auditory nerve, and at the other with the stretched membrane.

"In the so-called vestibulum, also, where the nerves expand upon little membranous bags swimming in water, elastic appendages, similar to stiff hairs, have been lately discovered at the ends of the nerves. The anatomical arrangement of these appendages leaves scarcely any room to doubt that they are set into sympathetic vibration by the waves of sound which are conducted through the ear. Now if we venture to conjecture—it is at present only a conjecture, but after careful consideration I am led to think it very probable—that every such appendage is tuned to a certain tone like the strings of a piano, then the recent experiment with a piano shows you that when (and only when) that tone is sounded the corresponding hair-like appendage may vibrate, and the corresponding nerve-fibre experience a sensation, so that the presence of each single such tone in the midst of a whole confusion of tones must be indicated by the corresponding sensation. Experience then shows us that the ear really possesses the power of analysing waves of air into their elementary forms."
—" *Popular Scientific Lectures,*" by *Professor Helmholtz,* pp. 83-85.

Dr. Tyndall expresses the same thing in his own beautiful language thus :—

" Finally, there is in the labyrinth an organ, discovered by the Marchese Corti, which is to all appearance a musical instrument, with its cords so stretched as to accept vibrations of different periods, and transmit them to the nerve filaments which traverse the organ. Within the ears of men, and without their knowledge or contrivance, this lute of 3,000 strings has existed for ages, accepting the music of the outer world, and rendering it fit for reception by the brain. Each musical tremor which falls upon this organ selects from the stretched fibres the one appropriate to its own pitch, and throws it into unisonant vibration. And thus, no matter how complicated the motion of the external air may be, those microscopic strings can analyse it and reveal the constituents of which it is composed."—" *Lectures on Sound,*" by *Professor Tyndall,* p. 409.

ART AND SCIENCE.—*Quality of Voice.* Mr. Sedley Taylor so well describes the origin of quality in the human voice that I can only quote his words. Every singer should study them well.

" The apparatus of the *human voice* is essentially a reed (the vocal chords), associated with a resonance cavity (the hollow of the mouth). The vocal chords are elastic bands, situated at the top of the wind-pipe, and separated by a narrow slit, which opens and closes again with great exactness, as air is forced through it from the lungs. The form and width of the slit allow of being quickly and extensively modified by the changing tension of the vocal chords, and thus sounds widely differing from each other in pitch may be successively produced with surprising rapidity. In this respect the human ' reed ' far exceeds any that we can artfically construct. The size and shape of the cavity of the mouth may be altered by opening or closing *the jaws*, raising or dropping *the tongue*, and tightening or loosening *the lips*. We should expect that these movements would not be without effect on the resonance of the contained air, and this proves on experiment to be the fact. If we hold a vibrating tuning-fork close to the lips, and then modify the resonating cavity, in the ways above described, we shall find |that it resounds most powerfully to the fork selected when the parts of the mouth are in one definite position. If we try a fork of different pitch, the attitude of the mouth, for the strongest resonance, is no longer the same. Hence, when the vocal chords have originated a reed-sound containing numerous well-developed partial-tones, the mouth-cavity, by successively throwing itself into different postures, can favour by its resonance, first one partial-tone, then another; at one moment *this* group of partial-tones, at another *that*. In this manner endless varieties of quality are rendered possible. Good vocalization, therefore, requires the resonating cavity to be so placed as to modify in the way most attractive to the ear, the quality of the sounds produced by the vocal chords." —" *Sound and Music,*" *pp.* 134, 135.

Quality of Tone in Instruments.

—In Mr. Sedley Taylor's work "Sound and Music," will be found the most clear and patient exposition of this subject which I have seen. I here add a few hints on the quality of instruments, condensed from Helmholtz's great work, and to this I append a quotation from an article, by Dr. W. Stevens Squire, in the *Quarterly Journal of Science*, No. 8. These quotations will enforce and develop the principles already announced.

Simple or nearly Simple Tones.—Tuning-forks held before resonance-tubes produce the *simplest* tones which can be obtained separately. The deep tones are obscure, the upper tones soft, without any trace of cutting or harshness. All simple tones have the same character at the same pitch however they may be produced, or whatever be the substance of which the resonance-tube is composed. Flutes have very nearly simple tones, the overtones being both few and weak. The vowel OO (in " too ") is very nearly a simple tone. Bottles with large bodies and small necks, made to resound by blowing a stream of air over the mouth, give simple tones accompanied with a rushing sound of the wind. Wide-stopped pipes of organs have practically simple tones, accompanied by the same rushing sound.

Compound Tones containing High Dissonant Partials.— The overtones of these tones are so high and so dissonating that they are usually disregarded in considering the qualities of the tone, and looked upon as a tinkling or jarring, which is unavoidable, but which is no part of the musical tone itself. Tuning-forks, when struck and placed on a sounding-board which strengthens the whole tone and does not select a single partial as the resonance tube does, have usually the fundamental and a few very high and tinkling overtones, which, as the fork is struck, are heard even more distinctly than the fundamental, but rapidly die away. Calling the fundamental C, the first overtone of a fork is about Ab^1, and the second about D^3. Elastic plates struck by a hammer, as in the glass, metal, or wood harmonicon, have the primary and some high dissonating overtones. When these high tones do not die off rapidly, there is a continuance of the effect known as a metallic ring. Bells have their fundamentals accompanied by overtones, whose relative vibrational numbers are as 4, 9, 16, 25, 36, &c., and not unfrequently, the fundamental itself is absent or weak. Thus a C_1 bell gives about D, C^1, $G\sharp^1$, D^3. The overtones vary with the form of the bell and the thickness of the margin. Unsymmetrical bells will give two series of partials. Stretched membranes, as in tambourines and drums, have high dissonating overtones, which rapidly disappear. Thus, if the membrane is tuned to C_1, the partials C_1, Ab_1, $C\sharp$, D, G, Bb, or thereabouts, may be heard for an instant. When tuning-forks, plates. bells, &c., are set in vibration by a violin bow, the dissonating partials may be cut off by touching the vibrating body in the proper place, but there remains a violent scratching effect due to the other dissonating partials, created by the intermediate action of the bow.

Tones of Stretched Strings.—The harp and the guitar give the primary strong, but the accompanying partials are determined by the instrument with which the strings are struck and the part of the string to which it is applied. The softest tones are produced by pulling with the soft part of the finger. Chipping with the nail gives high dissonant partials, or a metallic effect. A quill or a metal plectrum is disagreeable for the same reason. The pianoforte has different qualities of tone according to the different pitch of the primary dependent on the formation of the hammer, its weight, and softness. The following results were obtained from the calculations and experiments of Professor Helmholtz:—Bass, C_3 to C: The partials 2 and 3 are nearly $2\frac{1}{4}$ times as powerful as the primary tone ; the partial 4, about equal to the primary, but the partial 5 is only a quarter as strong, and the higher partials are scarcely perceptible. Treble, in the neighbourhood of G: The partial 2 is not quite twice as strong as the primary ; the partial 3 is about as strong as the primary ; the partial 4 has only about one-sixth the strength of the primary, and the higher partials are nearly imperceptible. Higher treble, in the neighbourhood of C^2: The partial 2 is nearly the same as the primary ; the partial 3 not more than one-eleventh of the strength of the primary ; the partial 4 not more than a fortieth : and the other partials are nearly imperceptible. The above results are very important in determining the effects of various partials on the piano, and their difference from the effects of the same partials on an organ or harmonium. If the string is struck with an extremely hard hammer, instead of one covered with elastic felt and leather, the partials 2 and 5 have *three* times as much force as the primary ; and the partials 3 and 4 have *five* times the force of the primary : the partial 6 is as strong as the primary, but as the string is struck at about one-seventh of its length, the partial 7 disappears. If the string is pulled instead of being struck, the intensity of the partials 2, 3, 4, 5, 6 are about $\frac{1}{4}$, $\frac{1}{9}$, $\frac{1}{16}$, $\frac{1}{25}$, $\frac{1}{36}$ that of the primary respectively. Hence the primary is heard much better when the string is pulled than when it is struck. On the violin, when the bowing is good, all the partials exist as far as the natural stiffness of the string will allow, and they diminish in intensity as they increase in pitch, in the proportion of 1, $\frac{1}{4}$, $\frac{1}{9}$, $\frac{1}{16}$, $\frac{1}{25}$, &c., respectively. These higher partials are easily perceived, if they are first heard as flageolet-toned harmonics. The latter can be readily obtained as far as the sixth harmonic, and the tenth may be reached with some trouble. The lower tones speak best when bowed at about $\frac{1}{10}$ or $\frac{1}{4}$ of the vibrating length from the bridge, and the upper tones at $\frac{1}{4}$ or $\frac{1}{5}$ of their length from the same. The primary is relatively stronger than on the piano or guitar, the lower overtones relatively weaker, but the higher partials, from the sixth to the tenth, or thereabouts, are much more distinct, and produce the peculiar sharpness and often cutting quality of tone. If the bowing and the instrument are both good, the tone is pure, musical, and unbroken. Every scratch of the bow gives rise to sudden alterations. The scratching effect of a violin is, therefore, due to irregular interruptions of the system of vibration into which the string, and, therefore, the wood, is thrown. Hence, one good effect of having well-seasoned wood, and of having a violin which has been used by good bowers, which trains the wood to vibrate uniformly. The relative intensities of the partials are slightly modified by the resonance of the air enclosed by the sounding-board of the instrument.

Masses of air enclosed in vessels of various shapes can be made to vibrate and give distinct musical tones, and generally will resound to several distinct simple tones, but the relative pitches of these tones depend upon the size and shape of the tube in a remarkable and very complex manner. Only some of the cases admit of mathematical consideration ; most of them must be determined by experiment. If, then, a noise of any kind be made near the mouth of a tube or vessel of air, and any of the partial tones of which the noise consists corresponds to the simple tones to which the vessel can resound, those simple tones will be greatly reinforced, and will ring out loudly and distinctly. If these simple tones have their pitches as 1, 2, 3, 4, 5, 6, and not higher, the result is a beautiful compound musical tone. Sometimes higher partial tones may be produced, and the result is a noise—as may be heard in banging a door at the entrance of a long passage. Usually only much fewer simple tones are produced.

Wind instruments consist of a resonance tube of constant or variable lengths or shape, with some apparatus at one end for making a noise—that is, a number of simple tones, or a very complex compound tone. This apparatus consists either of a sharp edge over which a thin stream of air is blown, or of a vibrating reed or membrane. Of the first kind are the greater number of organ-pipes, flageolets, flutes, and whistles. Of the second kind are reed organ-pipes, harmoniums, concertinas, clarinets, oboes, bassoons, trumpets, trombones, and the human larynx. In flute-pipes, as the first series may be called, there is always present a peculiar hissing or rushing sound, occasioned by the wind splitting on the thin edge, and generating closely-beating partial tones, only one or more of which is reinforced by the resonance tube.

To determine what tones would be reinforced by a given resonance tube (or the proper tones of the pipe) a series of tuning-forks may be held over the end, when only those forks which correspond to the tones of strongest resonance will have their tones increased. The character of the quality of tone of these pipes depends essentially on the partial tones of the wind-rush above described being sufficiently near to the proper tones of the pipe to be reinforced, in addition to the fundamental tone. It is only in narrow cylindrical open pipes, as those of flutes and the "violin-principal" of organs, that the higher partial tones of the tube exactly corresponds to the higher partial tones of the fundamental tone. By blowing stronger, and thus increasing the pitch of the wind-rush, the higher partial proper tones of the pipe can be made to speak without the lower or fundamental tones. A flute with all the holes closed gives D; blown more strongly, gives D^1; still more strongly, A^1 and D^2. Now D, D^1, A^1, D^2 are the 1st, 2nd, 3rd, and 4th partial tones of the compound tone D. Hence, in narrow cylindrical pipes not only the fundamental tone, but also a series of upper partial tones are reinforced by the resonance of the tube, when the blowing is strong, so that the wind-rush contains many higher tones. Hence in "violin-principal" and similar organ-pipes, partial tones up to the 6th may be distinctly heard (by proper aids) when the blowing is strong. On the other hand, in the wider pipes the adjacent proper tones of the tube are all somewhat higher than the corresponding partial tones of the fundamental tone, and hence these are much less reinforced by the resonance of the tube. These wide pipes form the chief mass of sound or "principal stops" on the organ, and have the advantage of not jumping up an octave or more when blown strongly. In wooden principal pipes, in addition to the first partial or fundamental tone, the second partial—or octave—is clear, but the third partial—or twelfth—is weak, and the higher partial tones are imperceptible. In the metal principal pipes, the fourth partial tone—or double octave—is perceptible. The quality of tone in these pipes is fuller and softer than in the "violin-principal." When softly blown, the upper partial tones on the flute-stops on the organ, and the German flute, lose strength more rapidly than the fundamental tones, and the quality of tone becomes weak and soft.

The conically-narrowed pipes of the organ-stops, called *Salicional*, *Chamois-horn*, and *Flageolet* (Spitzflöte) in Germany have their upper opening about half the diameter of the lower, and have the peculiarity of making some of the upper partial tones (the 5th to the 7th) proportionally distincter than the lower. The quality of tone is consequently poor, but peculiarly bright.

Narrow stopped cylindrical pipes have proper partial tones answering to the *uneven* partial tones of the fundamental tone—that is, to the primary or fundamental tone, the twelfth or 3rd partial tone, the double octave third or 5th partial tone, &c. On the other hand, *wide* stopped pipes have their adjacent proper tones perceptibly higher than the corresponding partial tones of the fundamental tone, and the latter partial tones are consequently hardly reinforced at all. Hence wide covered pipes softly blown give the fundamental tone as almost a pure simple tone. Narrow ones allow the twelfth—or third partial tone—to be heard distinctly, and hence their name, *Quints*; and when they are strongly blown they have also the 5th partial tone very distinct.

Wooden pipes do not give so sharp a wind-rush as metal pipes; they also do not withstand the tremor occasioned by the waves of sound so well as the latter, and this seems to destroy the upper partial tones by friction. Hence wooden pipes give a softer or obscure and less brilliant tone than metal pipes.

Reed pipes are of three kinds. (1) The organ reed pipes and harmonium reeds, in which a tongue of metal moves freely through an opening, so that it alternately closes and opens it, giving rise to puffs of air, as on the siren, and consequently to a very discontinuous form of vibration, which answers to an extremely complex composition of simple vibrations, and consequently gives a compound tone with a great number of partial tones. Hence the great roughness of harmoniums, in which the resonance tubes practically do not exist. On concertinas each tongue is enclosed in a box, the dimensions of which is important, as it serves as a resonance tube. The strength of the upper partial tones of a reed and their proportions to the primary, depend greatly on the constitution of the reed, its position in the frame, the closeness with which it fits, &c. The reeds which strike the frame instead of passing through give the harshest tone. Hard unyielding material, as brass and steel tongues, makes the puffs of air more discontinuous than soft yielding material. This is probably the reason why the human larynx gives the softest of all reed-pipe tones. The resonance tube is of great importance in modifying the tone. It must be considered as a tube closed at the end where the reed is placed.

(2) The tongues of the clarinet, oboe, and bassoon are similarly constructed of elastic reeds. The tongue of the clarinet is broad, and is fastened before the corresponding opening of the mouth-piece. It would strike if it made great excursions, but its excursions are limited by the pressure of the lips, and it is only allowed to diminish the aperture sufficiently without striking. In the oboe and bassoon two reeds are placed opposite each other at the end of the mouth-piece, separated by a small slit, and are pressed together so as to close it, when they swing inwards by the action of the breath.

These wooden wind instruments have each a single tongue to serve for a whole series of tones, whereas the first class of instruments has a separate reed for each tone. But the tongues of this second series are made of light elastic wood which are easily set in motion by the changing pressure of the vibrating mass of air, and follow its vibrations. Hence these instruments, in addition to the very high tones which correspond to the proper pitch of their reeds, are able to produce other much deeper tones, the pitch of which depends upon the sufficiency of the alternation of pressure produced by the vibration of the mass of air in the resonance tube at the insertion of the reed, to set the reed in vibration. This condition is satisfied by the proper tones of the resonance tube considered as closed at the point where the reed is inserted. In practice the proper tones of the reed are not used at all, because they are very high and screaming, and their pitch would not be sufficiently steady, especially when the reed is wet. The tones used are only those deeper tones which depend on the length of the column of air, and correspond to the proper tones of the closed tube.

The tube of the clarinet is cylindrical, and its proper tones correspond to the primary, 3rd, 5th, 7th, &c., partial tones of the fundamental tone. By blowing stronger we can jump from the fundamental tone to the twelfth or the double octave third. The acoustical length of the tube can also be altered by opening the vent-holes in its side, in which case the column of air between the mouth-piece and the nearest open vent-hole may be generally assumed to be all that is put in vibration. The quality of tone in this and similar instruments alters considerably with the mode of blowing, and tones of different pitch, when they require the opening of the side vent-holes, have very different qualities even on the same instrument. The opening of these side vent-holes is by no means a perfect substitute for the shortening of the length of the tube, and the reflection of the waves of sound at these openings is not precisely the same at the free open end of the tube. The partial tones of a tube which is limited by an open side vent-hole must differ considerably from harmonic purity, and this will have considerable influence upon its resonance.

The tube of the oboe and bassoon is conical. Conical tubes, closed at the vertex of their cone, have proper tones similar to those of open cylindrical tubes of the same length. Hence the tones of these two instruments are nearly the same as those of open pipes. By blowing stronger they give the octave, twelfth, second octave, &c., of the fundamental tone. The intermediate tones are produced by the side vent-holes.

(3) Membranous tongues consist of two membranes closing at a narrow slit over a tube. They consist of the lips and the vocal ligaments of the larynx; the former are used in playing brass instruments, the latter in singing. The lips are slightly elastic membranous tongues or reeds, laden with much inelastic watery tissue, and consequently would vibrate very slowly when isolated from a tube. On account of the little resistance which they offer they are readily brought into vibration by the alternating pressure of the vibrating column of air when used for wind instruments.

The old horns and trumpets consist of a long conical coiled tube without keys or pistons. They can only produce such tones as answer to the proper tones of the tube, which in this case are the upper partial tones of the fundamental tone. As the fundamental tone of such a long tube is very deep, the upper partial tones lie tolerably close together in the middle regions of the scale, and hence give most of the degrees of the scale. Thus, the tube of the French horn is about 27 feet long; its proper fundamental tone is Eb_3, but this and its octave Eb_2 are not used, the practical scale being Bb_2, Eb_1, G_1, Bb_1, Db, Eb, F, G, Ab, Bb, &c., where the Db is too flat and the Ab too sharp, for the true major diatonic scale of Eb. The trumpet was limited to these natural tones. In the French horn the hand could be inserted in the bell to diminish the terminal aperture; in the trombone the tube could be lengthened or shortened, and in this way missing tones could be supplied, and those which were too sharp or too flat for the scale improved. In later times, keys have been added to trumpets and horns, increasing the number of tones, but somewhat impairing their power and brilliancy. The vibrations of the air in these instruments are extremely powerful, and only firm, smooth, unpierced tubes can resist them completely without destroying any of their power. In using brass instruments the different form and tension of the lips of the blower serves to determine which of the proper tones of the tube shall sound; the highest of the individual tones is almost independent of the tension of the lips.

In the human larynx, on the other hand, the vocal ligaments, which here form the membranous tongues, alter and determine themselves the pitch of the tone. The hollow spaces filled with air in connection with the larynx are not adapted for making much change in the tone of the vocal ligaments, their walls are too yielding for them to allow vibrations of the air to take place within them powerful enough to force the vocal ligaments to assume a period of vibration which does not suit that which is required by their own elasticity. The opening of the mouth is too short and usually too widely open to serve as a resonance tube which could materially influence the pitch. In addition to the variable tension of the vocal ligaments (produced not merely by separating their points of attachment, but by voluntary tension of the muscles they contain), their thickness may be apparently altered. Below the proper elastic bundles of fibres and muscles of the vocal ligaments is much soft watery inelastic tissue, which probably acts to weight the elastic bands and retard their vibrations in singing the breast voice. The falsetto probably arises from withdrawing the mass of mucous membrane below the ligaments, and thus rendering their edge sharper and the weight of their vibrating portion less, without altering their elasticity. By artificial aids we may detect very high partial tones in deep powerful bass notes sung to the higher vowels, and in somewhat forced *forte* tones in the upper parts of the scale of any human voice high partial tones of the octave C^3 to B^3 (the highest octave of modern pianos) may be more distinctly heard than in any other instrument. The strength of the highest upper partial tones is very different in different individuals. In bright sharp voices it is much greater than in dull soft voices. In the sharp voices the cause of their quality of tone may perhaps depend upon the edges of the vocal ligaments not being smooth or straight enough to close exactly up to a narrow straight slit without striking, so that the larynx resembles more nearly a striking tongue which has a much harsher quality of tone than the free tongue. In hoarse voices the cause is probably that the glottis is not entirely closed during the vibration of the vocal ligaments. At any rate, corresponding results are obtained by making similar changes in an artificial glottis. For strong and yet soft qualities of voice it is necessary that the vocal ligaments, even when vibrating most powerfully, should come close to one another with their edges in a straight line, so as completely to close the glottis, without striking against one another. If they do not close completely the stream of air will not be completely interrupted, and the tone will not be powerful enough. If they strike, the tone will be harsh as for striking reeds. On examining the vocal ligaments in action, by means of the laryngoscope, the accuracy with which they close for vibrations which extend over their entire breadth is very striking.

The voice is set somewhat differently for speaking than for singing, which occasions a much harsher tone in speaking, especially for the open vowels, and produces a sensation of greater pressure in the throat. Probably the vocal ligaments strike in speaking. When the mucous membrane of the larynx is catarrhal, little patches of mucus may be seen by the laryncoscope to enter the glottis. These, when too great, disturb the motion of the ligaments, and by making it irregular, produce irregular harsh jarring or hoarse qualities of tone.

" The upper tones [partials] in the sound of an instrument of percussion depend upon—

1st, The kind of blow.

2nd, The place where the blow is delivered.

3rd, The thickness, rigidity, and elasticity of the string.

As far as the kind of blow is concerned, the string can either be drawn aside and then released, as in the harp or guitar; or by means of a plectrum, as in the ancient lyre and the modern Hungarian zitter; or the string may be struck with a hammer, as in the piano. It is easy at once to see that the effects will be very different. When the string is drawn aside, the whole string is removed from its position of equilibrium, so that when it is released the vibration will be chiefly confined to the string as a whole, that is, the fundamental will far exceed in power the upper tones. If, on the contrary, the string is struck by a hammer which springs away immediately, it is only just that portion which was immediately in contact with the hammer that is set in motion.

" Immediately after the blow, the other part of the string is at rest, and is only disturbed by the wave which is set up at the point of percussion, and which is propagated to the end of the string, and reflected back again like a wave on a trough of water, producing a long series of upper tones the intensity of which may equal or even surpass that of the fundamental. The harder and lighter the hammer, the more quickly will it be thrown off, and the shorter will be the length of string displaced at the moment of impact, so that the fundamental might be quite inaudible, and the sound shrill, thin, and of disagreeable quality. To obviate this, it has been found advantageous to cover the hammers with soft felt. At the moment of first impact the felt is compressed so that the force is gradually applied, and it is only when a considerable length of the string is in motion that the whole of the force has been expended and the hammer thrown off. The thicker the felt and the heavier the hammer the longer will it remain in contact with the string; accordingly these conditions are observed in the lower octaves of the pianoforte, where the strings are long and heavy, and a proportionately greater mass must be set in motion in order to get rid of the high upper tones which would spoil the rich deep quality required. The time that the hammer is in contact with the string to a great extent regulates the upper tones produced, for it is clear that there will be a tendency to produce just those tones which require an excursion of the string in one direction in the time, or in an even multiple of the time, that the hammer is pressing the string in one direction.

" The place at which the blow is delivered exercises an important influence in this respect, as none of those tones which have a node (or place of rest) at this point can be produced. On the other hand, those which have their maximum of oscillation about this point will come prominently forward. Thus, if the string be struck exactly in the middle, the fundamental which has its greatest amplitude here will be most powerful, but the next octave will be wholly wanting; the 12th, *i.e.*, the 5th of the higher octave (the third tone) will be prominent, but the second octave will not be produced; that is, the tones of the even numbers will be absent, but those of the uneven numbers will be present. The effect of this is to give the sound a dull nasal character. Now the first six tones come exactly into what is called the major chord, that is, they are all thirds, fifths, and octaves, but the seventh tone, which is a minor seventh, and the ninth, which is a major second, do not come into the chord. Theory, therefore, indicates that the place at which the string should be struck is that at which these tones have a node. Such a point is situated about the seventh from the end of the string, and this is the place actually adopted by the manufacturers. No theory has led them to this, but by blind experimenting they have arrived at the same practical conclusion that theory points out.

"Lastly, the thickness and material of the strings have considerable influence on the quality of the sound, for very stiff strings cannot give such high upper tones as thinner ones, because they are not capable of subdividing themselves into such minute flexible portions. With a very thin wire, such as is used for artificial flower-making, it is possible to obtain the 18th tone if the string is 7 or 8 yards long, but these high tones no longer belong to the major chord, and produce that peculiar wiry tone characteristic of instruments such as the zitter, with very thin wires. The elasticity of gut strings is far less than that of wires of similar thickness, so that the high upper tones disappear at once, and the sound is fuller and rounder.

"The theory of fiddles is not so complete as that of the piano, as the peculiar action of the bow, which is not well understood, will greatly influence the quality of the sound. The string is drawn by the friction of the bow from its position of equilibrium, and as soon as the tension overcomes the friction it is suddenly released, so that the motion rather resembles that of a tilt hammer, slow in the one direction, but quick in the other The fundamental is proportionately stronger in these instruments than in those in which the string is struck near the end, as in guitars and pianos; the lower overtones are weaker, but the higher tones, from the sixth to about the tenth, are much more distinct, and to these are due the peculiar clearness of the sound. The form of the vibration is in the main tolerably independent of the place where the bow is used, still minute variations arise from this cause. If, for example, the bow is drawn across a portion of the string which corresponds with a node of one of the higher tones, that tone will be wanting, and variations in the quality are partly dependent on this circumstance. So that if the bow is used too near the finger board, the end of which is about one-fifth of the length of the string from the bridge, the fifth or sixth tone will be absent, which ought otherwise to be audible, and the sound will be duller. The usual position of the bow is about one-tenth from the bridge, for *piano* passages rather farther, for *forte* rather nearer. If the bow is used very near the bridge, about one-twentieth, it is possible to produce by a gentle and rapid movement only the higher octave, so that a node is produced in the middle of the string, just as if it had been lightly touched by the finger at that point, and, between this point and the usual place every possible mixture of the primary tone and its higher octave may be obtained.

"In the quality of the tone of the violin, much is supposed to depend upon the wood of which it is made, and this is unquestionably true. Still both age and long use of the instrument tend to increase the elasticity of the wood, which is, perhaps, one reason for the preference accorded to the instruments of the old makers. The sound of the violin does not come to us direct from the strings, but from the body of the instrument. The one leg of the bridge rests on a rod of wood joining the upper and lower surface, the other rests unsupported on the upper wooden surface, and this conveys to it the vibrations of the strings, which are again transmitted to the air by the greater surface of the wood. But a hollow space enclosed by elastic walls like those of the violin must have certain proper tones which may be evoked by blowing into the openings. Savart found this to be for the violin C¹ and for the violoncello F. This will have the effect of strengthening those tones which approximate to those of the hollow space, and it is found both in the violin and violoncello that these tones come broadly out. As the lowest note of a violin is G, it is only the upper tones of the three lowest notes which will be increased by resonance, while of the other notes generally, the fundamental will be augmented rather than the upper tones, as they approximate more to the peculiar tone of the body of the instrument."— "*The Quality of Musical Sounds,*" *by W. Stevens Squire, in the "Quarterly Journal of Science," No. 8.*

Effect of Partials on Chords.—

Nearly all good tones, especially those of the human voice, are compound tones. When, therefore, such tones are placed one above the other in chords, it becomes necessary to consider how far the partials of these tones help or hinder the harmony of the chord, for it is obvious that if any partial of a lower tone vibrates in unison with one of the higher primary tones of a chord, it will reinforce that tone. And if, on the other hand, the partial vibrates as an adjacent dissonant tone, it will give more or less of roughness to the chord—will "put a drag" on its wheels. Our studies of this subject will be greatly facilitated by the following considerations:— First, that the very slight intensity of the higher partials taken in connection with their absence from tones of the best quality, enables us to put out of our calculations all but the first five or six; and, second, that the wide intervals of the earlier partials throw up the partials of the higher tones of a chord out of the ear's reach— thus the second, third, fourth, and fifth partials of a tone in the middle of the bass compass, lie in the range of the soprano, but those of a tone in the middle of the tenor compass throw all but *two* of their number above the common range of the soprano. We may, therefore, yet further limit our enquiries to the partials of the bass tone in a chord, neglecting the less effective partials of the higher tones. We must also remember that the lower the bass tone is in pitch, the greater the number of partials which it brings to bear on the chord. The diagrams on the following page show at a glance the effect of the partials of a bass tone on major, minor, and diminished chords in all their positions or inversions. The chord D is taken as the example of major chords, L of minor chords, and T of diminished chords. The chords F and 8 would have served the purpose of the diagram as well

EFFECT OF PARTIALS ON CHORDS.

The Roman Numerals show the Partials of the Bass Tone. Each Chord is shown in its three positions, a, b, and c.

MAJOR.	MINOR.	DIMINISHED.
a b c	a b c	a b c
3 6 6/4	3 6 6/4	8 6 6/4

as D; R and M as well as L, and *SE* as well as T. The partials of the bass tone are represented by Roman figures, as at p. 14. A reference to the scale on the left-hand of each diagram will show what scale-tone the partial represents, while the Roman figures will indicate to the mind their decreasing loudness. A slur, or tie, points to the dissonating partials and the tones with which they dissonate. It must not be supposed that this diagram represents the *invariable* effect of the partials on the chords enumerated; first, because in actual music all the tones of a chord are not so fully given, and some particular tone, which a partial would strengthen or roughen, may be absent, and, second, because when the bass tone is lower, the partials will be more numerous, and when it is higher, less so. Such a diagram can only represent *the average consequences* (as far as partials are concerned) of using such and such a form of chord.

SCIENCE AND ART.—*Chords and Positions.* Major chords, it will at once be seen, assert their superiority to minor chords. In their first position, all the strong partials of the bass are perfectly consonant with the chord: they simply strengthen it. But in the first position of the minor chords, the Vth partial of the bass makes a sharp "out-of-key" dissonance with the chord. In the double minor or diminished chords, not only the Vth, but also the IIIrd and VIth partials make similar dissonances. Thus the study of the effects of partials on chords shows us the reason for the preference accorded by musicians to the major chord over the minor, and to the minor over the diminished chord. Coming to the positions of the major chord, we see that, while in the "*a*" position there is no material dissonance between its tones and the partials of the bass, in the "*b*" position the IIIrd partial makes a sharp semitone dissonance, and in the "*c*" position a tone dissonance. We can see from this why musicians do not use the inversions of a major chord except in apologetic circumstances. See "Construction Exercises," pp. 10, 24, 73. Again, with regard to the positions of

the minor chord—in the "*a*" position, there is a dissonating "out of key" Vth partial, the dissonance being at a semitone; in the "*b*" position a IIIrd partial dissonates, but only at the interval of a tone; while in the "*c*" position, a IIIrd partial dissonates at both a tone and a semitone distance. Thus, while on the whole the "*b*" position is not so inferior to the "*a*" position as in major chords, the "*c*" position of minor chords is relatively worse than in major. If this fact does not give a preference to the "*b*" position among minor chords, it, at any rate, accounts for the very great freedom with which it is used. See "Construction Exercises," pp. 30, 35; compare p. 40. If we compare the "*b*" position of minor chords with that of major chords, it is plain that, as far as the partials of the bass are concerned, the minor chords have the advantage. Turning to the diminished chord, we find the IIIrd partial dissonating in each position; in the "*a*" position at the distance of a semitone and out of key; in the "*b*" position" at a tone distance, in the "*c*" position at a tone and semitone distance, but not out of key. These facts partly account for the well-known habits of this chord—the preference given to its second position, the free use of its third position, and the avoidance of its first. See "Construction Exercises," p. 35.

From the resemblance of the first six partials to a major chord, several writers on the theory of music have been led to imagine that the "whole system of partials" should be received by us as *Nature's model* of a chord, and upon this idea they have built up heavy and complex theories, claiming the authority of Nature for them. But every musician ought to perceive that the fact of the higher partials being dissonant among themselves, and some of them *out of tune* with the scale, while quite suitable to their proper quality-giving purpose, utterly unfits them to be a model of full-voiced harmony. Let us make full use of these beautiful constituents of tone in our musical theory, but do not let us set up for them an authority which they do not claim, and which music does not follow.

CHAPTER III.

DIFFERENTIALS, AND WHAT THEY TEACH.

IF two tones, somewhat high in pitch, be sounded together pretty loudly on a harmonium, American organ, or, better still, on an English concertina, a third tone will be heard, which cannot be detected when either of the two tones is sounded by itself. Thus, if $C^2 = 1,024$ and $F^2 = 1,280$ be sounded together, $C = 256$ will be heard also ; if $C^2 = 1,024$ and $D^2 = 1,152$ be simultaneously produced, $C_1 = 128$ will be produced. The vibration number of this third tone is equal to the difference of the vibration numbers of the tones that generate it. In the above examples, for instance, $256 = 1,280 - 1,024$, and $128 = 1,152 - 1,024$. Hence these "third tones" are usually termed Difference Tones or Differentials ; they have also been termed "Resultant Tones" and "Grave Harmonics." They were first discovered by Sorge, a German organist, in 1745, and brought into general notice by Tartini, an Italian violinist, in 1754.

The differential may be readily heard, and tested, on the instruments just mentioned, but in calculating the tones of the instrument with which it should correspond, allowance must be made for the degree in which such instruments are "tuned out of tune" by the prevailing system of Equal Temperament. Thus in a recent experiment, the pitch-tones D and E were held down in the highest octave of a harmonium. The resulting differential ought to have corresponded with the fourth C *below* them, but so sharply was the E tuned, and so much greater, therefore, was the vibrational difference, that the differential corresponded more nearly with the tone above (D). Two high-pitched powerful whistles made to vary only a little in pitch will produce a very low, but well-heard, differential. We have heard a similar differential from two strong soprano voices. Some time ago, a double flageolet was exhibited in various parts of the country, the player on which prided himself on producing a very audible "sub bass," by means of these differentials. But it was necessary to make the flageolet-tones unbearably ear-piercing in order to bring out the differentials into great distinctness, and when brought out they did not make, and could not make, a proper bass. Even on the organ there has been an attempt to produce a new stop, without additional pipes, by the help of the differentials. It was known that when two tones are sounded, a perfect

fifth apart (as d s and l, m), the differential produced is an octave below the lower tone, and it was at once concluded that if the bass were played in fifths we should get a strong "sub-bass" an octave lower, which would be useful in harmony ; but it was found that, to make this "differential-bass" loud enough to be heard, the consecutive fifths above it must be made too strong to be borne. All attempts to drag these modest differentials and partials out of their proper sphere must necessarily fail.

EXPERIMENTS.—Mr. Ellis recommends the use of two G flageolet fifes. They can be blown loudly, so as to produce very audible differentials. The scale of these instruments is as below, only two octaves higher. Their lowest tone really begins with the highest here given. It is, therefore, the G^1 above the treble staff. The fingering is also given below.

G¹ A¹ B¹ C¹ D¹ E¹ F♯¹ G² A² B² C² D² E² F♯² G²

Two octaves higher than these notes.

THE FINGERING OF THE FLAGEOLET.

G^3	:	0	2	3	0	0	6
$F♯^2$	:	0	2	3	4	0	0
E^2	:	1	0	0	0	0	0
D^2	:	1	2	0	0	0	0
C^2	:	1	2	3	0	0	0
B^2	:	1	2	3	4	0	0
A^2	:	1	2	3	4	5	0
G^2	:	0	2	3	4	5	6
$F♯^1$	:	0	0	0	0	0	0
E^1	:	1	0	0	0	0	0
D^1	:	1	2	0	0	0	0
C^1	:	1	2	3	0	0	0
B^1	:	1	2	3	4	0	0
A^1	:	1	2	3	4	5	0
G^1	:	1	2	3	4	5	6

The fifes may not be tuned to the "philosophical pitch" (that is, C being produced by 256 vibrations in a second), but assuming that they are, and that all the tones are correct, the table on page 28 gives the vibration numbers of the higher tones. A simple set of subtraction sums will show us what differentials can be produced by these fifes. The following diagram gives a few examples. In the Staff notation, let the open notes represent the loudly-blown generators and small-headed notes the diffentials. In the Tonic Sol-fa notation, let the small notes below represent the differentials. In both notations this ` means a little flatter and this ′ a little sharper than the note written.

Secondary Differentials.

It is easy to see that a differential tone may produce, when coupled with a principal tone, another tone, which may be called a Secondary Differential. Thus, if $G^3 = 3{,}072$ and $E^3 = 2{,}560$ be sounded, the first differential $C^1 = 512$ $(3{,}072 - 2{,}560)$, will make with the lower principal E^3 $(2{,}560 - 512 = 2{,}048)$ a secondary differential C^2. These secondary differentials are very weak to the ordinary ear. Still feebler differentials have been discovered by Helmholtz, which may be called tertiary. They are produced by principal tones and secondary differentials.

Summation Tones.

It may here be mentioned that Professor Helmholtz has discovered another kind of tone—the product of two principal tones. This tone corresponds not with the difference, but with *the sum* of the vibrations of the principals. Thus, if we suppose C (256) and E (320) to be sounding together, a very minute tone is generated at $(256 + 320 = 576)$ D^1. Again, if A (432) and E^1 (640) are sounding together there will be a tiny summation tone $(432 + 640 = 1{,}072)$, which will be a trifle flatter than $C\sharp^2$. These summation tones are generally too high and always too faint to be of service in our musical studies.

SCIENCE AND ART.—*Effect of Differentials on a Chord.* Like the partials, these differentials sometimes strengthen a tone of the chord, and sometimes they are out of the chord and out of the key. Their intensity is not great. It varies with the intensity of the producing-tones. But they are effective, especially when they dissonate with a tone of the chord, or with one of its partials. Those are best heard which spring from high and loud producing-tones. For simplicity

VIBRATION NUMBERS.

d^3	G^3	$=$	3072
t^2	$F\sharp^3$	$=$	2880
l^2	E^3	$=$	2560
s^2	D^3	$=$	2304
f^2	C^3	$=$	2048
m^2	B^2	$=$	1920
r^2	A^2	$=$	1728
d^2	G^2	$=$	1536
t^1	$F\sharp^2$	$=$	1440
l^1	E^2	$=$	1280
s^1	D^2	$=$	1152
f^1	C^2	$=$	1024
m^1	B^1	$=$	960
r^1	A^1	$=$	864
d^1	G^1	$=$	768
t	$F\sharp^1$	$=$	720
l	E^1	$=$	640
s	D^1	$=$	576
f	C^1	$=$	512
m	B	$=$	480
r	A	$=$	432
d	G	$=$	384
t_1	$F\sharp$	$=$	360
l_1	E	$=$	320
s_1	D	$=$	288
f_1	C	$=$	256
m_1	B_1	$=$	240
r_1	A_1	$=$	216
d_1	G_1	$=$	192

EFFECT OF DIFFERENTIALS ON CHORDS.

MAJOR.

MINOR.

DIMINISHED.

MAJOR CHORDS.

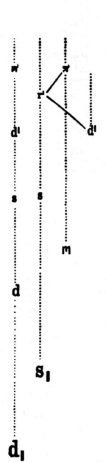

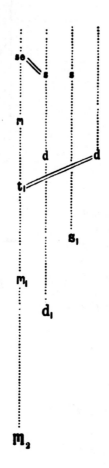
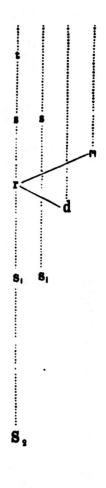

d¹	s	d	m
m	m	s₁	d
s₁	d	d₁	s₁
d₁	d₁	m₂	s₂

s	d	ᵗa₁	ᵗa₁
m	s₁	ᶠe₁	m₁
s₁	d₁	d₁	d₁
d₁	d₂	d₂	s₂
d₂		s₂	d₂

MINOR CHORDS.

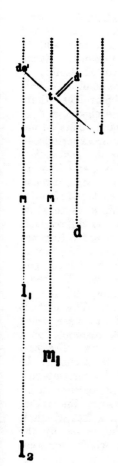
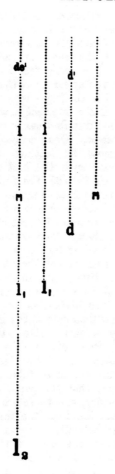
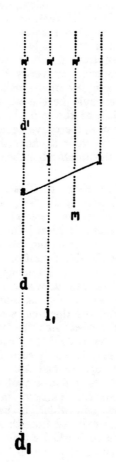
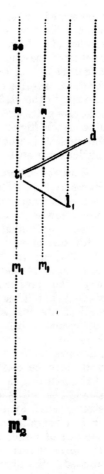

KEY E♭.	KEY E♭.	KEY C.	KEY A♭.
l	m	l	d
d	d	m	l₁
m₁	l₁	l₁	m₁
l₂	l₂	d₁	m₂

of calculation and convenience of comparison we take the vibrational numbers used before, and on p. 29 we employ the chord D to represent major chords, L to represent minor chords, and T diminished chords. The differentials are represented by smaller notes placed below the chord. To the left are seen the numbers, by means of which the vibration numbers are calculated, so that the student may verify the calculations. If we had taken any other number for d, the results of course would be the same; in fact, in the staff notation, at the right-hand side, the notes are represented, for convenience, at a much higher pitch; in order to hear the differentials it would be better to play the chords much higher still in pitch.

Roots of Chords.—In "How to Observe Harmony," p. 2 (see also pp. 44, 92, 93), the root of a chord is defined as the tone which stands lowest, when the chord is placed in its closest position of thirds one over the other. With this closely corresponds the definition of Dr. Stainer, in his "Theory of Harmony," paragraphs 34 and 39. This definition answers well the practical purposes of the harmony student, but it may be asked, are there not some statical reasons why this lowest tone of two superposed thirds should be called the root? How far this is the case may be easily seen by reference to the tables on pp. 25 and 29. It will there be seen that if we define a root as that tone in a chord whose partials best strengthen all the others, and which is best strengthened by the differentials of the others, such a definition would prove markedly true in the case of major chords, and partly true in that of minor chords, but would break down when applied to the diminished chords. It is perhaps in consequence of this that the diminished chord has been treated by most theorists as only a part of the dominant chord, the root being omitted. But a tree with the root omitted is a curious image, and as the diminished chord is really used independently of the dominant, and often used quite differently when thus apart from its imagined root, I think it better to give it a separate name, with this explanation.

Sonorousness of Chords.—I propose to put together the effects of Partials and Differentials in strengthening a chord, and to call the combined effect *Sonorousness.* Every musician must feel that, while the *chief* effect of chords arises from their relation to other chords and to the key—which *the mind* perceives—there is also a *physical* power in some chords, and in some distributions of chords, which others do not possess. Good composers know by experience—almost by instinct—both how to *approach* a chord with the best mental effect, and how to *strike* it with the fullest physical sonorousness. In the tables on pp. 30, 31, common types of major and minor chords are drawn out, so as to show the combined effect of partials and differentials on them. The chords under consideration are printed in bold type at lower part of the tables, the partials of their tones being above them, and the differentials in small type below. The tenor and bass are represented as sung, and not an octave higher, as usually printed. The partials that dissonate at the interval of a tone are joined by a single line; those that dissonate at a semitone distance by a double line. The bass notes are of the same pitch throughout. In studying these tables, it must be remembered, first, that the partials generally decrease in intensity, and therefore in importance, the farther they are from the fundamental, a fact which is symbolically represented in the tables by the decreasing size of the letters which represent them; second, that a semitone dissonance between partials is much harsher than a tone; third, that all the possible differentials are given in the table, but that few are audible, and even these are very faint; and fourth, that the tables only approximately express an average result— what particular partials are present in any tone, and with what intensity, varying with the instrument and with the performer.

CHAPTER IV.

BEATS, AND WHAT THEY TEACH.

Beats : their Nature and Disagreeableness.—The word "beat" is an unfortunate one in this connection; it leads the imagination to expect some vigorous action, whereas it is cessation of action which we have chiefly to think of. The phrase "Interference of Sound-impulses" would be better understood. This subject of interferences causing the phenomena usually called beats is easily explained. When a ball is struck by two equal blows, but in opposite directions, the result on the ball is—*no movement*. When two equal waves of water, the one in its upward and the other in its downward impulse, meet together, the result is—*no wave*. One force simply neutralizes the other. It is just so with the waves or vibrations or impulses of musical sound. When two equal sound-waves come together at the same moment, so that the condensation of one coincides with the rarefaction of the other, the result is—*no sound*. This will always be the case when two tones *very near to one another* in pitch are sounded together. At certain intervals of time the vibrations of the two will thus "interfere," causing a momentary silence or stop. This complete or partial stopping of the sound causes, when the sound itself returns, the effect of a thump or beat. This phenomenon of the interferences, followed by the recurrences of sound, is called the "beating" of one tone against another. Professor Tyndall puts this point very clearly as follows:—

"Each of the two forks now before you executes exactly 256 vibrations in a second. Sounded together, they are in unison. Loading one of them with a bit of wax, it vibrates a little more slowly than its neighbour. The wax, say, reduces the number of vibrations to 255 in a second, how must their waves affect each other? If they start at the same moment, condensation coinciding with condensation, and rarefaction with rarefaction, it is quite manifest that this state of things cannot continue. At the 128th vibration their phases are in complete opposition, one of them having gained half a vibration on the other. Here the one fork generates a condensation where the other generates a rarefaction; and the consequence is, that the two forks, at this particular point, completely neutralise each other. From this point onwards, however, the forks support each other more and more, until, at the end of a second, when the one has completed its 255th and the other its 256th vibration, condensation again coincides with condensation, and rarefaction with rarefaction, the full effect of both sounds being produced upon the ear. It is quite manifest, that under these circumstances we cannot have the continuous flow of perfect unison. We have, on the contrary, an alternate rising and falling of the sound. We obtain, in fact, the effect known to musicians by the name of *beats*, which, as here explained, are a result of interference."—"*On Sound*," *by Professor Tyndall, pp.* 366, 367.

It is easy to see why this beating of the tones is disagreeable to the ear. "Any uniform unbroken sensation," says Mr. A. J. Ellis, in agreement with Professor Helmholtz's views, "is pleasing and soothing. Any broken, jagged sensation, so to speak, is annoying. Compare the steady light of a lamp and the flickering of a gas jet when some water has got into the pipe. Compare riding in a well-hung gentleman's carriage and in a springless cart. When two sounds proceed uniformly and evenly together, either with no breaks, or with breaks so rapid that they cannot be distinguished separately, the ear is pleased and satisfied; the nerves have their desired stimulus. When two sounds *beat* perceptibly, the nerve is at one moment violently excited, at the next left unsatisfied by the sudden cessation of the exciting cause."

Their Varying Effects.—Any student can try the experiment of beats on a harmonium, or on a piano, or even with two stringed instruments, or two human voices. If he sounds two tones close together on the lowest part of his instrument, he will hear the "beating" very distinctly, and be able almost to count the interferences. The effect is something like that of closing the mouth while singing the open AA —thus, AA-OO-AA-OO, &c. The little step, or semitone, at this pitch sounds very disagreeable, and the full step, or whole tone, almost equally so. If he sounds two similar tones an octave higher, he will notice that the interferences are more frequent. They are more frequent because the vibrations of the two tones are themselves more frequent. If he tries the same experiment another, and yet another, octave higher, he will notice the interferences to be more and more frequent, and less and less disagreeable. When the beats reach the rate of about 120 or more per second, they cease to be unpleasant. Besides this difference in the effect of beats, when their producers are high or low in pitch, it may be noticed that when the beats are exceedingly slow the ear does not object to them; they produce only a "tremolo" effect. Three or four beats in a second may not trouble the ear, but thirty or forty do. *Beats are the source of all discord in music.*

D

The number of beats per second is the same as the difference between the vibrations of the beating tones. Thus C below the bass staff is produced by 64 vibrations, and the D next above by 72. They would therefore, when sounding together, give 8 beats a second, which, if the tones were loud, would be unpleasant. C-one (C_1) against D-one (D_1) would produce ($144 - 128 = 16$) 16 beats in a second. This would be quite disagreeable. The middle C beating against the D above it would produce ($288 - 256 = 32$) 32 beats in a second. This is the very acme of disagreeableness. One-C (C^1) against one-D (D^1) would produce ($576 - 512 = 64$) 64 beats in a second. This, though not so bad, is still within the range of marked dissonance. Two-C (C^2) against two-D (D^2) would produce ($1,152 - 1,024 = 128$) 128 beats in a second, and that is almost beyond the reach of disagreeableness.

As the number of *beats* in a second, resulting from two dissonant tones, is the same as the number of *vibrations* in a second of the differential which may result from any two tones, either dissonant or consonant, Dr. T. Young attributed the generation of differentials (or, as they were then called, third-tones) to the beats having become too rapid to be distinguished. "This theory is disproved," says Mr. Ellis, "first, by the existence of differential tones for intervals which do not beat; and, secondly, by the simultaneous presence of distinct beats and differential tones, as I have frequently heard on sounding high F and F♯ together on the concertina, when the beats form a distinct rattle, and the differential is a peculiar, penetrating, but very deep hum." In fact, a differential is a sound, or, at least, a perception of sound, whereas the beat is chiefly to be considered as the interruption of sound.

It should also be observed that the beats of a "false unison" (that is, one tone being a little sharper than the other) are very slow even in the higher octaves. They are scarcely noticed. They seem only to add to the sharp and piercing quality of the tone.

ART AND SCIENCE.—The Celeste stop on the harmonium is made upon this principle; it consists of a second set of reeds tuned a trifle sharper than their companions. The shrill effect of the uncultured voices of children in a choir is ascribable to the same cause; it is false unison.

Beating Distance.—While, then, tones a quarter of a komma apart do not beat painfully, on the other hand, tones which are a minor third apart do not beat at all. We are here speaking exclusively of simple tones—that is, of tones without partials. Beats commonly attain *their maximum of roughness* when the two producing tones are about a little step, or a semitone, apart. For a full step the roughness is decidedly less marked, and when the interval reaches a minor third, it is gone. For tones of medium pitch, therefore, "the beating distance" is two or three kommas less than a minor third. Among simple tones no two can be dissonant unless they stand within this "beating distance" of one another, or unless beats result from their differentials.

The Beats of Partials and Differentials.

—If, instead of using the harmonium, stringed instruments, or human voices for his experiments, the student employs only the dull, pure tones of two wide stopped organ-pipes, or two flutes, he will find that the beatings cease to be perceptible to the ear just before the interval between the two tones reaches a minor third, although on instruments like the harmonium, the violin, and the voice, the beatings are still heard when the two tones are at wider intervals. How is this? It is because these last-named instruments have in the quality of their tone those "partials" which have already been explained, and *they* may "beat" against one another, or against the principal tones, so as to cause discord. Thus even a major third, struck at a low pitch on the harmonium, will sound very coarse, not because the two tones themselves beat, but because the IVth partial of the lower tone beats against the IIIrd partial of the higher tone. But if a major third is struck on the higher part of the instrument, these little partials would be inaudible, and the dissonance gone. In the following diagrams, we see them rising higher and higher into the region of inaudibility. In the case first named (the major third being low down in the bass), the dissonance of partial III in one tone against partial IV in another would make ($512 - 480$) 32 beats in a second, and, the producing tones being loud, the partials would be correspondingly loud. In the second case, the beats of the same interval would beat ($1,024 - 960$) 64 times in a second, and being with their producers higher in pitch would be less loud. In the third case, the beats would be so frequent ($2,048 - 1,920$), 128 in a second, as to be indistinguishable, and the pitch so high that they would be inaudible. It should here be noticed that, when two tones beat, the audible parts between the silences are louder than either tone separately. Hence the beat-rattle is audible even when the tones that beat would be separately inaudible. This increases the importance of the beats from differential tones.

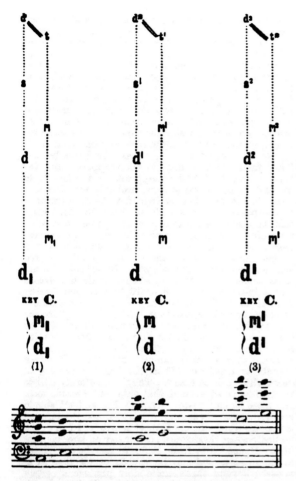

ART AND SCIENCE.—This explains why, in the early days of church music, when only bass and tenor voices were used, the major third was considered a dissonance. It also explains why close harmony for the left hand (bass) on the organ (which has in the dull pure quality of its pipes few partials) is quite allowable, and why the same harmony on the harmonium (which is full of partials) is very disagreeable. This also explains why dissonances can be more freely used high in pitch than low. A notable illustration of this is found in Mendelssohn's trio for female voices, "Lift thine eyes." The hearer feels that when listening to it he has reached the highest point of musical sweetness, but if he is a harmonist, he is surprised, on analysis, to find it full of dissonance. If he has the opportunity, let him try the same piece an octave lower, with male voices, and he will find that the dissonance is developed, and the sweetness almost disappears.

The following quotations will impress these doctrines on the mind:—

"Beats may be produced by all sonorous bodies. These two tall organ-pipes, for example, when sounded together, give powerful beats, being one of them slightly longer than the other. Here are two other pipes, which are now in perfect unison, being exactly of the same length. But it is only necessary to bring the finger near the embouchure of one of the pipes, to lower its rate of vibration, and produce loud and rapid beats. The placing of the hand over the open top of one of the pipes also lowers its rate of vibration, and produces beats, which follow each other with augmented rapidity as the top of the pipe is closed more and more. By a stronger blast the two first harmonics of the pipes are brought out. These higher notes also interfere, and you have these quicker beats."—*"On Sound," by Professor Tyndall, pp.* 367, 368.

"Thus, when one simple tone is being heard, we by no means *necessarily* obtain an increase of loudness by exciting a second simple tone of the same pitch. On the contrary, we *may* thus weaken the original sound, or even *extinguish it entirely*. When this occurs we have an instance of a phenomenon which goes by the name of *Interference*. That *two sounds should produce absolute silence* seems, at first sight, as absurd as that two loaves should be equivalent to no bread. This is, however, only because we are accustomed to think of sound as something possessing an external substantial existence; not as consisting merely in a *state of motion of certain air-particles*, and therefore liable, on the application of suitable forces, to be absolutely annihilated. A single tuning-fork presents an example of this very important phenomenon. Each prong sets up vibrations corresponding to a simple tone, and the two tones so produced are of the same pitch and intensity. If the fork, after being struck, is held between the finger and thumb, and made to revolve slowly about its own axis, four positions of the fork with reference to the ear will be found where the sound goes completely out. These positions are midway between the four in which the plane sides of the prongs are held straight before the ear. As the fork revolves from one of these positions of loud sound to that at right-angles to it, the sound gradually wanes, is extinguished in passing the interference-position, reappears very feebly immediately afterwards, and then continues to gain strength until the quarter of a revolution has been completed. The case of co-existent unisons has now been adequately examined: we proceed to enquire what happens when two simple tones *differing slightly in pitch* are simultaneously produced.

"Beats are also frequently to be heard in the sounds of church bells, or in those emitted by the telegraph wires when vibrating in a strong wind. In order to observe them in the last instance, it is best to press one ear against a telegraph-post and close the other; the beats then come out with remarkable distinctness. It should be noticed that, when we are dealing with two composite sounds, several sets of beats may be heard at the same time, if pairs of partial-tones are in relative positions suited to produce them. Thus, suppose that two clangs coexist, each of which contains the first six partial-tones of the series audibly developed. Since the second, third, &c., partial-tones of each clang make twice, three times, &c., as many vibrations per second as their respective fundamental tones, it follows that the differences between the vibration-numbers of successive pairs of partial-tones belonging to the two clangs will be twice, three times, &c., the difference between the vibration-numbers of the two fundamental tones. Accordingly, if the fundamental tones give rise to beats, we may hear, in addition to the series so accounted for, five other sets of beats, respectively twice, three, four, five, and six times as rapid as they."—"*Sound and Music,*" by *Sedley Taylor, pp.* 154, 155, *and* 161, 162.

"Hence, while every separate musical tone excites in the auditory nerve a uniform sustained sensation, two tones of different pitches mutually disturb one another, and split up into separable beats, which excite a feeling of discontinuity as disagreeable to the ear as similar intermittent but rapidly repeated sources of excitement are unpleasant to the other organs of sense; for example, flickering and glittering light to the eye, scratching with a brush to the skin. This roughness of tone is the essential character of dissonance. It is most unpleasant to the ear when the two tones differ by about a semitone, in which case, in the middle portions of the scale, from twenty to forty beats ensue in a second. When the difference is a whole tone, the roughness is less; and when it reaches a *third* it usually disappears, at least in the higher parts of the scale. The (minor or major) *third* may in consequence pass as a consonance. Even when the fundamental tones have such widely-different pitches that they cannot produce audible beats, the upper partial-tones may beat and make the tone rough. Thus, if two tones form a *fifth* (that is, one makes two vibrations in the same time as the other makes three), there is one upper partial in both tones which makes six vibrations in the same time. Now, if the ratio of the pitches of the fundamental tones is exactly as 2 to 3, the two upper partial-tones of six vibrations are precisely alike, and do not destroy the harmony of the fundamental tones. But if this ratio is only approximately as 2 to 3, then these two upper partials are not exactly alike, and hence will beat and roughen the tone. It is very easy to hear the beats of such imperfect fifths, because, as our pianos and organs are now tuned, all the fifths are impure, although the beats are very slow. By properly directed attention, or still better with the help of a properly-tuned resonator, it is easy to hear that it is the particular upper partials here spoken of that are beating together. The beats are necessarily weaker than those of the fundamental tones, because the beating upper partials are themselves weaker. Although we are not usually clearly conscious of these beating upper partials, the ear feels their effect as a want of uniformity or a roughness in the mass of tone, whereas a perfectly pure fifth, the pitches being precisely in the ratio of 2 to 3, continues to sound with perfect smoothness, without any alterations, reinforcements, diminutions, or roughnesses of tone. As has already been mentioned, the siren proves in the simplest manner that the most perfect consonance of the fifth precisely corresponds to this ratio between the pitches. We have now learned the reason of the roughness experienced when any deviation from that ratio has been produced."—"*Popular Scientific Lectures,*" by *Professor Helmholtz, pp.* 100, 101.

"When two simple tones which are not of the same pitch are sounded together, they will alternately reinforce and enfeeble each other's effect, producing a libration of sound, termed a *beat.* The number of these beats in one second will necessarily be the difference of the pitches of the two simple tones which may be termed the beat *number.* As for some time the two sets of vibrations concur, and for some time they are nearly opposite, the compound extent

will be for some time nearly the sum, and for some time nearly the difference of the two simple extents, and the *intensity* of the beat may be measured by the ratio of the greater intensity to the less. But the beat will not be audible unless the ratio of the greater to the smaller pitch is less than 6 : 5, according to Professor Helmholtz. This is a convenient limit to fix, but it is probably not quite exact. To try the experiment, I have had two sliding pipes, each stopped at the end, and having each a continuous range of an octave, connected to one mouthpiece. The tones are nearly simple; and when the ratio approaches to 6 : 5, or the interval of a minor third, the beats become faint, finally vanish, and do not reappear. But the exact moment of their disappearance is difficult to fix, and indeed seems to vary, probably with the condition of the ear. The ear appears to be most sensitive to the beats when the ratio is about 16 : 15. After this the beats again diminish in sharpness; and when the ratio is very near to unity, the ear is apt to overlook them altogether. The effect is almost that of a broken line of sound, as —— —— ——, the spaces representing the silences. Slow beats are not disagreeable; for example, when they do not exceed 3 or 4 in a second. At 8 or 10 they become harsh; from 15 to 40 they thoroughly destroy the continuity of tone, and are discordant. After 40 they become less annoying. Professor Helmholtz thinks 33 the beat number of maximum disagreeableness. As the beats become very rapid, from 60 to 80 or 100 in a second, they become almost insensible. Professor Helmholtz considers 132 as the limiting number of beats which can be heard. They are certainly still to be distinguished even at that rate, but become more and more like a scream. Though F$\sharp^3$ and G^3 should give 198 beats in a second if C = 264, and the interval is that for which the ear is most sensitive, I can detect no beats when these tones are played on two flageolet fifes. Hence beats from 10 to 70 may be considered as discordant, and as the source of all discord in music. Beyond these limits they produce a certain amount of harshness, but are not properly discordant."—"*Musical Chords,*" by *A. J. Ellis, from the Proceedings of the Royal Society,* 1864.

"According to Professor Helmholtz's observations and theory, beats can only be heard when the two systems of vibrations which produce them can set the *same* part of the internal ear in vibration with sufficient intensity to be perceptible. It also appears that if the interval of two tones is nearly a minor third, or greater than a minor third, the *same* part of the ear will not be put into sensible vibration by *both* tones. *Hence, if two tones differ by an interval of a minor third or more they will not beat perceptibly.* Tones differing by a greater interval are heard by different parts of the ear, and do not beat. As regards the mental effect produced by the consonance of two tones, it is agreeable when they are in unison. It is not at all disagreeable when they beat slowly, as 2 or 3 times in a second. When the beats increase to 12 or 16, the continuity of tone is utterly broken, and we have an unpleasant flutter or rattle. As the beats increase in rapidity they become very harsh; and at from 30 to 40 in a second they are unendurable, except for a short time. After this they are less annoying, and when very rapid they only approach to a slight scream. But the mental effect is much influenced by the intensity of the beats, and this depends greatly on the interval. The interval of a greater semitone, 16 : 15, is harsh at every pitch. The interval of a

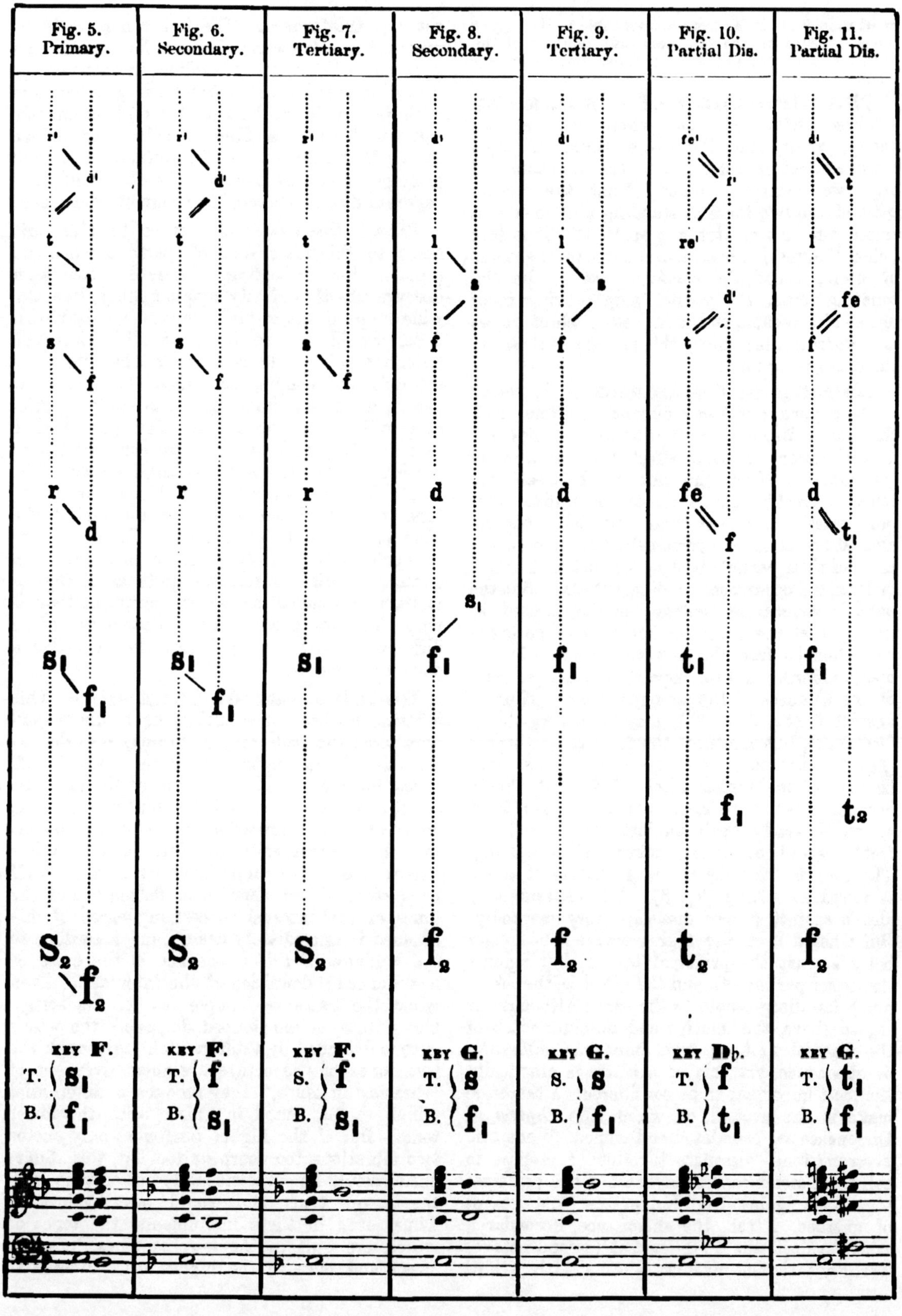
Fig. 5. Primary.
Fig. 6. Secondary.
Fig. 7. Tertiary.
Fig. 8. Secondary.
Fig. 9. Tertiary.
Fig. 10. Partial Dis.
Fig. 11. Partial Dis.
KEY F.
KEY F.
KEY F.
KEY G.
KEY G.
KEY D♭.
KEY G.

great tone, 9 : 8, is far from disagreeable in the higher tones, because of the faintness and rapidity of the beats ; it is harsher in the lower tones, but never very harsh.

The Differentia of Dissonance.

—These undoubted facts, which any ear can verify, show that there are three principal considerations in reference to the dissonance of any two "simple" tones. First, the *relative pitch* of the two tones as standing a little step, a small step, or a greater step apart, the little step being disagreeable even when high in the range of pitch ; second, the *absolute pitch* of the dissonating tones, the greater step proving itself not so disagreeable at the highest pitch of voices and instruments ; third, the *relative loudness* of the dissonating tones.

Degrees of Dissonance.

—Increased loudness always makes a dissonance strong, and, therefore, dissonating "principal" tones are quite different in their effect from dissonating "partials." When the interval between two tones is greater than a minor third, dissonance must arise from one of their "partials" beating against one of their "principals," or from two or more of their partials beating against each other, or from the occurrence of differentials. But the partials *decrease in loudness*, as they ascend, so greatly that the *tenth* has (on an average taken by Helmholtz from the best instruments—instruments differing in this respect) only *one per cent.* of the loudness of the principal tone. Thus, s_2 against f_2 (fig. 5, p. 37), may be a very strong dissonance, but s_2 against the f_1 an octave higher (fig. 6) must be a much feebler one, not only because of the higher pitch of f_1, but chiefly because it is not the s_2 but the second *partial* of s_2, which really beats against the f_1, and the feeble partial, of course, makes feebler beating. The case is the same if the s instead of the f is raised an octave (fig. 8). In the same way also d against r may dissonate very markedly. But when d is in the higher octave it no longer beats against the principal tone r, but against its second partial (r^1), and the effect is, therefore, much less disagreeable to the ear. Although, as shown above, the relative and absolute pitch of the dissonating tones form important *differentia* of dissonance, yet this of *loudness* is practically the most important to be considered. I therefore make it the ground on which the *Degrees* of Dissonance are calculated and named. When two *principal* tones dissonate together, I propose to call the dissonance Primary ; when one principal tone beats against the IInd partial (first octave) of another, I call the dissonance Secondary ; when against the IVth partial (second octave) Tertiary ; when against the VIIIth (third octave), Quaternary. The last can scarcely be regarded as a dissonance, because few instruments have the VIIIth partial audible in their klang. As a differential tone (though varying in loudness with the loudness of its producers) is commonly equal in force to a IInd or IIIrd partial, we shall call the dissonance of a differential with a principal tone, Secondary. Another kind and degree of dissonance should be distinctly described.

Partial Dissonance.—I propose to give this name to the dissonance of partials when no principal tone is beating. These dissonances on instruments of perfectly simple quality, like the wide stopped organ-pipe, or the gently-blown flute, would not be heard at all. Thus the tritone t_1 to f produces no beats when its tones are dull and simple, but when they are compound, as on most instruments, the IIIrd partial of t will beat against the IInd partial of f (see fig. 10), and as these are early and loud partials the roughness will be considerable. The result is the same when, f being the lower tone, the IIIrd partial of f beats against the IInd partial of t (see fig. 11). The dissonance of such early partials is much stronger than quaternary dissonance, and quite as strong as tertiary dissonance, unless one principal tone is very low in pitch. The dissonance of a differential with a partial may also be called a partial dissonance.

Definiteness of Interval.

— This doctrine of dissonance enables us to understand why some intervals are, in tuning, regarded as more definite and unchangeable than others. If, in the interval of an octave, one of the tones be a little too sharp or a little too flat, the ear detects the fault immediately. It is so, though to a less extent, with the fifth, and to a less extent still with a major or minor third. In all these cases, if you sharpen or flatten one of the tones of the interval, a certain degree of dissonance is immediately heard ; and according to the loudness of this dissonance is the more or less marked "definition of the interval." Even when the tones are simple (as on the softly-blown flute, or the stopped diapason), the octave is thus defended by a differential. Although the two tones of the octave are themselves out of "beating distance," they produce a differential which should sound in unison with the lower tone. But if the higher tone were only one or two vibrations too sharp or too flat, this differential would be proportionately out of tune with the lower tone, and would beat against it. Thus, even in these instruments, the tones of which are dull in the lower pitches, however sweet and pure in the higher, the differential

DEFINITENESS OF INTERVALS.

Octave	Fifth.	Fourth.	Major Third.	Minor Third.	Major Sixth.	Minor Sixth.
KEY C.	KEY C.	KEY C.	KEY C.	KEY E♭.	KEY C.	KEY A♭.
d / d,	s, / d,	f, / d,	m, / d,	d, / l₂	l, / d,	d, / m₂
d,	d₂ (d,)	f₃	f₅	f₄	f₂	s₃

helps to mark out the octave to the ear, and to guard its just intonation by dissonance on either side. In the case of the fifth, with these simple-toned instruments, the boundary is still guarded, though only by means of secondary differentials, which being of less power, cause a less painful roughness when the interval is made untrue; and the interval of a fourth is similarly defended, but not by so strong a guard.

"With simple tones, all intervals from the minor third nearly up to the fifth, and from a little above the fifth up to the major seventh, ought to sound equally smooth. This conclusion is probably very inconsistent with the views of musical theorists, who are apt to regard concord and discord as entirely independent of quality, but it is strictly borne out by experiment. The intervals lying between the minor and major thirds, and between the minor and major sixths, though sounding somewhat *strange*, are entirely free from roughness, and, therefore, cannot be described as dissonant. Helmholtz advises such of his readers as have access to an organ to try the effect of playing alternately the smoothest concords and the most extreme discords which the musical scale contains, on stops yielding only simple tones, such, *e.g.*, as the flute, or stopped diapason. The vivid contrasts which such a proceeding calls out on instruments of bright *timbre*, like the pianoforte and harmonium, or the more brilliant stops of the organ, such as principal, hautbois, trumpet, &c., are here blurred and effaced, and everything sounds dull and inanimate, in consequence. Nothing can show more decisively than such an experiment that the presence of overtones confers on music its most characteristic charms."—"*Sound and Music,*" *by Sedley Taylor,* p. 185.

When, as in most instruments, partials as well as differentials come into play, the definiteness of intervals becomes much more marked.

It may be seen from the diagram on p. 39 that *the octave* is guarded at one extremity by a IInd partial, and at the other by a first differential. If, the lower tone having 144 vibrations per second, the upper one were tuned to 290 instead of 288 (that is, two vibrations per second too sharp), the differential 146 (290 — 144) would produce, with the lower tone, two (146 — 144) beats per second, and the IInd partial of lower tone, 288 (144 × 2), would give the same number of beats (290 — 288) with the higher one. If, on the other hand, the upper tone were tuned too flat, say by two vibrations per second, that is, 286 instead of 288, the differential would be 142 (286 — 144), which would give two beats per second (144 — 142) with the lower tone, and the IInd partial of the lower tone, 288 (144 × 2), would beat at same rate with the flat octave, 286. Similar consequences would arise if the interval were sharpened or flattened by only one vibration a second instead of two. Besides this, the less loud, but quite *sufficiently* loud, early partials (II of the higher tone, and IV of the lower), would also be put out of their

strengthening unison, and made to dissonate. Thus it is plain that the octave cannot be put out of tune without two powerful guardians ringing the alarum bell, and a couple of weaker voices also crying out their warning.

The just intonation of *the fifth* is also strongly guarded. Its loudest defence is in the unison of a IInd with a IIIrd partial. These are quite loud enough to make a perceptible roughness when this interval is flattened, as it generally is upon the piano. The first differential is an octave below the lower tone, and quite out of beating distance with either of the principals. But the secondary differential, made by this last, taken with the higher of the primaries, and marked on the diagram by brackets, would beat with the lower primary, if the interval were put out of tune. There are, therefore, two guardians of the fifth, but they are not nearly so powerful as those of the octave. It may also be noticed that the fifth has a partial dissonance of a IIIrd against a IVth, but both partials being high and distant, and their interval being a greater step, and not a little step, the effect of this dissonance is only to give a little tartness to the interval.

ART AND SCIENCE.—Tuners have long ago found out that they must tune their octaves perfectly, that the octave is the most definite of all intervals, and will not bear to be tampered with. They have also, though compelled by the necessities of their "temperament" to flatten the fifths, formed the habit of first tuning that interval perfect, and then flattening it a little. They find this the easiest way to reach their object, because a perfect fifth is so well defined to the ear. Aiming at a flat fifth would be aiming nowhere. The thirds, as we shall afterwards see, make much less complaint than the fifth when they are put out of tune, and, therefore, tuners of tempered instruments take much greater liberties with them. They are commonly much too sharp.

This analysis will also illustrate the importance of the fifth in the history and the art of music. It will easily be understood how, in the first rudimentary attempts at harmony (since thirds had been forbidden), bare fifths, though of no great loudness, were allowed to float, like partials, above a strongly-sustained melody; how afterwards, when more parts were introduced, and those parts made co-equal in loudness, the fifths were felt to stand out in too hard and definite a manner, and were forbidden; how, when closes at the end of a line of harmony came into use, the chord of the fifth going to that of the key-tone was felt to be so full of the key, so decisive, that that chord was called the dominant; and how when, much later on, the skilful transition from one key to another began to be practised, the key of the fifth was chiefly used, because the fifth stands out in so definite a relation to the key-tone. It will also be understood how the octave tends to repetition rather than change, and although a more definite interval than the fifth, does not allow itself to be repeated among other harmonies without causing confusion of parts. Consecutive fifths make the parts stand out hard and distinct; consecutive octaves make the parts, as such, disappear. See "How to Observe," pp. 13, 15; and "Construction Exercises," pp. 17, and 25-27.

The fourth is the inversion of the fifth, but it is far more weakly defended by its differentials. Exactly where the fifth is strong in its partials, the fourth has a dissonance; and where the fifth has a distant and insignificant dissonance, the fourth has a distant and insignificant consonance. It is essential to the interval that the IInd and IIIrd partials should beat, and the perfect unison or otherwise of the IIIrd and IVth partials will not be so much noticed, while the much louder IInd and IIIrd are beating beneath them. It should be noticed that this interval is as much a "partial dissonance" as the tritone noticed above. We do not commonly name it so because there is this distinction between the so-called "perfect fourth" and the tritone, that in the tritone the dissonance is the harsh one of a little step, while in the fourth it is the mild one of a greater step.

ART AND SCIENCE.—Even before these revelations of science, the instincts of art had discovered the inferiority of this interval, and it is surprising that some musicians should go on classing it among the *perfect* intervals. I had often wondered why my best teacher in harmony so constantly told me to avoid making a fourth between the bass and the part above it, unless accompanied by melodic progressions which would apologise even for a dissonance. I now see the reason. This "partial dissonance," though weak in the higher pitches, becomes louder and more important when low in the range of pitch. I also see why, in the commonest case of a fourth taken from the bass (that is, the third last chord of a tonic cadence, D*c*), the higher tone d is so commonly prepared and resolved like a dissonance. (See "How to Observe," p. 9.) When d is really dissonating against r in such early partials (which, being low in pitch, are more important), it is quite as well that the d should be prepared and resolved. It is interesting to notice that when the d is once prepared and resolved, it is quite easy to let the r come out as a principal tone instead of a partial; and this is frequently done when *S is used in this place instead of D*c*.

If the *major third*, with its inversion the minor sixth, and the minor third, with its inversion the major sixth, are studied on the diagram, they will be found to agree with the fourth in this, that they all have partial dissonances, but only the sixths have beating partials of equal loudness with those of the fourth. The major third and its inversion have a stronger dissonance than the minor third and its inversion. Both the thirds have their partial dissonance made louder by inversion. The major third has a worse *sort* of partial dissonance than the minor third, and the fourth has a much louder partial dissonance than either of them.

ART AND SCIENCE.—It is remarkable how the love of theory in the human mind has sometimes hindered the development of Art. The Greek philosophers reckoned thirds to be dissonances, because the relation of the lengths of string which produced them was not so simple as that of octaves, fifths, and fourths. The Greeks almost worshipped simplicity of ratio, and, therefore, men of science and cultivation did not use the thirds, and their inversions, the sixths, for consonance. Thus, the power of science prevailed in Greece, and it was not till the Middle Ages that thirds, and, later on, sixths, were admitted in Europe to be consonances. And still, to distinguish them from octaves, fifths, and fourths, they were called *imperfect* consonances. When harmony began to be used, it was a long time before thirds were allowed in the last chord of a cadence, and then only *major* thirds were permitted there. It was not until comparatively recent times that the minor third was used in this place.

Dissonating Intervals Wider than a Second.—It has already been shown that the only dissonating interval among simple principal tones is the second—that is, either the step (sometimes called a tone), or the little step (called a semitone). It has also been shown that the second is still dissonant when augmented by one, two, or even three octaves (becoming a ninth, a sixteenth, and a twenty-third), in consequence of one of the partials of its lower tone beating against the higher. The same is true when the second is inverted, so as to become a seventh, and when that seventh is augmented by octaves (so as to become a fourteenth and a twenty-first), and for the same reason. But on the stopped diapason and flute (without partials), after the second there is only one interval—the sharp seventh—which is dissonant; and it is made so by a differential. Let us take the diagram on page 29, and calculate the differential of the sharp seventh—d' to t'. It will be 1,080 — 576 = 504, which we see to be only a trifle flatter than **ta**—that is, one step below the lower principal, and quite able to beat against it. But if we take the flat seventh (**s**$_1$ to **f**), or the ninth (**d** to **r'**), or any of the intervals just named, and calculate their differential tones, we shall find that none of them come within beating distance of either of the principals. The only two that approach dissonance are the flat twenty-first and the sharp twenty-first, which are just out of beating distance. (Thus, *flat seventh* = **f'**, 768 — **s**, 432 = 336, which is an acute **r**, nearly a fourth below the **s**. *Ninth* = **r'**, 648 — **d**, 288 = 360, which is **m**, a major third above **d**, and a flat seventh below **r'**. *Flat twenty-first* = **f'**, 768 — **s**$_2$, 108 = 660, which is only a slightly acute **r**, not two kommas less than a minor third, and so out of beating distance. *Sharp twenty-first* = **t'**, 1,080—**d**$_1$, 144 = 936, which is a slightly acute **la**, just out of beating distance, like the last.) As, however, nearly all instruments possess the partials, more or less developed, this deficiency of dissonating power in simple tones need not trouble us.

ART AND SCIENCE.—If the student has access to an organ, let him play the following example of primary, secondary, and tertiary dissonance—first, on the stopped diapason; second, on the open diapason; and third, on the open diapason with principal. Let him keep his attention on the dissonance itself, and the loudness of its beats in each case. When he uses the open diapason, he will have a second partial to create the secondary dissonance. When he employs the principal or octave stop, that secondary dissonance becomes primary. And, if he employs the stop called the fifteenth, even a tertiary dissonance becomes primary. This should be well understood by organists when playing music which abounds in dissonances.

PRIMARY.   SECONDARY.   TERTIARY.

KEY **C.**

Dissonance in Chords.—Thus far we have studied the dissonance of two tones one against another, without any regard to the chord in which they may appear. We have seen that, for practical purposes, dissonance may be defined as the beating of one tone against that which stands next to it in the scale—that is, the

"beating of seconds;" that the seconds of a little step—a semitone—are more severe in their effect; that dissonances are most noticed in the lower and middle parts of the musical scale, and in any part of the scale when the producing tones are most loud; that the dissonance is retained in nearly all instruments when the second is inverted and becomes a seventh, or is enlarged and becomes a ninth, and so on, though in less and less degree of force; and that the intervals of the diminished fifth, the tritone, and the fourth produce dissonance of early partials which are very strong. Let it be noticed that these are facts, not theories—simple, proved facts, which we are bound to recognise, and not dogmatic statements. Now, when we are beginning to apply these facts to dissonance *within a chord*, we are met with a difficulty, one created by the commonly accepted theories. Shall we regard the dissonance simply *as an intruder* into a well-known consonant chord, or shall we imagine that we have got hold of a new chord altogether—a chord of a new structure—for which a new origin must be found, and new explanations given? If there were any real facts showing a new origin to such chords, and suggesting a new structure, we should feel bound to throw away all this information, and follow the newly-discovered facts; but this is not the case. The main structure of such chords is found to consist of our old friends the thirds, fifths, and octaves, with their strengthening partials, and their confirming differentials. And one of the tones forming the dissonance is so obviously foreign to the chord, that it is commonly heard to make its entry, and always its exit, in a melodic form of its own—a melodic phrase not interfering with the harmonic progression, and separable from it. If, on the other hand, we adopt the mode of looking at the subject which the discoveries of Helmholtz most naturally suggest, we shall simply have to ask ourselves the question, What new phenomena does this intruder bring into the chord along with its dissonance? We shall also be emancipated from the old theories (not facts and observations) on which the doctrine of discords has commonly been built. We shall no longer bewilder our minds with the various systems of *unheard*, though ingeniously imagined, Roots. Nor shall we follow any further the *ignus fatuus* of the so-called "Harmonic Chord" and "Chord of Nature." A chord is a combination of "principal" and co-equal sounds. But the harmonic "partials" are only dependent and subordinate *parts* of an original sound, and they die away in loudness so rapidly that even the Vth of them has only four per cent. of the loudness of a real tone, and when we come to the VIIth, VIIIth, IXth, and Xth, on which the discord theories are founded, we find only one or two per cent. of the original intensity. If these partials had been meant for a model of chords and discords, they would certainly have been made *louder*. Moreover, some of these high partials, on which theorists have so much relied, are actually out of tune with *the scale of real tones*, although they are perfectly proportioned as quality-giving tones of some one principal tone. Nor shall we try to square our practice with the theories which make the roots of chords depend on their differentials. The theory-lovers seem to forget that differentials are (like the partials) not roots, but *products* of tones. They have no existence of their own, and to ascribe to them the creative power of roots is surely illogical. It would be equally wise to maintain that the ivy and the mistletoe tell us the root of the oak. Of the older theories of piling up thirds one above the other until we get chords containing all the notes of the scale, Richter, in his "Manual of Harmony," Chap. IX, says, "They are a relic of the old so-called thorough-bass doctrine, which was fond of conceiving of every combination of notes, *however accidental it might be*, as an *especial chord*, the treatment of which was to be taught. Thereby the whole doctrine of harmony was made more difficult and diffuse." He also speaks of the "Strange and frightful form of the chords of the eleventh and thirteenth, which in four-voiced music cannot be used through the *necessary* omission of many of the notes," and recommends that these discords should be treated as *Incidental Intrusions* into a chord, rather than as making a separate chord of their own. Dr. Stainer speaks of the Fundamental Theory thus :—

"It will probably have been noticed that suspensions have not had the important position assigned to them in this work which they usually hold in treatises on harmony, by being separated from the tonic or dominant series to which they belong, and explained under various heads. Formerly, discords were divided into two great classes, fundamental discords and discords of suspension. This system arose from two causes : first, because authors had come to an erroneous conclusion that certain discords, being the intervals produced by a mathematical ratio, were specially entitled to be called fundamental ; secondly, because it was found that tonic discords (discords of the tonic series) were generally prepared, and it was hence supposed that they never could or would be used without preparation. Whereas, in fact, as far as mathematical ratios are concerned, both tonic and dominant discords are of equal importance, and the preparation of tonic discords is not a legal necessity, but a mere habit now almost extinct. Finding, therefore, that dominant series of discords were often used without preparation, and the tonic series nearly always with preparation, some authors constructed the following definition of a fundamental discord :—'A discord that can be used without preparation.' Of course, numerous instances of unprepared tonic discords were quoted by the unconvinced, to prove the badness of the definition, but all arguments, founded though they were on facts, were crushed by the remark that such progressions could only be written *by licence*. The attempts made in some works to distinguish between 'fundamental discords' and 'discords' which ought to be of 'suspension,' but which *by licence* are 'unsuspended,' are more amusing than profitable. Again, some have drawn a distinction between a suspension and retardation, the former being a prepared discord resolved downwards, the latter a prepared discord resolved upwards.

"When, after long habituation to the musical effect of a particular suspension, the ear has become ready to adopt the discord *without* preparation, such a chord must not be called a suspension *unsuspended by licence*, but must be treated as a legitimate combination of sounds."—"*A Theory of Harmony*," *by Dr. Stainer, 3rd ed., pp.* 93, 94, *and* 96, 97.

The following quotations from Dr. Marx's great work on "Composition," and Mr. G. F. Graham's article in "Encyclopædia Britannica," will interest the student :—

"It was customary to distinguish between *consonant* and *dissonant* intervals, and between *concords* and *discords*, as they were termed. The octave, major fifth and fourth, major and minor thirds and sixths, were termed consonant intervals ; the rest were called dissonant intervals. Amongst the chords, the major and minor triads, with their inversions, were called *concords*, and the others *discords*. And now it was laid down as a general rule, that every dissonant interval— that is, every seventh or ninth in a chord of the seventh or ninth—must be *prepared*. The preparation consisted in this, that the dissonant interval had appeared in the preceding chord as a consonant interval ; thus, the seventh in the chord G, B, D, F, as the octave in F, A, C, or the third in D, F, A. Without entering into a minute critical examination of this rule, we will enquire into its reason, and thence examine how far it is true. The reason was, that those so-called discords were felt to be the most attractive, and therefore, in some sense, the most striking intervals of their chords, and that these chords themselves were less capable of giving satisfaction than the major triad and its inversions. Now the impression of such striking sounds is certainly softened, when the latter have already appeared in a more quiet combination ; or, at least, when the chords which contain such sounds are well connected with the preceding harmony ; and we have everywhere endeavoured to show that there is more unity and a smoother flow of modulation when the harmonies are well combined. But we know that it is by no means suited to the purpose of music to select and employ only the mildest combinations of sounds, that it has to represent ideas and feelings of every shade and description, and therefore requires all kinds of means, the harshest and most startling, as well as the mildest and most common. Thus, it may sometimes be necessary to soften or prepare the so-called dissonances ; while at other times it may answer our purpose best to introduce them suddenly, and without any preparation. Here, then, every *general* rule, excepting the universal law to do always what is proper, is an error. Accordingly, we find that the old rule alluded to has.

in point of fact, been constantly contradicted by all composers, while the more intelligent theorists of the old school have narrowed it more and more by exceptions or licenses. It was found that a discord need not always be prepared, but that it was often sufficient if only the root, or any other interval of the dissonant chord, had previously appeared ; or, which amounts to the same, if there were any combination between the harmonics. It was farther discovered that a softening preparation was not equally necessary to all dissonant chords ; and the dominant chord, and the chord of the diminished seventh in particular, were allowed to make their entry unprepared. Here and elsewhere, an excuse, or rather a subterfuge, was sometimes resorted to, which, though it is based upon a mere superficial view of the nature of art, and has been often enough refuted, is again occasionally brought forward, with the obvious intention of re-establishing its validity. Theorists make a distinction between a *free* and a *strict style* of composition ; in the latter, which is designed principally for church music, *all* rules—i.e., those respecting the preparation of dissonances—are to be strictly observed ; while, in the free style, a considerable relaxation of the rigour of the law is held to be allowable ; as if those rules, were they at all right and proper, ought not to hold good under any other species of composition, as well as in church music, and as if church music did not require *all* available means in order to do justice to the immense task imposed upon it, just as well as any other branch of composition ! However, this is not the place to enter upon a lengthened argument on the question ; all we have at present to aim at, is to acquire an unrestrained command over every form and combination presented to us.

"To us these rules and exceptions are no longer necessary. We know how to combine our harmonies where it is required ; but if it accord with the idea of our composition, we shall not hesitate to introduce *any* chord or interval without a preparation. If, nevertheless, at any time a question should arise whether a certain chord does not require to be treated more carefully than the rest, the development of our chord itself will point out to us where such might be the case, for we have always started from the most simple and nearest combinations, and only gradually proceeded to the more distant ones. We know that, in the order of succession, the two triads, with their inversions, come first, next the dominant chord with its inversions, then the diminished triad ; after this, the two chords of the ninth, with their derivative chords of the seventh and inversions ; and, lastly, the modified chords of the seventh and ninth : and that the chords become less satisfactory and more startling at every step of our progress in this development. If, therefore, a particularly mild and smooth modulation be required, we shall naturally be careful to introduce the more remote harmonies in the most gentle manner possible ; but, where it is necessary, we shall not lack the courage to treat even the most remote and harsh chords with boldness and freedom." —" *School of Composition*," by Dr. A. B. Marx, pp. 452, 453.

"With regard to *passing* notes, notes of *grace*, *anticipations*, *substitutions*, *altered*, or *chromatic* notes, and so on, the truth seems to be, that theorists have always found them inexplicable upon their favourite principle of the fundamental bass ; and that, not knowing how to account for them rationally upon that principle, they have been obliged to treat all such sounds that occur in melody and in harmony as sounds that have no foundation in the *real* structure of the composition ; and to assign to them, by way of salvo, any names that might pass current in an obscure and erroneous terminology. But if theorists *will* adhere to the received systems of fundamental basses, they ought to be able to apply these systems to *all* the phenomena of melody and harmony. This is not the case ; for it is utterly impossible to refer *all* the combinations of modern (or even of ancient) harmony, to the received systems of fundamental basses. Every candid and intelligent musician will admit this to be true. Among all the systems of fundamental basses, Serre's theory (formerly alluded to) seems the most plausible, although still very imperfect. He assigns to a chord, one, or two, or three fundamentals, which are to correspond to the diatonic or chromatic nature of the sounds and intervals of the chord. But other theorists have their fundamental *suppositions* and *substitutions ;* their *after* notes : their *changing* notes ; their *passing* notes ; their *altered* notes : their *appoggiature ;* their *suspensions ;* their *anticipations ;* and, in short, such a chaos of hypothetically un-essential and *unreal* things, that it is no wonder if the study of harmony is looked upon with horror and despair by all students who are trained in the ordinary schools of composition.

"It is wrong to say that the *ear* recognises or suggests what are called *suppositions* and *substitutions* in fundamental basses ; sounds that are not heard, but are ascribed, by erroneous theory, to such and such chords. The ear hears none of these imaginary and hypothetical things. Were it otherwise, and to carry this hypothesis to the *reductio ad absurdum*, the ear ought to hear all the chords that can possibly be applied to the accompaniment of any given melody. In fact, if two voices, or two instruments, perform a duet, for example, the lower part is felt to be the bass for the time being ; and there is no other part felt, or *supposed*, or *substituted*, by the ear. The imagination may suggest an additional part below the lower part, or above the higher part, or intermediate ; but this has nothing to do with the theory of the fundamental bass. If another lower part is added to this same duet, then the ear feels *that* part to be the bass ; and supposing a fourth or a fifth part, and so on, added still lower, then such added part becomes the bass, in so far as the ear is concerned. If the lowest part is overpowered by the upper ones, then the ear pays no attention to it, but to the predominant upper or middle part or parts. Experiment will prove this. If a melody is performed by a single voice or instrument, or by a great number of voices or instruments in unison or in octaves, does the ear supply a fundamental bass, or any bass at all? Surely not. As to what are called *passing* notes, chromatically *altered* notes, *suspensions*, *anticipations*, and so on, in melody or harmony ; all these *sounds* are just as *real* as any other sounds that are heard in the course of the melody or of the harmony ; and if theorists adhere to the received fundamental bass system, then *every* sound that is heard in a melody, or in any part of a harmony, must have its own fundamental bass, just as much as *any other* sound that exists in the melody or the harmony. This inference is inevitable from rational logic."—" *Theory and Practice of Musical Composition*," by G. F. Graham, Esq., pp. 29, 30.

The history of theories in harmony is well given by Fetis :—

"The history of harmony is one of the most interesting parts of the general history of music. Not only is it composed of an uninterrupted succession of discoveries in the collective properties of sound—discoveries which owe their origin to the desire of novelty, to the boldness of some musicians, to the improvement of instrumental music, and, without doubt, also to chance—but there is a portion of this history which is not unworthy of interest; it is that of the efforts which have been made to combine together, in a complete and rational system, all the scattered facts presented by practice to the greedy curiosity of theorists. And it is to be remarked that the history of the theory is necessarily dependent upon that of the practice; for, as fast as the genius of composers hazarded new combinations, it became more difficult to combine them in a general system, and to discover their origin. The numerous modifications which the chords underwent so much changed the character of their primitive forms, that we ought not to be astonished if many errors have been committed in their classification.

"Until about the end of the sixteenth century, none but consonant chords and some prolongations, which produced prepared dissonances, were in use. With such elements, the harmonic forms were so limited that no one thought of uniting them into an organised science, or even imagined that there could be any systematic connection between the chords then in vogue. The intervals were considered two by two, and the art of employing them according to certain rules constituted the whole learning of the schools. Towards the year 1590, a Venetian, named Claude Monteverde, for the first time, made use of natural dissonant chords and of substitutions; from that time the dominion of harmony was greatly extended, and the science which resulted from it became an object of attention to masters in the art. It was about fifteen years after the happy attempts of Monteverde, that Viadana and some Germans, who contest the invention with him, thought of representing harmony by figures, and for that purpose were obliged to consider each of the chords by itself. The name of *chord* was then introduced into the vocabulary of music, and harmony, or *continued bass*, as it was called, became a branch of the science of music. For nearly a century things remained in this state, though numerous elementary works were published during that interval, with a view to clear away the difficulties of this new science.

"An experiment in physics, pointed out by a monk, named Father Mercenne, in 1636, in a large book, filled with trifles more curious than useful, under the title of *Universal Harmony*—an experiment repeated by the celebrated mathematician Wallis, and analysed by Sauveur, of the Academy of Sciences—afterwards suggested to Rameau, a skilful French musician, the origin of a system of harmony, in which all the chords were reduced to a single principle. In this experiment, it had been remarked that, when a string was made to vibrate, there were heard, beside the principal sound, produced by the entire length of the string, two other feebler sounds, one of which was the twelfth, and the other the seventeenth, of the first—that is to say, the octave of the fifth, and the double octave of the third—which produced the sensation of the *perfect major chord*. Rameau, availing himself of this experiment, made it the basis of a system, the structure of which he explained in a *Treatise on Harmony*, which he published in 1722.

This system, known under the name of *System of Fundamental Bass*, had a prodigious currency in France, not only among musicians, but among people in general. From the moment that Rameau had adopted the idea of making certain physical phenomena the source of all harmony, he was obliged to have recourse to forced inferences; for all harmony is not included in the perfect major chord. The perfect minor chord was indispensable; and he imagined some sort of tremulous motion of the sonorous body, which, according to his idea, produced this chord to an attentive ear, but in a manner less distinct than the perfect major chord. By means of this arrangement, he had only to add to, or take away from, the sounds of the superior or inferior third of these two perfect chords, in order to find a great part of the chords then in use; and, in this way, he obtained a complete system, in which all the chords were connected together. Though this system rested on a very frail basis, it had the advantage of being the first to exhibit something like order in the phenomena of harmony. Rameau had, too, the merit of being the first to perceive the mechanism of the inversion of chords, and therefore deserves a place among the founders of the science of harmony.

"By this factitious production of chords, he destroyed the relations of succession, which are derived from their tones, and was obliged to substitute, for the laws of those relations, the rules of a fundamental bass, which he formed of the low sounds of the primitive chords—fanciful rules, which could only have a forced application in practice.

"At the time when Rameau produced his system in France, Tartini, a celebrated Italian violinist. proposed another, which was also founded upon an experiment of vibration. By this experiment, two high sounds, vibrating in thirds, produced another low sound, which was also the third of the lower one of the two, which again produced the perfect chord. Upon this, Tartini had established an obscure theory, which Rousseau, though he did not understand it, preferred to that of Rameau, but which never had any success. Systems of harmony had become a sort of fashion. Everybody had one of his own, and found somebody to puff it. In France, there appeared, almost at the same time, those of Ballière, of Jamard, of the Abbé Roussier, and many others, which are now deservedly forgotten.

"Marpurg had attempted to introduce the system of Rameau into Germany, but without success. Kirnberger, a celebrated composer and a profound theorist, had just discovered the theory of prolongations, which explains, in a satisfactory and natural manner, some harmonies, of which no other theory can give the law. At a later period, Catel reproduced in France this same theory, in a simpler and clearer manner, in the *Treatise on Harmony* which he composed for the Conservatory of Music; and, if I may be permitted to speak of my own labours, I will say that I have completed this same theory by an explanation of the mechanism of substitution, and of the combination of this same *substitution* with prolongations and *alterations*."—"*The Music-Lover's Handbook,*" *pp. 21-25, an abridgment and translation of "La Musique mise à la portée de tout le monde," by François Joseph Fétis.*

Of the modern theories of discords, I like those best (though not for teaching purposes) that give the composer the greatest liberty. This is exactly the best thing for the artist; but it does not help the learner. For the artist, liberty; for the learner, *guidance*. Let the artist boldly produce whatever he finds to be beautiful and expressive, and then let the scientist find out the reason, and build upon it that theory which will best help the learner to remember, to think, and to work. Dr. Stainer's description of a dissonance corresponds very nearly to our own :—

"If any interval smaller than a third be heard, it requires to be adjusted to a third before the ear is satisfied. For instance, if C and D be struck on a pianoforte or harmonium, we must either move the C to B, making a third between B and D, or move the D to E, making a third between C and E. This unsatisfactory effect of an interval smaller than a third is termed 'discordant;' and the whole chord which contains it, a 'Discord.' The removal of the unsatisfactory effect by altering the chord so as to leave the ear satisfied, is termed a 'Resolution.'—"*A Theory of Harmony*," by Dr. Stainer, p. 16.

Even before the discoveries of Professor Helmholtz were made known, I had adopted from Gersbach the simpler mode of analysing discords, and by means of the first edition of "How to Observe Harmony" had proved to a large number of students that the discords used by classical writers *can* be thus analysed. Yet although in this, as in many other cases, practice had gone before philosophy, it was comparative groping in darkness and doubt. Now the light has come, we shall go forward with bolder and surer steps. In "How to Observe Harmony" (p. 90), I have developed this theory of discords at some length, and have proposed a new classification of them, which is founded more on Æsthetic than on Statical principles; and in the "Construction Exercises," p. 133, I have treated the subject much more fully, analysing every discord which is to be found in the Text Book and in the Historical Specimens, from Bach to Beethoven. We have here only to deal with the statics of the subject, although we are closely bordering on the realms of taste and feeling. Helmholtz says :—

"Æsthetics endeavour to find the principle of artistic beauty in its unconscious conformity to law. To-day I have endeavoured to lay bare the hidden law, on which depends the agreeableness of consonant combinations. It is in the truest sense of the word unconsciously obeyed, so far as it depends on the upper partial tones, which, though felt by the nerves, are not usually consciously present to the mind. Their compatibility or incompatibility, however, is felt, without the hearer knowing the cause of the feeling he experiences. These phenomena of agreeableness of tone, as determined solely by the senses, are of course merely the first steps towards the beautiful in music. For the attainment of that higher beauty which appeals to the intellect, harmony and dysharmony are only means, although essential and powerful means. In dysharmony the auditory nerve feels hurt by the beats of incompatible tones. It longs for the pure efflux of the tones into harmony. It hastens towards that harmony for satisfaction and rest. Thus both harmony and dysharmony alternately urge and moderate the flow of tones, while the mind sees in their immaterial motion an image of its own perpetually streaming thoughts and moods."— "*Popular Scientific Lectures*," by *Professor Helmholtz, p.* 105.

Melodic Apologies for Dissonance.

—Closely connected with this idea of flow of feeling in music, and the power of dissonance to incite and move onward the musical strain, is that melodic entry and exit of a dissonance, which is called its preparation and resolution. Although the subject belongs to the æsthetics rather than to the statics of music, it is necessary for the student to understand it before proceeding further. It is universally acknowledged that no dissonance must be left to stand alone in a chord; it must be led (like a blind man through a narrow passage) in or out, or both, either by a tone of its own pitch, or by its next neighbours above or below. The commonest melodic phrase which thus supports and excuses the intruder, is that which was the earliest form of discord. The dissonance is introduced (or prepared) by a tone on its own level, and received out of discord (or resolved) by a tone which stands waiting a step, or a little step, below it. The following example shows the melodic phrase, supposing the notes with stars above them to be the intruders :—

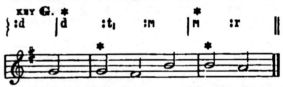

Professor Helmholtz says, "The pitch of dissonance is best secured (made safest) by its being heard before as a consonance. Such a dissonance is very powerful in giving the idea of driving on. But to do this it must be on a strong pulse and firmly struck." Palestrina, his teachers and contemporaries, began this kind of dissonance, and it is curious to notice that for a long time they were afraid to separate the dissonating tone from its preparation. It had to be introduced as a held tone or a syncopation, thus :—

Indeed, it seems probable that this sort of prepared dissonance was suggested and discovered by the early love of syncopation. Palestrina however, found that the ear would bear a break for striking afresh between the preparation and dissonating tones. This kind of dissonance was found to be so agreeable that it was constantly used on the strong pulse or beat where it would be loudest. These are commonly called discords by suspension. The next melodic phrase which excuses a dissonance, is the following :—

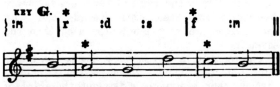

Palestrina uses this kind of stepwise passing-tone, but chiefly, if not entirely, as a mere light part-pulse passing-tone, thus :—

It was some time before musicians ventured boldly to use this passing dissonance even on the weak pulse, where it is least heard. I have followed some of the German writers in calling a dissonance on a strong pulse, or beat, a Fore-stroke, and one on the weak pulse an After-stroke. The first form of dissonance named we call a Horizontal Forestroke. It is seldom used on a weak pulse. The second we call a Down-ward Oblique Forestroke when on the strong pulse, a Passing-tone when on the weak pulse. Modern writers employ the oblique forestroke with considerable freedom on the weak pulse, and often with good effect on the strong pulse also. An upward oblique preparation is some-

$$\{:s \ \ |l \ :-.t \ |d^l \ \|$$

times used. It was long before a dissonance was allowed in any chord unprepared. When the commonest of all, the dominant seventh, was first tried it raised a storm of reprobation from the strict grammarians. Others followed slowly, as musicians ventured out of the beaten track, and trusted their ears. The *resolution* of dissonances is almost always by a step downward. Professor Helmholtz says that in discords the dissonating tone is isolated—cannot take its natural leap by consonance—is left, therefore, to its stepwise motion, that *downward* resolution gives the idea of yielding after a struggle, and therefore dissonances are not resolved upward except in rare cases. I have noticed that when two voices are singing a dissonance the one which holds the higher note can sustain its tone more

steadily than the other. This suggests that the lower tone should yield by going downward. When the second is inverted to a seventh the dissonance is between a principal tone and a more quickly-vibrating partial. How far a mere partial can have ascribed to it this power of sending an opponent down, instead of itself moving up, I cannot say, but in practice the power is exercised. In modern music many discords are unprepared, but none, except in uncommon cases of tertiary and quaternary dissonance, are unresolved. Even the student of musical statics will find it useful to bear in mind these æsthetic apologies for dissonance. That which statically forms the harshest dissonance, æsthetically requires the best apology.

Dissonating and Resisting.—When a dissonance comes into a chord, how are we to know which is the intruder, and which only the resisting tone? First, it is generally easy to see which of the tones stands in the relation of root to the others of the chord—that is, at the bottom of two thirds—and which tones appear to spring from that root. Thus in ⁷S, why is f the dissonance—the intruder—and not s? Because s₁, t₁, and r stand in the acknowledged relation of root, third, and fifth, and f is left alone. Again in ⁷D, which is the intruder? If it were only d against t₁, or t₁ against d, one would be as much the dissonance as the other; but in *the chord*, it is at once seen, and felt by the ear, that m and s hold relation to d as their root, and we feel that t is "left alone"—is the foreign element in the chord. Second, in those cases, in which—taken as they stand—it is doubtful which are the chord tones and which the dissonances, judge the composer's feeling on the question by noticing which tones he has prepared and resolved, for *they*, in his mind, were the dissonances.

New Phenomena.—When a dissonance comes into a chord it does not bring to that chord *only* dissonance. In some cases it adds to the consonance a third or a fifth which the chord did not possess before; in other cases it drives out a valuable third, and adds only a hard fifth or fourth. Although the effect of a dissonance in a chord depends mainly on the æsthetic question, "What tone of the scale is it that is about to distinguish itself, and vivify its mental effect by percussion and resolution?" yet the statical question just raised is of great importance. For example, let us take the dissonance of d against r (the key-tone against the supertonic) in the chord of the supertonic. Directly it enters this chord it

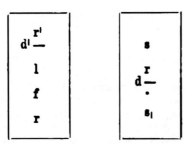

covers its own dissonance by a flood of consonance, with its third or sixth (l), and its fourth or fifth (f). But when this same dissonance enters the chord SOH, the dominant, it strikes out the third of the chord itself and brings no compensation, but an ineffective fourth with the **s** below, or the hard fifth with the **s** which may be above. The consequence is that when "**d** against **r**" enters, as a primary dissonance, into the chord of SOH, it is much more harsh than when it occurs in the chord of RAY. The same comparative effect is felt when the dissonances are both secondary or both tertiary. Try the following example:—

The student cannot fail to notice that although the mental effect of the whole phrase is still that of a key-tone with its strong determination, yet the statical effect of the percussion itself is very different in the two chords. In the first case the dissonating tone is the seventh of a chord, in the latter case it is the fourth. It will easily be seen from this why dissonant fourths have always to be horizontally prepared, and why sevenths are often allowed to enter without even an oblique preparation. It will also be understood why the sevenths are very far more frequently used than other discords, and why the fourths are very much less used than the sevenths.

The seconds, in the primary degree, have the same objection against them as the fourths—that is, they commonly strike out the third of the chord and introduce only a fourth or a fifth, with this addition, that they cannot get a proper downward resolution, and have to move up. The seconds, however, in the secondary and tertiary degree, displace not the third, nor the root, but the *octave* of the root; and then they can resolve downward. When they thus resolve downward we call them ninths. The primary second seldom occurs but on the dominant. There are, however, exceptional cases, to be afterwards shown.

SECONDS.		SIXTHS.	
	m'		l'—
	r'		
			m'
s		d'	d'
	.	l —	
r	s	s	s
.		m	m
l|		d	d
s|	d		

The sixths, if they drive out the fifths, are not dissonant, for they have nothing above them to strike against; and if the fifth remains, they have only an upward resolution. They, however, are like the sevenths in this respect that they bring a new third and a new fifth into the chord, and almost claim the position of a new root. It is, perhaps, this doubtfulness of character, as well as their upward resolution, which makes them so little used in the primary degree. In the secondary or tertiary degree (as thirteenths) they can displace the *octave* of the fifth, without losing all their dissonance, and resolve downward. Coupled dissonances require separate treatment: most of them enter a chord in thirds, sixths, fourths, and fifths with one another, and bring into it their own mutual consonance, and a few of them are mutually dissonant as they enter, but make consonance with the tones among which they intrude.

Statical Study of Discords.

Let us study the discords in the order in which I have just spoken of them, observing how they are treated in respect of degree, accent (or force), preparation, and resolution; and noticing, as we pass, the æsthetic question—which tones of the scale are most used to bear the discords before us? The student of composition must, however, be warned that this is not the best order of study for him. He must not suppose that he can use his sevenths, fourths, &c., wherever he likes. He has to remember that the proper effect of a discord is not in the disturbance which it makes, but in the rest which it leads to. By far the greatest number of dissonances are only so many entrance gates into that place of repose which our ears and our feelings recognise as the tonic chord. There are a very much smaller number of such bold entrances into the dominant chord, and still fewer into the subdominant or its representatives. The young modern composer, therefore, who, above all things, must keep the key clear, will learn how, by these preliminary clashes and challenges, to confirm the effect of tonic, dominant, or subdominant, on the ear. See "How to Observe Harmony," and "Construction Exercises." All this, however, has to do with matters of taste and feeling—with music *as it moves.* We must confine ourselves as closely as possible to music *as it stands.* We have to study the dissonant clashes themselves, rather than the skilful manner in which they are used to enlighten and quicken the harmony. In order to give the student the assurance that the following analysis is thorough, I have taken nearly all the examples of discords selected from classic writers which are to be found in Mr. Macfarren's "Six Lectures on Harmony," in Dr. Stainer's "Theory of Harmony," and in Dr. Hiles' "Harmony of Sounds," and have analysed them. A few which were duplicate cases, or merely ornamental part-pulse and weak-pulse dissonances, I have omitted. I have also omitted a few condensations of symphony-scores, from which we do not get the real effect, and some other examples from instrumental music, because the preparation and resolution are not easily traceable through being written in arpeggio, or other similar form.

The Sevenths. — The sevenths are, for æsthetic reasons (see "How to Observe," and "Construction Exercises,") chiefly used on the dominant. The great acceptableness of this dissonance is shown by its being taken as a primary, both unprepared and on a strong accent. See Illustration 1, which also shows a "secondary" use of this dissonance. A quaternary case will be found in Il. 2.

The seventh on the minor dominant ^{7m}M can be heard as primary in Il. 3, and as secondary in Il. 4. Although this seventh has not the smoothness of a downward leading-tone and a little step, like that of the major mode, yet, for æsthetic reasons, it is comparatively more used than its companion ^7S. See "Const. Exs.," p. 93; and "How to Obs.," pp. 79 and 95.

E

The next seventh in frequency of use is that on the major supertonic. In Il. 5 it is primary, on a strong pulse horizontally prepared. This is almost as common as the secondary case in Il. 6. A very uncommon case is that of Il. 7, where the dissonance is resolved in another part, and that the most prominent; but in its own part the dissonance moves to the tone above. It also comes from or is prepared by the tone below; in this irregularity of progression it is supported by another part moving in sixths with it. Cases of this kind very seldom occur except in the tertiary or quaternary degree.

that the resisting-tone is well prepared. This seventh on the supertonic, like that on the dominant, is more used in minor than in major.

The seventh on the leading-tone is difficult to find with the dissonance in the bass, and in the primary degree. See Il. 10. In Ils. 11 and 12 the commoner cases are seen. For convenience of melody, this dissonance may be prepared in the secondary and tertiary degrees as well as the primary; but it is generally unprepared and pungent. In these respects it differs from the habits of the supertonic of the minor mode, although it is statically the same thing.

The same thing occurs in the minor mode. See a "secondary" case in Il. 8. In Il. 9 there is a very rare case—primary unprepared, and with the dissonance in the bass. It should be noticed, however,

The Consonant Seventh.—The only chord of the scale which can have a consonant seventh, is that on the leading-tone of the minor mode, '8E, commonly called the chord of the diminished seventh. Æsthetically, it corresponds with 'T in the major mode. Its f is out of beating distance with se. This is a peculiar chord. It consists of three minor thirds. It has much sweetness, but both the ear and the student's calculation will show that it has among its early partials much dissonance.

The seventh on the major tonic ('D) is not much used on the strong pulse; but here are two decided cases: Il. 13 is secondary, Il. 14 is tertiary. Its pungency—the interval being only a little step—makes it very undesirable as a primary dissonance.

The corresponding minor 'L or ᴹL is variable. Il. 15 is a clear case from Bach.

The seventh on the major submediant, ('L), is rarely found. See a secondary case in Il. 16.

The corresponding minor ('F) is shown in Il. 17. It is here tertiary.

The seventh on the major subdominant 'F presents an interesting study in the two cases from Bach. In Il. 18 the dissonance is tertiary, the preparation oblique, and the resisting-tone moves; while in Il. 19 the dissonance is primary, with a better preparation, but with the resisting-tone standing. It is not common for this dissonance to appear on the strong pulse. See for this and the corresponding minor ('R), "Const. Exs.," and "How to Observe."

Il. 19. KEY A♭.   *   BACH.

The Fourths.—The fourth on the dominant is, next to the sevenths on the dominant and on the supertonic, the most common of dissonances. Probably because it is always regularly prepared and resolved, the writers of the books above referred to did not think it necessary to select examples in the major mode.

The corresponding minor ('L') is shown in its rarer appearances in Ills. 23 and 24, in both of which the third is retained. In Il. 23 the dissonance is secondary against the fifth, tertiary against the third, that third being in the bass. In Il. 24 the dissonance is primary against the fifth, and secondary against the third, the dissonance itself being in the bass.

The usual form of the corresponding minor, 'M, is given in Il. 20, in which the third is, as usual, driven out.

Il. 23. KEY D. *Lah is B.*   BACH (Passion Music).

Il. 20. KEY E♭. *Lah is C.*   * HANDEL.

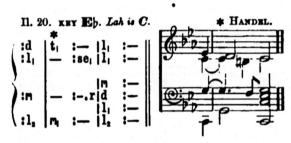

Il. 24. KEY A. *Lah is F♯.*   BACH ("Confiteor").

The fourth on the major tonic ('D') appears in its common form in Il. 21, driving out the third of the chord; but in Il. 22 there is a very uncommon case, in which the dissonance is secondary, but the third is retained *above* the dissonating tone. Commonly, when the third is retained the dissonance is not only secondary or tertiary, but the third stands at a good distance *below* the dissonating tone.

The Ninths and Seconds.—The common case of the ninth on the tonic as a secondary dissonance (resolving downwards) with the resisting-tone continuing, is in Il. 25. A very exceptional case, which, according to our definition, should be called a ninth, but which had better be called a "downward second," is found in Il. 26. It should be noticed that in this case the resisting-tone moves.

Il. 21. KEY A.   MENDELSSOHN.

Il. 25. KEY A.   *   SCHUBERT.

Il. 22. KEY D.   * BEETHOVEN.

Il. 26. KEY A♭.   MENDELSSOHN'S "St. Paul."

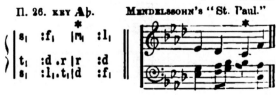

The ninths on the dominant (⁹S and ⁹ᵐM), on the subdominant (⁹F and ⁹R), and on the major supertonic (⁹R), are not fully elucidated in the books above referred to. Their theory of dissonances as suspensions or fundamentals made it seem to the writers unnecessary to do so. But a ninth when *unprepared* comes more directly within the scope of these books, and they supply an example in Il. 27. A very rare case of ⁹R secondary is the following, in Il. 28.

The Sixths. — The doubtful character of these dissonances we have already studied above. The ordinary cases of the sixth on the tonic major and minor (⁶D and ᵇᵃL) resolving upwards may be studied in "How to Obs.," and in "Const. Exs." The books also supply us with the less common examples of this dissonance self-resolved downward. In Il. 29 we have ⁶D secondary, and in Il. 30, the corresponding ⁶L, employing the minor (natural) sixth of the minor mode. This keen dissonance is rare.

The sixth on the subdominant (⁶F) may be heard in Il. 31. It is on a weak pulse, and follows the common rule of upward resolution. This chord, as well as the corresponding minor (⁶E), is, except for its resolution, dubious. It might be mistaken by the ear at its percussion for ⁷R♭, and ⁶R might be mistaken for ⁷T♭, which is statically the same thing. This dubiousness accounts for the rare employment of the chord in the major, and its disuse in the minor.

The Ninths and Sevenths. — These, when on the dominant (on which they are chiefly used), commonly strike out the fifth of the chord, but they introduce their own third. And when the dissonating tones are far apart there is a certain richness of effect produced by the thirds and sixths, although if the tones of the chord were placed stepwise they would form four consecutive tones of the scale. Il. 32 affords an example of this chord in the major, without the omission of a single tone.

An exceptional case—according to our definition, called ²⁷S (in which the ninth *can* be used as a second, and resolves upwards, and which we should therefore call an "upward second")—is shown in il. 33. See "How to Obs.," p. 101; and "Const. Exs." p. 139.

Il. 33. KEY D♭.   BALFE.

The nine-seven on the tonic (⁹⁷D and ⁹⁷L) are very harsh and unwelcome to the ear, because they strike out either the third or the root of the chord.

The Ninths and Fourths, chiefly used on the tonic (⁹⁴D and ⁹⁴L), may be seen in their commonest forms in "How to Obs.," p. 97; and in "Const. Exs.," pp. 140 and 141. These ninths and fourths, whether they resolve upward or downward, strike out the third of the chord itself, although they bring in another third. A less complete case of ⁹⁴D is shown in Il. 34, where statically the chord is ⁷R, but where the ear is æsthetically compelled to recognise a dominant chord moving to its tonic, and overflowing into it. A similar example in the minor ⁹⁴L of overflowing without the omission of the fifth is seen in Il. 35.

Il. 34. KEY B♭.   BEETHOVEN.

Il. 35. KEY G. *Lah is E.*   MENDELSSOHN.

While on this subject of the dominant overflowing into the tonic chord, we may study in Il. 36 the only case of a three-fold dissonance ⁹⁴⁹⁹L. See also "How

to Obs.," and "Const. Exs.," where the corresponding major ⁹⁷⁴D may also be examined. Statically considered, these chords may be read in different manners, but æsthetically the ear feels that we have come to the tonic chord.

Il. 36. KEY C.   MOZART.

The ninths and fourths on the major subdominant (⁹⁴F) find an illustration in il. 37.

Il. 37. KEY F.   MENDELSSOHN.

The Fourths and Sevenths are not very welcome to the ear because they drive out the third, and only introduce a new fifth. However, when the fourth comes in with the seventh, it may be unprepared. See for ⁴⁷M, Il. 38. Compare "How to Obs.," both for this and the corresponding major ⁴⁷S.

Il. 38. KEY C. *Lah is A.*   MENDELSSOHN.

Fourths and sevenths where—in a dominant cadence—the tonic chord seems to overflow may be seen in Il. 39, where the chord is evidently ⁴⁷SE.

Il. 39. KEY F *Lah is D.*   BEETHOVEN.

The fourth and seventh on the supertonic (⁴⁷R) is shown in Il. 40.

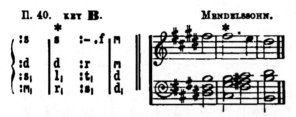

Il. 40. KEY B.   MENDELSSOHN.

The Sixths and Sevenths form very dissonant chords, for though they drive out only the fifth of the original chord, they introduce a dissonance of their own. Nevertheless it may be found even with the sixth unprepared and in the bass. See for ⁶⁷S, Ils. 41 and 42; and for ⁶⁷ᵐM, Ils. 43 and 44.

Il. 41. KEY C.   MENDELSSOHN.

Il. 42. KEY G.   SCHUMANN.

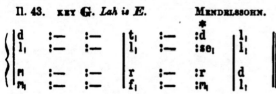

Il. 43. KEY G. *Lah is E.*   MENDELSSOHN.

Il. 44. KEY D. *Lah is B.*   SCHUMANN.

Chromatic Chords.

—Only a very few, and those rarely used, of the chromatic chords differ in structure from those with which we are already familiar. The chromatic effect of these chords depends on their first *disturbing* the sense of key-relationship, and then by an unexpected resolution *restoring* it; and this is an æsthetic rather than a statical question. The student who examines all the "Illustrations" in "How to Observe Harmony," will find that, statically considered, these chords correspond either with major chords, or minor chords, or diminished chords, or dominant sevenths, or diminished sevenths, or sevenths on the leading-tone of the major mode. Even the "Neapolitan sixth," he will find to be a plain major chord. The German sixth is statically much the same as the dominant seventh, containing, like it, a dissonant seventh and a diminished fifth. The augmented sixths are, statically speaking, sevenths. They would beat, if placed in their normal position, against the root of the chord at the distance of a tone. They are, however, always secondary or tertiary dissonances. The French sixths are like the German, except in their having that tone which stands at the interval of a tritone from the root, instead of a perfect fifth, thus making a dissonance against the third, as well as one against the root. The peculiarity of the Italian sixth is that it has neither a fifth, like the German, nor a fourth, like the French. These statical facts would lead to the conclusion, justified by the ear, that the German chord is the strongest; the Italian, especially with its double third, the sweetest; and the French the harshest.

THE AUGMENTED SIXTHS.

GERMAN SIXTHS.				ITALIAN SIXTHS.				FRENCH SIXTHS.			

KEY **G**.

fe	s	d	d	d	m	l	se	r	m	t,	d
d	d	l,	l,	fe,	s,	re	m	d	d	l,	l,
ma	m	re	m	d	d	l	t	fe	s	re	m
la,	s,	f,	m,	la,	s,	f	m	la,	s,	f,	m,

fe ma **LA**   re **F**   fe **LA**   re **F**   fe **LA**   re **F**

The same with the Major Third at the bottom and the Essential Sixth at the top.

fe	re	fe	re	fe	re
ma	d	•	•	•	•
				r	t
d	l	d	l	d	l
la	f	la	f	la	f
fe	re	fe	re	fe	re

CHAPTER V.

STATICS AND ÆSTHETICS—THE BORDER-LAND.

WE have now to study some important subjects which lie on the outer verge of Statics and on the threshold of Æsthetics. It is well, therefore, to remind ourselves of the proper relation between the two. Professor Helmholtz tells us that "the ideas of what is physically 'pleasant' or physically 'unpleasant' depend on physical facts, but how much of the pleasant or the unpleasant the ear will require or endure depends on the historical and national developments of taste. Hence it is that the various systems of keys and of harmonic progressions do not rest only on the unchangeable natural laws, but also on æsthetic principles which, with the development of man, have necessarily changed and will change." There have always been some general and necessarily true principles more or less known, but accidents of natural character and circumstances have overruled all. It should also be remembered that our likings and dislikings depend very much upon what we have been accustomed to; so that many crudities have lived in musical practice long after their unsuitability or untruthfulness has been discovered. It is thus that different nations form their various habits of enjoying or performing music. Every style thus originated has its own consistency and its own interest, being developed by the tentative, empirical processes of artists finding what pleases them best. If science can find out the motive forces, mental or physical, which have governed the artist in this process, and can discover the end which he aimed at, it will make the path of progress easier for all future artists.

First Idea of a Tonic.—Partials and differentials have always existed, and have influenced the feelings—through them the opinions —of men, even while they themselves were little understood, or entirely unknown. Thus it was that the first idea of a tonic, or governing tone, came to be formed. In the writings of the *mathematical* musicians of Greece, there is no developed idea of a tonic. It is true they had their "given" string—their proslambanomenos —which we now understand in that light. But it was Aristotle, the æsthetic, who first perceived the dependence of the other tones of the scale upon one central tone. Professor Helmholtz quotes his "Problems," to understand which it is necessary to know that the Mese, or middle string of the Greek lyre, represented the key-tone of what we should now call the Minor mode, and was understood to be the octave of the proslambanomenos. Aristotle says, "When, after having tuned all the strings, one changes the *middle* string, and then uses the instrument, why do they *all* sound wrongly tuned, not only when one strikes that middle tone, but all through the melody, while if, instead of this, one changes any other string, the difference is noticed when he uses that string, and that string only, the whole of the melody not being put out of tune? Does not this take place with good reason, for all good melodies often use the middle tone, and no other tone in equal degree?" He then compares the middle tone with conjunctions in grammar, or *binding* words, suggesting that the middle string binds together the sense and effect of the whole melody. In another passage Aristotle answers the same question by saying, "Is it because good tune is enjoined for *all* the strings—for all a certain relation to the middle tone—and by this middle tone the place of all is determined? But when the foundation of right tuning (that which keeps the music together) is taken away, no proper order is perceived." We must agree with Professor Helmholtz, that in these sentences, the æsthetic meaning of a tonic is as well described as it can be. To this may be added, that the Pythagoreans compare this middle tone with the sun, and the other tones with the planets. The Greeks seem also to have begun a song usually with this middle tone, which we now call the tonic, and commonly to have ended their tunes with the fifth above or the fourth below, which we now call the dominant. It is more according to our modern feeling to close on the tonic as well as to begin with it. But the ancient practice of ending on the dominant has its parallel in modern affirmative declamations and recitatives, in which the voices end on the dominant, leaving the instruments to close on the tonic cadence.

The word "Tonic" was employed by Aristoxenes, the earliest writer on music whose works have been handed down to us, to describe one of those arrangements of tones in a scale which he called *genera*. Later, it was used to describe the principal tone of a tune—that from which the whole music is evolved, and to which it returns again—that governing tone just spoken of. The Arabs, the Indians, and the Chinese wrought out their theories of scales with extraordinary subtlety, and they all appear to acknowledge various "modes" of using the tones of their scales, so as to bring into prominence some one or other of its tones, and make it the ruling tone of a musical passage. Hence we have the various Greek modes, followed afterwards by the Ecclesiastical modes, all of which have parallels at the present time in the practical music of the less civilised nations of the world, and in the musical systems of the Eastern civilisations. Various and contradictory names were given to these modes, with which it is not necessary to trouble the reader. It is enough to say that the favourite modes were those founded on the second and sixth of the scale, both of which have a minor third at their beginning. The ancient nations were fond of minor modes.

THE MODE OF THE SECOND OF THE SCALE.

THE MODE OF THE SIXTH OF THE SCALE.

There was another mode, which the monks called the "lascivious," or the secular mode, because it was used for dances and bright songs. It is the mode founded on the first of the scale, which has a major third at the bottom. This is the mode in which the chief part of modern music is written.

The word "Dominant" was at first used to represent the predominating tone—that which was most used—in a chant, commonly the reciting tone. After a time, when students began to notice the remarkable power of the over-fifth in melody, the term was applied exclusively to the fifth above the tonic, or to its lower octave, the fourth below. The fall of a fifth is like the IIIrd partial lost in its principal —a part dissolved into its whole. It is a fall of the most definite of all intervals except that which is a mere octave or repetition. It is to the *over*-fifth, and not to the under-fifth, that this peculiarity belongs. See "Definiteness of Interval," p. 39. There is also something in the higher and brighter pitch which gives to this over-fifth (and its shadow, the under-fourth), so great a power to single out and distinguish the tone it falls upon. The following are some of the illustrations given in "Standard Course," pp. 83, 84. In the mode of the sixth of the scale (LAH) we have the tonic defined thus :—

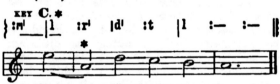

In the mode of the second of the scale we have the dominant defined thus :—

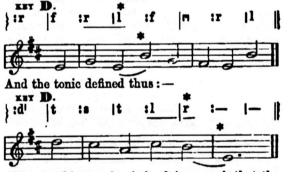

And the tonic defined thus :—

However this may be, it is plain enough that the mind feels and acknowledges the power of the over-fifth. But the idea of a tonic and its accompanying dominant was far more weakly developed in ancient one-voiced music than in modern harmony. Its melodies followed the words, and therefore needed little else for their artistic bond. It was not till Rameau—only a hundred and fifty years ago—developed the first theory of chords and their relations that the words "tonic," "dominant," "subdominant," and "leading-tone" came to be accepted in their present meaning. In the following paragraphs I shall try to show some of the underlying physical truths which have unconsciously ruled the feelings of artists in perceiving and acknowledging the relations which these words express.

Chord of "First Impression."—

Immediately that we come to modern harmony we are met by this apparent puzzle, Why is one chord taken for a tonic rather than another? Thus, the following four chords consist of precisely the same sounds in all three of the examples given.

KEY G.

:s	m	:l	s
:m	d	:f	m
:d	d	:f₁	d

KEY C.

:r¹	t	:m¹	r¹
:t	s	:d¹	t
:s	s	:d	s

KEY D.

:d¹	l	:r¹	d¹
:l	f	:ta	l
:f	f	:ta₁	f

Which is the true interpretation of them? Of course, when you see them written, you see also the key which the composer had in his own mind. But how does the unaided ear decide? There is apparently nothing in the notes themselves to tell us the key. But it is a principle of mental philosophy that a *first impression* rules us unless its pre-eminence is worthily disputed. The first mass of colour which strikes us in approaching a picture lays hold of our mind, and we immediately begin to compare any other colours with that; we make it our criterion. So, the first chord, especially if it be a full major chord, which plays its vibrations upon the ear—the chord of first impression—is naturally accepted as the principal chord, that by which other chords are to be measured and judged. Therefore, in the case given above, the first interpretation is the right one. Gottfried Weber, in his "Theory of Musical Composition," was the first, and, as far as I know, is still the only writer who explains to us the true principles of "the attunement of the ear to a key." He says:—"When our ear perceives a succession of tones and harmonies, it naturally endeavours to find, amidst this multiplicity and variety, an internal connection—a relationship to a common central point. For as, in every art, the mind spontaneously desires to find a certain unity in the multiplicity—a centrality of the manifold parts, so it does here. The ear everywhere longs to perceive some tone as a principal and central tone, some harmony as a principal

harmony, around which the others revolve as accessories around their principal; that is, around the predominant harmony. Thus it is natural that in the beginning of a piece of music, when the ear is as yet unpreoccupied with any key, it should be inclined to assume as the tonic harmony any major or minor chord that first presents itself." Nor need we wonder at this when we remember how great and far-reaching is the full klang, with partials and differentials above and below, of a major or minor chord. It is Music pitching her tent — driving her stakes and stretching her chords—over some definite spot in the region of sound. It sets apart and appropriates—it clears a space for the performance which is to follow.

Idea of a Dominant.—

The melodic idea of a dominant—that of a tone at the interval of a "definite fifth" above the tonic, becomes more important when introduced into harmony. We have shown that chords are really *tones made stronger*. In all major chords, and, to a less degree, in minor chords, the root is bonded to its third, fifth, and octave by the partials it throws up; and the third, fifth, and octave are bonded

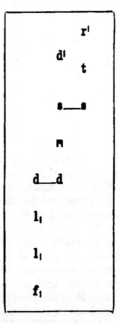

to the root by the differentials they throw down. (See diagrams, pp. 25 and 29, "Effect of Partials and Differentials.") Everything strengthens the root. A chord built upon any tone adds to the power of that tone; develops its force and effect, and makes it more definite. Therefore, whatever power a tone at a certain interval in melody possessed, that power it wields with much weightier force when it becomes the root of a chord in harmony. Notice that the chord of the under-fifth cannot have the same defining and controlling power which is exercised by the over-fifth, for it does not attach its root, but only its fifth, to the tonic; and the root itself, for which the whole chord exists, is dissonant with the tonic chord. Whereas the chord of the over-fifth attaches itself by its root, and with its greatest strength, to the tonic chord, and does so at the interval which defines that tonic even more clearly than a repetition of the tonic itself. In other words, it adds force to the interval which even in melody is felt to be a dominant.

Idea of Subdominant.—Although, when a certain chord is already preconceived as the chord of first impression, its over-fifth is more important than its under-fifth, yet the interval of a fifth taken by itself has a defining power whether we take it upward or downward, and next to the over-fifth is the most

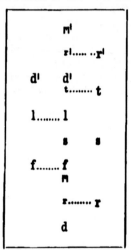

important interval in relation to the tonic. The tonic chord takes hold of the dominant by its root, or stem, and of the subdominant by its highest branch. In other words, the chord of the over-fifth guards and defines the tonic by its *strongest* tone, and the chord of the under-fifth by its tone *next* in strength. No other chords support the fifth and the root of the tonic so clearly. The mediant places its root on the third of the tonic chord, and the submediant uses its third to strengthen the root of the same chord; but the third has not the definiteness and force of the root and fifth. It should be noticed that there may be much ambiguity of key when only the tonic and dominant have been heard, but that immediately the subdominant comes in, the scale is complete—every tone of it occurs in these three chords—and there can be

no ambiguity. Hence it is that these three chords are so much used in the closes of lines and in other places where it is important to establish the sense of key.

The Under-fourth and Over-fourth.—The under-fourth has just been called the shadow of the over-fifth. It is so because it exercises the same power as the over-fifth, only in a smaller degree. It is in its IInd and

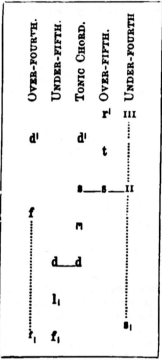

IIIrd partials (octave and octave-fifth) that the under-fourth agrees with the over-fifth, and so becomes a weaker dominant. A similar remark applies to the chords of the over-fourth, and of the under-fifth. Thus we have seen that when a chord is once accepted as a tonic, or ruling-tone, it is quickly surrounded by a four-fold guard—the dominant and its attendant, the under-fourth, standing at the right hand of the king; the sub-dominant and its attendant, the over-fourth, standing near the throne on the left.

The Bonding Power in Chords.—In the progression from one chord to another the natural sense of unity is gratified if the second chord carries with it some one tone or more as a reminiscence of the previous chord, and this is called the "bonding of chords." How much this is practically felt by musicians will be seen at once by examining any composition at hand. In the following examples the staff

three
lines
it to

er-
ween
be-
fth.
and

tation gives the chant just as it is, all the **nes** being freshly struck with each new chord; **d** the Tonic Sol-fa notation shows by con- **nuation**-marks how much the tones of one **ord** are carried on to the next. The reader **ill** see at once how the chords overlap each **her.** It is like the bonding of a brick wall.

KEY D.   BATTISHILL.

d¹	s :—	d :—	— l :s	f :—	m :—
m	— :r	d :—	— — :—	— :t₁	d :—
s	— :—	m :—	s f :s	l :s	— :—
d	— :t₁	l₁ :—	m f :m	r :s₁	d :—

KEY E♭.   J. BARNBY.

s	m :s	f :—	m r :f	m :r	d :—
m	d :r	d :—	— l₁ :—	t₁ :—	d :—
s	d¹ :t	l :—	s f :r	s :f	m :—
d	— :—	— :—	f₁ :—	s₁ :—	d :—

KEY E.   E. G. MONK.

m	— :l	s :—	— — :f m	r :—	m :—
d	— :—	— :—	r s₁ :d	— :t₁	d :—
s	l :—	d¹ :—	s m :d	l :s	— :—
d	l₁ :f	m :—	t₁ d :l₁	f₁ :s₁	d :—

KEY E.   DR. HILES.

d¹	r :m	— :r	l s :d	r :m	d :—
s₁	— :ta₁	l₁ :—	d — :—	— :t₁	d :—
m	f :s	l :—	r m :—	s :f	m :—
d	— :—	f₁ :—	fe₁ s₁ :l₁	s₁ :—	d :—

These are the *direct* bonds with which the warp and woof of harmony are woven. But even when the binding-tone is not struck in the same part and octave as in the previous chord, the ear still recognises an *indirect* bond between the two chords. In Battishill's chant there is such a bond between the tenor of the fourth chord and the bass of the fifth. In Monk's chant there is an indirect bond between the bass of the sixth chord and the tenor of the seventh, and also between the bass of the seventh chord and the tenor of the eighth. The student will observe how much the horizontally-prepared dissonances promote this bonding of chords; and those who have followed the previous discussion, and who recognise the kingly power of the tonic, will be prepared to acknowledge between the dominant and subdominant (which have no direct bond the one to the other) an *implied* bond, because they are both so strongly bonded to the tonic.

This sense of sameness and immobility in chord progression is strongest when a new chord brings with it *two* tones of the old chord. All the cases of this double bonding are as follows :— D and L,—D and M,—S and T,—S and M,— F and R,—F and L,—R and T,—ʰM and SE,— ʰM and ʰD,—T and SE. So that if we wish to go from the chord of S, for instance, with the least possible change of effect, we should move to T; if from the chord of F, we should go to R; and so on.

The bonds next in strength to a double bond are those which carry the very root of the last chord into the second place of honour—the fifth —in the new chord; or *vice versa*, take the fifth of one chord and use it as a root for the next. All the cases of this strong single bond are as follows:—D and S,—F and D,—S and R,—T and F,—M and T,—R and L,—L and M,—L and ʰM, ʰM and T,—ʰD and SE,—SE and R. But it must not be concluded that the best progressions are those in which the chords have the strongest bonds; first, because, in modern music, relation to the tonic overrules all other considerations— that is to say, the ear and taste desire this more even than the bonding of chords; second, because the sense of continuity and unity is not the only thing wanted in chord progression: variety and change are also required. The still lake of closely-bonded harmony gives us too much rest and sameness; we desire more stirring chords; we long for the current of the ever-changing river.

The Moving Power in Chords.

—Professor Helmholtz has shown that dissonance is the chief moving power in chords. It creates a feeling of unrest, which demands motion to another chord for satisfaction. Even a slight shade of dissonance is sufficient to accomplish this object. There are three kinds of dissonance which accomplish this object. First, all those discords which we studied in the last chapter, and which cry out for resolution, are moving powers, too strong and obtrusive, indeed, to be incessantly used; second, the use of a minor chord after the clear klang of a major chord gives just enough of that sense of discomfort which stimulates motion, for the minor chords are, as we have noticed, more or less self-dissonant; third, the sort of dissonance we feel when we pass, in melody, immediately from one tone to another, which, *if in harmony*, would dissonate with it, possesses considerable power. This melodic dissonance is increased, and becomes a strong motive power, when there are *two* such tones in the second chord, and when they beat against *the root* of the previous chord. Thus, when the chords of S or T follow the chord of D, they sound t and r in melodic dissonance with the d just heard. All the progressions which involve such a double melodic dissonance against a previous *root* are as follows:—D to S,— D to T,—S to F,—S to R,—F to D,—F to M,— R to D,—R to L,—L to S,—L to M,—T to L,— T to F,—M to R,—M to T,—*L* to *M*,—*L* to *SE*, —*SE* to F,—*SE* to R.

Thus we see the bonding and the moving powers in chord-progressions as far as musical statics can teach them. But the student must not suppose that, when he desires motion, any one of the "moving" progressions will do as well as any other, or that when he desires a quiet and unpronounced change of chord, any one of the "bonded" progressions will do as well as any other. All these different "bonded" and "moving" progressions are only the possible materials, out of which the great æsthetical principle of key-relation makes its selection. In every progression, whether of rest or motion, the modern composer has a distinct object. He feels himself going to or from the tonic, dominant, or subdominant of the mode. It was not so in the old days of mere counterpoint, or the movement of "part" against "part," before chords and their progressions were much studied; then, chords went anywhere. Professor Helmholtz quotes from a "Stabat Mater" of Palestrina's, and says:—"In the beginning

(where we should expect some decision of key), he gives a series of chords of the most various keys from A major to F major; and not till after all this does the tonic occur—the tonic, which a modern composer would have to put on the first strong beat of the first measure! In this kind of music we miss—first, the bold assertion of the tonic chord; and second, the related succession of chords, — those chords following each other which have a common tone. We miss those *chains* of chords related to one another and to the key which we find in modern music." He shows how, in the seventeenth century—partly through the revived opera, which demanded "accompanied recitatives" and "figured basses," and bold effects, and partly through the wide spread of psalm-singing by great masses of people requiring plain harmonies —the separate stroke of the chord began to be studied. "The modern principle of tonality in chords," he continues, "has been *in practice* scarcely two hundred years, and received its theoretical development little more than one hundred and fifty years ago, from Rameau. We now set up the axiom as a fundamental principl· of the European tone system, that the whole mass of the tones and harmony-links is to be *placed in close and always clear* relationship to a freely chosen *tonic;* that the tone-mass of the whole passage must evolve itself out of this, and return to it again. This is not a physical, but an æsthetic principle. We cannot prove its correctness *a priori*, but must test it by its results."

Classification of Chords. — In

speaking of key-relation and of the classification of chords, it is important to explain the distinctions which I venture to make between SCALE, KEY, and MODE. By *scale*, I mean, if no qualifying word is used, the diatonic scale which was described in the first chapter, at *whatever pitch* it may be placed. By *key*, I mean that same scale placed at *some definite pitch*, as "key C," "key G," &c., or holding some definite relation to a previously fixed key, as "first sharp key," "first flat key," as will presently be seen By *mode*, I mean the *manner* in which this great scale is used for the purpose of bringing out the mental effect of one or other of its tones. In modern music, only two modes are used: the Major Mode,—that of DOH,—and the Minor Mode,—that of LAH, and this Modern Minor has almost always one altered tone to make it suit the requirements of the ear in harmony, as will hereafter appear. The Major Mode is identical with the common scale, and where I speak of a key, I always mean to imply the Major Mode, unless the contrary is stated. Thus, "Key A" means the common scale placed at the pitch of A and in the Major Mode, with Doh for its tonic; and "Key A, *Lah is* F♯," or "Key A, minor mode," means the common scale with Doh at the pitch of A, but used so as to develop the mental effect of Lah, and having Lah for its tonic.

Now, it is the *mode* which rules the progression of chords, and marshals them to suit its purposes. Different modes use different chords, though the static and æsthetic principles on which they are marshalled are the same in all. Let us see how the various qualities of bonding and moving among chords fit and prepare them to be thus marshalled. A little study of the simplest and commonest harmony progressions in modern music will show that their idea is this: first, a central chord, with its attendant dominant and subdominant chords; and second, subordinate chords, differing either from the dominant or subdominant only in a single tone, and capable of being substituted for them, wherever convenience of parts, or variety of effect, or better bonding to the following chord may require; so that each of these attendants on the principal chord has its own train of assistants; the chords on the dominant side representing, in relation to the tonic, the more stirring effects, and those on the subdominant side, the quieter changes. Confining ourselves first to the major mode, if we place the tonic chord in the centre of a diagram, it is natural to place the dominant, and the chords which we know to be used as its substitutionals, on the right-hand, while we place the subdominant and its substitutionals on the left; and this classification of chords would represent the actual usage of modern music. (See "How to Observe Harmony"). It is interesting to observe that there are double bonds between the dominant chord and those on the leading-tone and mediant, so that a composer may pass from one to another of these chords with the least possible change of effect. We find the same double bonding between the chord of the subdominant and those of the supertonic and submediant. Moreover, double bonds may be felt when the chord D (tonic) moves either to or from the chords of L (the submediant), and M (the mediant); but it is so rarely advisable (except in surprise cadences, sequences, and fugal passages) to substitute anything in the place of the tonic, that I prefer regarding these two chords, one as belonging to the dominant family, and the other to the subdominant. All this will be clearly seen from the diagram on p. 64. This diagram would have *looked* more symmetrical if I had made the chords M and T change places; but I have tried to represent the actual usage of chords, and T is certainly much more frequently

employed than M as a substitute for S. By this arrangement, also, the memory localises the two mediants as "outside chords," far less used than the others, and then occasionally as a substitute for the tonic as well as for the dominant or subdominant to which they respectively belong. We adopt the same classification with the chords of the minor mode, and when the sharp seventh of that mode is introduced we find an exactly corresponding system of bonds. This classification of the chords in a mode undoubtedly corresponds with the practice of good composers, and I hope it will prove an assistance to the young student in the comprehension of harmony relations.

Idea of Leading-tone.—In addition to the relation of chords by bond or dissonance which has been sufficient to give us this classification, there is another, which applies only to one progression in a key or mode, and does not arise from the structure of the chords themselves, but from the possession, by the first of them, of a particular tone of the scale—that which is called "the leading-tone." Every singer must have noticed how natural it is in singing up or down the scale to take a "little step" after two full steps. Thus,

}| d :r |m :f |m ‖

is more natural than

}| d :r |m :fe |m ‖

and even

}| f :s |l :ta |l ‖

suggests itself quite easily to the ear instead of

}| f :s |l :t |l ‖

Going downward, we have the same feeling.

}| m :r |d :t₁ |d ‖

is better than

}| m :r |d :ta₁|d ‖

and

}| t :l |s :fe |s ‖

comes quite as naturally as

}| t :l |s :f |s ‖

THE HARMONY CHART.

	f	f		•	f	
m			m			m
	r̀			r	r	
d	•	d	d	•		
			t	•	t	t
l	l	l		•		
			s	s		s
	f	f		•	f	
m			m			m
	r̀			r	r	
d	•	d	d	•		
			t	•	t	t
l	l	l		•		
			s	s		s
	f	f		•	f	
m			m			m
	r̀			r	r	
d	•	d	d	•		

L	R	F	D	S	T	M

	f	f	f		m	m		•	
	r̀	r̀			•	r	
d		•	d		t	t		d
l	•	l	l				
				se	se	se
f	f	f		m	m		m
	r̀	r̀			•	r	
d	t	•	d		t	t		d
l	•	l	l				
				se	se	se
f	f	f		m	m		m
	r̀	r̀			•	r	
d	t	•	d		t	t		d
l	•	l	l				
				se	se	se
f	f	f		m	m		m
	r̀	r̀			•	r	
d		•	d				d

F	T	R	L	se M	SE	se D

SUBMEDIANT.	SUPERTONIC.	SUBDOMINANT.	TONIC.	DOMINANT.	LEADING-TONE.	MEDIANT.	SUBMEDIANT.	SUPERTONIC.	SUBDOMINANT.	TONIC.	DOMINANT.	LEADING-TONE.	MEDIANT.

This may arise from the æsthetic desire for variety in the melodic steps, or from the underlying statical fact that the perfect fourth (d to f, or f to ta, or m down to t₁, or t down to fe) forms what we may call a better melodic harmony than the tritone, or the diminished fifth (d to fe, or f to t, or m down to ta₁, or t down to f). This is the more likely, because the feeling I have described is always stronger when the "starting-tone" going upwards, d or f; and going downwards, m or t) is on a strong accent, and thus dwells in the ear so as to seem present with the tones which follow. The fact, however, is undoubted that, after two steps of melody, the ear naturally desires a *little* step, and if, instead of this, a third full step is taken, naturally feels that there is something *marked* and emphatic in the "reach" upward or downward of that last step. Hence it is that the seventh has sometimes been called "the sharp of the scale," and the fourth "the flat of the scale." Of course this emphatic exciting or depressing effect is all the more noticeable if some *new* flat or sharp is introduced into the music; but of this, more presently. It should also be noticed that the sense of tension, of which we are conscious in taking the full, instead of the little, step is always relieved when the seventh is heard "leading" up to the octave, or the fourth leading down to the third.

Of the two "leading-tones" the *upward* is the more effective, simply because it *is* upward. It is found in the chords of the dominant and of the leading-tone itself, and its tendency is so strongly felt by the ear, that these chords are nearly always followed by others (the tonic or submediant), which have the tone to which it leads. The *downward* leading-tone is in the chords of the subdominant and the supertonic. Two of the chords,—that of the leading-tone (T or SE) and that of the dominant seventh (^7S or ^{7m}M),—have *both* the leading-tones, and are therefore very effective in deciding the key. This force of the leading-tones does not "bond" chords by continuance of tone from one into the other, nor does it "move" them by dissonance, yet, in its own way, the "leading" from one tone to another both bonds and moves.

There is one chord—the dominant seventh—which combines not only both the leading-tones but also both the motive forces. By making the downward leading-tone into a dissonance, it adds, to the melodic tendency already felt, harmonic pressure, and makes the chord "cry out" for its resolution. It is a curious illustration of the slow development of musical truth, that this chord was scarcely used by Palestrina and the writers of the sixteenth century, except as a

prepared discord on the strong pulse or beat of the measure, and that on the weak pulse it was at first only allowed as a part-pulse passing-tone. The old harmonies of many of our psalm-tunes still in use show the remnants of the fearsome spirit. It was not till the last century that the chord,—on a weak pulse and unprepared as we now know it,—came into free and common use. Its great dynamic force—leading to the tonic—was not needed in the early days of counterpoint, because composers thought more of how one "part" moved in relation to the other (point against point), than of how the mode and key were established, and the force and beauty of chords best brought out. When changes of key and mode were little used (and then apparently more by accident, or for convenience, than by intention and for their own sakes), the want of a key-and-mode-deciding chord, such as the dominant seventh, could not be felt. Thus far, then, we have seen among the chords these three powers,—that of bonding, that of moving, and that of leading; we have found these powers to be partly statical and partly æsthetic; and we have noticed how they help to classify the chords in modal relation. Their importance will be more manifest in the study of cadences.

Disuse of the Mediant Chord.
—It will be seen that the chord on the mediant has the leading-tone, as well as that on the dominant. It has also double bonds with the tonic. Why is it not much used in modern music? The reason must be chiefly æsthetic, for in the early counterpoint it was freely used, and statically it is quite as good as any other minor chord. It was only when the *mode-relation* of tonic, dominant, and subdominant began to be more strongly demanded by the modern ear, that this chord was felt to be "unmeaning." See "How to Observe Harmony." Our simple statical studies show us at least these points of weakness about the chord—first, that it is similar to the tonic and dominant, having double bonds to both of them, and that as these chords speak out their mode-relation more clearly, they are sure to be preferred to it; and second, that the upward "leading-tone" is not in this chord associated either with *its opposite* leading-tone, as in the chord on the leading-tone T or SE, or with the dominant *root*, as in the chord on the dominant S or ^mM, so that its *leading* quality is not supported. In mode-relation it is "neither one thing nor the other." Further, in the chord ^mD, there is a bad partial dissonance. This will be seen by taking the vibration numbers for d and se from the table on p. 14; d = 288 and se = 450. Now the IInd partial of se = 450 × 2 = 900, while the IIIrd

partial of d = 288 × 3 = 864; therefore these two partials will give rise to 900 — 864 = 36 beats per second—about the worst possible dissonance in the middle region of pitch.

Idea of Cadence.

In Chapter II a theory is suggested of the first idea of cadence. That suggestion relates only to melody, and to the fact that its going *downward* leads naturally to the feeling of *rest*, especially when the melody falls on the chief tone of the scale. In harmony, the same idea is carried out, but with some difference. At first, the constant motion of the counterpoint, and the answering of part to part, left little or no place for those closes of "lines," or rhythmical divisions of the melody which we now call cadences. Rhythmical Form was then as little studied as Transition and Modulation. The counterpoint which stood for harmony was a continuous waving and intertwining of consonant melodies, seldom coming to a pause. Milton well expressed its finest effects when he described it as "Untwisting all the chains that tie the hidden soul of harmony." But even in this sort of music, there must be a final resting-place, and commonly one or two other places of pause in a piece. It is curious to note that the word "cadence"—or falling-place—was at first used, not for the final chord of the close, but for the discord and resolution (or going down) of the dissonating tone which habitually preceded it.

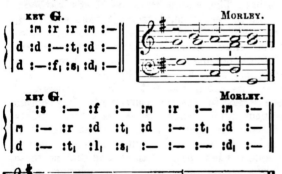

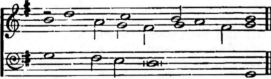

Soon the word came to be applied to the two or three chords which, at the close of a "line" or rhythmic division, both mark the key and claim for their line a certain relation to it, as tonic, dominant, or subdominant, and so on. In harmony it did not matter whether the melody ascended or descended so that the chords moved decisively to the characteristic cadence intended, except

that, in final cadences, it was still felt that a *descending* bass part is more effective than one which ascends. A brief study of the "Historical Specimens" will show that Palestrina and the men of his age—the first part of the sixteenth century—used very few cadences, and those chiefly cadences on the tonic. The following examples will show how the cadential syncopations come rolling in one after the other, until the tonic itself first demands a hearing as a dissonance, and then draws all the music to rest in the final chord.

From the same.
KEY **C.**

It is plain that the æsthetic object of all these dissonances approaching a close was "motion," to set off and signalise the coming "rest." These old writers used also the plagal cadence and that on the dominant as we use them, but much more seldom, and without preparing for them—as for the tonic cadence—by a series of dissonances. Instead of a dominant cadence, however, they sometimes treated the dominant as a tonic, and then came in the dissonances as before.

The Greeks, in their melodic music, while always beginning on the tonic, very commonly ended a piece of music with the dominant, and it is curious to notice that the early writers of counterpoint were slow to abandon this example. They close some of their pieces with a cadence on the dominant, and sometimes with a cadence on the tonic of the dominant (first sharp) key. So slowly did our modern feeling for the tonic establish itself.

FINAL CADENCE.

KEY **C.**   PALESTRINA.

KEY **F.** S.C.T.T.B.   VITTORIA.

English composers of the latter half of the same century—such as Tye, Edwards, Tallis, and Farrant—were bolder. They seem to have delighted in cadences on the dominant and on the dominant key, but made their *final* closes on the tonic. Thus, the contrast of cadences, and their relation to the mode, began to be felt, and *clearness of key* was more and more demanded. The *contrast* of these two cadences has a distinct statical cause. We have already noticed that in going from the dominant to the tonic (S to D, or *M* to L), as in the tonic cadence, we move from a chord with a "leading-tone" seeking resolution into one which is bonded to it by its fifth. It is motion seeking rest. But in going from the tonic to the dominant (D to S, or L to *M*), as in most dominant cadences, we move from the acknowledged resting-tone of the tune to a chord which has a restless leading-tone, and has "melodic dissonance" with *the root* of the chord last struck. The stirring effect of this cadence is even more manifest when the dominant follows the subdominant, with which its very root is melodically dissonant.

KEY **F.** C.T.T.B.   BIRD.

KEY **F.** S.C.T.T.B.   BIRD.

In watching the historical development of cadences, it is interesting to see how early a *bond* was added to the progression—subdominant, dominant, tonic (F S D, or *R ᵐM L*), by using, instead of the subdominant, the supertonic in its *b* position (or first inversion), and introducing the tonic-tone (d in 'R*b*, or l in 'T*b*) as a prepared and resolved dissonance, just as in the old cadences. Thus was secured, not, indeed, so firm a bass, but the bond of root to fifth, and also that other kind of bond, stretching across three chords, which is made by the preparation, percussion, and resolution of a dissonance, and the emphatic announcement of the coming tonic which that dissonance gives. But so strong was the feeling that this was the place for the subdominant, that that tone was still regarded as the root, and the r in major, and the t in minor regarded as the "added sixth."

S.S.C.T.B. ("*Fire, fire my heart.*") KEY **F**. MORLEY.

The free use of the dominant seventh also became an important factor in cadences. Although Monteverde, at the close of the sixteenth century, is credited with the bold introduction of the dominant seventh *unprepared*, it was not till the seventeenth and eighteenth centuries that its great use as a key-decider in tonic cadences was thoroughly understood. It is almost amusing to observe how slow composers were to use the now so common tonic chord in its *c* position, or second inversion, on the third last chord of a tonic cadence. It came in as an alteration of the old fourth on the dominant ('S).

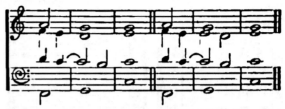

The theorists did not perceive that by this process the chord itself was changed, and the sixth of the dominant became the third of the tonic in its *c* position. By this means the dissonating tonic tone was lost, but instead of that we had the tonic chord, in its less sonorous position, announcing itself, like "coming events" which "cast their shadows before." We may also be reminded that the dominant *following* the tonic suggests the feeling of motion *forward*, and all the more "restfully" leads into the tonic again. Thus slowly did tentative Art discover the best and truest things, and yet more slowly does Science test and approve.

Cadential Habits.—It is not necessary to trace these ideas of the bonding, moving, and leading powers of chords through all the development of cadences. (See a practical development of this subject in "How to Observe Harmony," and "Construction Exercises.") But it is important to notice, that the care with which *tonic* cadences have been studied has led to the formation of habits so strong that certain progressions, which have been found best in these cadences, and are constantly used there, have come to be positively avoided outside of those cadences. Thus, the dominant seventh in its strongest position is so much used in tonic cadences, that it is now not commonly found in that position elsewhere. These *habits* of the ear, once formed, *compel* us to imagine a root, when it is omitted, if the incomplete chord occurs in some well-known *habitat* of that chord. It is thus when d is sometimes omitted from the cadential D*c*. It is thus, also, in two-part harmony, when a mere outline and shadow of the habitual progression of chords is able to suggest them to the mind. Our definition of the root of a chord, p. 32. will show that it is *not all* habit or imagination which makes us realise the presence of the true root when only dimly indicated in its proper place. This recognition of the power of habit will help us to see more clearly some of the following reasonings on Transition and Modulations.

Intrusion of Harmony on Melody.—When first harmony, in its crude form of counterpoint, began to be applied to the old-world melodies, it had a modifying influence upon them. There were melodic cadences and modes which it was difficult to dress in counterpoint, or to arrange in harmony. No one can glance over the ancient music, and the modern music of ancient nations contained in "Historical Specimens," without noticing that there are very many closes of lines to which our modern ears have become quite unaccustomed, chiefly because our modern harmony does not easily accommodate itself to them; and it is also well-known that our love of harmony has deprived us of the use of all the "modes" of the Great Scale, except that on the first and that on the sixth. There are things which melody can do, but which harmony spoils. Many of the ancient modal songs of Scotland, Ireland, Wales, and other nations lose at once their characteristic mental effect when harmony is added to them. And this is because certain requirements of the ear, in harmony, make it necessary either to alter the melodies themselves, and so destroy them, or to use in the harmony such accidentals and such progressions as give the melody a different meaning from that which first belonged to it. It seems that the ear early declared its preference for the major over the minor thirds in harmony, and especially required the major thirds in cadences, where the ear expects rest. These remarks find illustration in the Gregorian Tones, see "Historical Specimens," Nos. 25 and 31, from the old book of Antoine Bernabei, who flourished at the end of the seventeenth century. Here we have the tones as sung by the priests alone, followed by the same tones taken up by the choir, with thin harmonic accompaniments above and below. In the second tone, when the priest sings alone, he closes with the bold and touching cadence—

KEY B♭.
{ :d |t₁ :s₁ |l₁ ‖

But when the choir takes up the same chant in reply, the last tone but one is made sharp to suit the harmony; that is to give the ear the pleasure of a major chord on the dominant. But that sharp takes not only itself but the next tone out of the original mode and key, and totally alters their mental effect. In the first tone, the harmony shows us the early love of a major third even in closes, and the fourth tone shows us the half of a chant quite changed in its effect on the mind from that of the "sorrowful" sixth of the scale falling on the fifth to that of the more business-like second falling on the first. For a long time the minor third was avoided in a closing chord. Sebastian Bach often introduced the sharp third, even when it made an awkward and difficult melody for the voice, rather than have a

minor third in a long-drawn close; and Mozart, not liking the weird effect of this "Picardy Third," sometimes endured the hardness of omitting the third altogether. It is only of late years that we have grown accustomed to a minor third on the last chord. In earlier times, when the unprepared dominant seventh, which now clearly fixes the key, was not known, great importance was attached to the clear klang of the last chord, but now, by means of that chord, a sense of key can be maintained even with a close on a minor chord. This sensitiveness of the ear, along with the growing demand which harmony brought for the mode relations of tonic, dominant, and subdominant, gave harmony a "modifying" power over the structure and the effects of melody.

Harmony and the Modes.— Professor Helmholtz, in the closing part of his great work, has shown how the old modes with their characteristic mental effect were necessarily pushed out when harmony came; but he sees that, although we have thus lost many quaint and beautiful effects of melody, we have gained new powers of musical expression by means of transitions and modulations which can only be effected by keeping the ear close to the key, as that condensed melody, which we call harmony, always does. One composer after another tried his various ways of harmonising the modes, and those modes which it was found could not satisfactorily submit to the conditions of harmony fell gradually into disuse. Even Bach and Handel still tried occasionally to harmonise the mode on the second of the scale; but the teachings of Rameau left us only one major mode—that on the first of the scale—and one minor—that on the sixth. "Let us suppose," Professor Helmholtz says, "the old contrapuntists trying one melodic mode after another and seeking to fit on to it the clothing of harmony."

The mode on the first of the scale (D) was easily fitted, and its adaptation to the bright old melodies of the Meistersingers and other popular songs, which Luther used for his People's Chorales, greatly promoted the love of plain chordal harmony. Not only did its tonic carry a major chord, but its dominant and subdominant also, so that it possessed every advantage arising from the full sonorousness of these chords. Of no other mode can this be said.

The mode on the fifth of the scale (S) has also a major third for its tonic chord, and a major chord for its subdominant, but the more important chord of the dominant (R) is minor. Not only so, but it is without that important element of a dominant, the "leading-tone" already studied. Hence it was that the early writers of counterpoint, when harmonising a passage in the Soн mode, or one in which s was made emphatic and important, changed the f of its dominant into fe. They were thus able to obtain the progression ᵗʰR S, or D ᵗʰR S, and in this way Palestrina and others made cadences on S, as the tonic of the Soн mode, quite as early as they made the now common cadences on S, as the dominant of the Doн mode. See '' Historical Specimens." They soon felt, however, that by creating this artificial leading-tone they only secured a cadence exactly like the *natural* tonic cadence of the Doн mode, for D ᵗʰR S is exactly the same thing as the familiar and natural F S D. It produces no longer the effect of a Soн mode, but is in fact, what they did not then understand, an actual transition to the key of the dominant. There was nothing to be gained by continuing the use of a Soн mode which had to be thus harmonised.

The mode on the fourth of the scale (F) has indeed, like the last, a major tonic chord. It has also, better than the last, a major dominant chord (D). But this dominant chord is without a leading-tone, and there is no true subdominant. It has been shown that the power of dominant and subdominant depends upon the interval of a fifth ; and in this case, the fifth below f is a diminished, not a perfect, one. Even in the old times of melody this mode was but little used, because the defining power of the over-fifth and under-fifth is felt in melody, though not so strongly as in harmony. For similar reasons a mode upon the seventh of the scale was scarcely attempted ; the tonic would have been a self-dissonant chord, and it has no perfect fifth above.

The mode on the third of the scale has a minor chord (M) for its tonic, and a minor chord (L) for its subdominant. These alone would make the harmonisation of its cadences gloomy, and this effect would be increased when attempts were made to use the dominant (T), with its self-dissonant chord and its downward (added to the upward) leading-tone. It has a true dominant tone, but not a true dominant chord. Composers tried all ways of avoiding that which the ear obviously dreads—two unrestful minor chords in a close. Even so late as Mozart we find attempts to harmonise passages with the peculiarly sad effect of this mode, sometimes doing without a dominant chord — thus, *REb* ᵗʰ*M*— and sometimes altering the diminished dominant into a major chord. See " Agnus Dei," Mozart's *Twelfth Mass,* measures 9 to 12 and 47, 48. There are some beautiful specimens of this mode in the melodies of ancient nations. See especially the Indian melodies, ʿʿ Historical Specimens," where

we have not only constant cadences on the third of the scale, but as a "relief" in the middle of the tune, a lively play upon its dominant.

The mode on the second of the scale has minor chords for its tonic (R, or more properly RAH) and dominant (L), and a major chord for its subdominant (S). The two minor chords in the tonic close were unendurable. The first contrapuntists varied it by sharpening the third of the tonic, making ᵗʰR, and the third of the dominant (L), making ᵈᵉL. But when they had done this, the sound was that of a Doн mode cadence to a RAH mode passage (for ᵈᵉL ᵗʰR is the same thing as S D), and the characteristic effect of RAH was gone ! If, on the other hand, taking advantage of the allowance in the use of the old church modes to take the seventh of the scale either sharp or flat (t or ta) they changed the subdominant S into ᵗʰS, they found that the cadence produced—ᵗʰS ᵈᵉL R—had the same sound as R ᵗʰM L—the modern minor, and gave a LAH mode close to a RAH mode passage ! And this it did by two changes of tone instead of one. The following examples will show that this Doric mode (or Phrygian, as the Greeks called it) still struggled for existence among the unfriendly surroundings of harmony even to the days of Bach and Handel, and will show also, how impossible it is to produce, by cadences made sonorous *artificially*, the characteristic effects of either an ancient mode or a modern key.

The end of the Chorale, "Was mein Gott will," from the
ᴋᴇʏ A.   *St. Matthew Passion.*   ѕᴇʙ. Bᴀᴄʜ.

:f	ᴍ	:r	s	:f .ᴍ	ᴍ	:—	r
:l,	s,.l,	:t,.de	r	:r	r	:de	l,
:d .r	ᴍ .fe:s		r .ᴍ :f	t,	:ᴍ	fe
:l,.t,	d	:t,	ta, :l,	se,	:l,	r,

The close of " I will exalt him," from " Israel in Egypt."
ᴋᴇʏ C.   Hᴀɴᴅᴇʟ.

.d¹	:ta,.ta	l	:r¹	—	:de¹	r¹
.l	:l .s	s	:f	ᴍ	:—	f
.r¹	:r¹	—	:l	l	:—	¹l
.fe	:s	r	:—	l,	:—	r

We cannot then wonder that this mode, though existing long, has at last fallen into disuse. It refused to yield its characteristic effects when placed under the inexorable conditions of modern harmony. Modern taste rejects everything that is not harmony. I, for one, am sorry not to hear this old mode still used in pure *melody* with its fine expressive prayerful effects, as "Bangor" may still be heard among the hills of Wales, and as Burns must have heard "Martyrs" in the highlands of Scotland when he wrote the "Cottar's Saturday Night." Shame to say it, *both* the melodies have been altered by modern editors in the vain attempt to suit them to harmony, but the masses of the people in both countries still hold fast to their RAH mode. Why should everything in our church music be harmonised? As Melody refuses to yield up some of her finest effects when she stands alone, why should not Melody be humoured? Why not use some of the old chants and responses as Marbeck gave them, without flourishes and without accompaniment? Why should not the advocates of *unison* singing in psalmody introduce it first in connection with some of these fine old Doric tunes united to time-honoured psalms and hymns? Only, if this is attempted with an organ, do not let it go wandering about into every key and no key—trying to harmonise, but only confusing the ear. Let it play nothing beyond the "pedal," "diapason," and "principal" unison.

The mode on the sixth of the scale (L) proves to be the only *minor* mode which satisfies the modern ear when harmonised. It can be made to suit the requirements of a cadence with only one artificial change, that of sharpening the third of its dominant chord, and making M into ᵐM. When this was done with the RAH mode, there was heard a major subdominant as well as a major dominant, and these two major chords overshadowed, by their clear clang, the minor tonic. The LAH mode avoids this, and by its succession of minor, major, minor, retains the predominating minor character of the cadence, while it secures a leading-tone and a clear klang for the dominant chord. At first, indeed, the tonic itself was constantly made major, L being changed into ᵐL. In Bach's chorales we have,

in long-drawn-out closes, the ᵐL, which was called the Picardy third, and even as late as Mozart we sometimes find the third omitted (leaving a "bare fifth") in the closing chord, rather than use the minor third. But within this last hundred years we have learned to accept the minor tonic for this mode. This acquiescence, however, in a minor tonic with a major dominant was not yielded without the consciousness that the tonic was thus a little thrown into the shade by its dominant, and probably to counteract this effect, and to subordinate the dominant, the dissonant seventh is freely introduced in it—very much more constantly than in the dominant of the major mode. Another alteration common in the LAH mode—the sharpening of the *sixth*, changing f into ba—is made for the sake of melody, not harmony, in which, indeed, it is awkward. It is used to avoid the leap of a minor third in stepwise progressions like

}:l |se   :f   ‖

or

}:ᵐ |f :se |l ‖

But however thankful we may be for a minor mode which will, even proximately, suit itself to harmony, we cannot help feeling that fine old LAH mode psalm-tunes like "Windsor" have changed their manly sorrow for a sentimental grief when the artificial leading-tone comes in the melody. We therefore distinguish this "made up" harmonic mode from the ancient LAH mode by calling it the Modern Minor. These studies of cadences and of mode-relations will help us to understand the historical development and statical facts of modulation and transition.

Generation of Keys.—In modern music there has gradually grown up a great System of Keys around a central key of fixed pitch. The central key has for its key-tone C, and stands on the common staff notation without either sharps or flats in the signature. Taking the dominant of this and making it a key-tone, at the same time raising the fourth for a new leading-tone, we have the key of G. Taking again the dominant of this, we have in the same way the key of D, and so on. Returning to the central key C, and taking its subdominant, and using the flat seventh as a downward leading-tone to the third of the new key, we have the key of F. Taking in the same way the subdominant of F, we have the key of B♭, and so on. This generation of keys is shown in the diagram on p. 73. On this diagram the names of the major keys are placed above the staff notation signature, and the names of the minor keys below. I regard the relative minor as of more importance than the minor of the same tonic. More on this subject later on.

Statical Relation of Modes and Keys.

—Under the heading of "Classification of Chords" above, I have explained the distinction which we make between key and mode. This distinction becomes increasingly important as we study the principles on which *changes* of key or mode, or both, are made in the course of a single piece of music. Changes of key we call Transition; changes of mode, Modulation; changes of both key and mode, Transitional Modulation. By Minor Transition, we mean transition from the relative minor of one key to the relative minor of another key. A transition which makes it necessary to alter *one* tone of the original key by sharpening it (which is sometimes represented in the staff notation by the removal of a flat) we call a transition to the first sharp key. When *two* tones have to be sharpened, we call it transition to the second sharp key; and so on. When one tone has to be flattened (which is sometimes represented in the staff notation by the removal of a sharp), the transition is one to the first flat key; and so on. The mental effects of transition and modulation, and the actual practice of modern composers in the use of these contrivances, are carefully described in "How to Observe Harmony," and the manner in which the various changes are effected is shown in "Construction Exercises," with copious references to examples in "Historical Specimens." The question before us now is this, How far can musical statics supply the reasons why one "remove" is taken rather than another? It is easy to say that these different transitions and modulations are taken simply because the composer *likes* them, or because he wants such an effect in such a place. This is undoubtedly true; but are there not some physical facts which guide the composer, however unconsciously to himself, in the choice he makes? The natural immobility of the mind—its "*vis inertiæ*," as Gottfried Weber calls it—suggests the idea that keys and modes are bonded like chords. Our first principle, therefore, shall be, that those transitions and modulations are most easily accepted by the ear which require the *least change* of tones. A second principle is found in the *relative importance* of the bond; that of the new tonic with dominant and subdominant being the most important. A third and very important

principle is that the new *leading-tone* (whether upward in the sharp removes, or downward in the flat removes) shall be clear. For this purpose it is undoubtedly better—1st, that it should be a new tone; 2nd, that there should be no other new tone struck at the same time which might seem to dispute the leadership. The composer makes his transitions and modulations for certain effects. He thinks only of these effects, and is commonly guided by his ear alone. But, nevertheless, he is found to avoid some of these changes, and to use some, more than others. We shall see how far the statical principles just laid down have unconsciously guided him; and if these principles are true, then the learner will be saved the laborious process of finding out for himself, by years of experiment, what statics can show him in a few hours.

In the ancient one-voiced (Homophonic) modulation, the first rule was perfectly obeyed, because there was no change of tone at all; there was simply an effort—by accent, by cadence, by the defining power of the over-fifth—to bring out the mental effect of some new tone of the scale—to change the mode. When harmony in its first form—counterpoint—came into use, composers naturally employed the same kind of modulations with the addition of counterpoint. They confined themselves, as Dr. Burney says, to the old modes, and to such changes of key as could be made from the open key "by the sharps in the signature of the key of A." These changes would be **fe** for **f**, making a harmonic leading-tone to the Soh mode; **de** for **d**, making a harmonic leading-tone to the Ray mode; and **se** for **s**, making a harmonic leading-tone to the Lah mode. It is interesting to notice that these harmonised modulations to which the first writers of counterpoint confined themselves are still amongst the commonest changes that are now made, even in these days of greatest licence in alteration of key. Their "modulation" to the Soh mode we call transition to the first sharp key; their "modulation" to the Ray mode we call transitional modulation to the first flat key; and their modulation to the Lah mode we call by the same name—modulation.

The following analysis of all possible transitions and modulations as far as the fourth sharp and the fourth flat removes will be more interesting to the student than to the general reader. I have therefore placed it in small type. The general results of this analysis show a striking coincidence between the statical principles announced above and the actual practice of musicians. Even where it might be thought that æsthetics alone would rule, statics point in the same way. Thus, while natural feeling

THE SYSTEM OF KEYS AND JUST INTONATION.

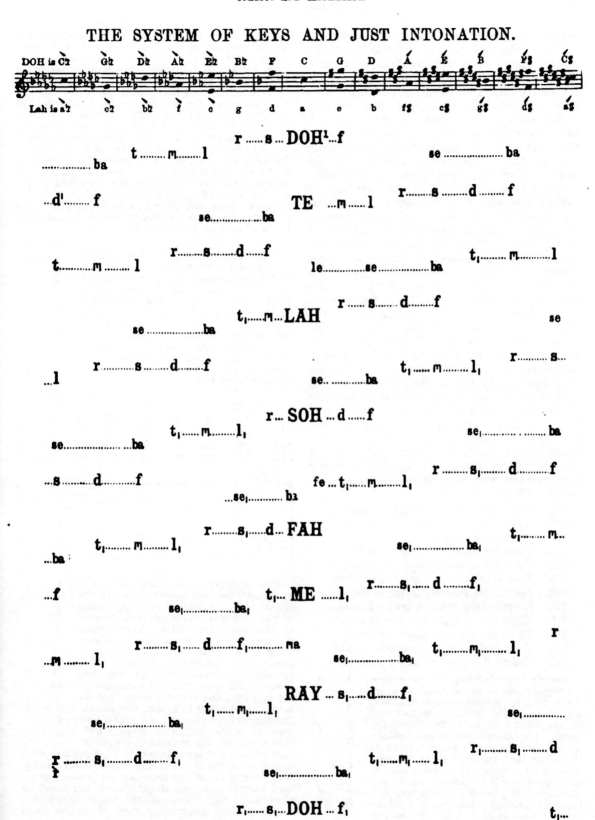

suggests that passing into the sharp removes and into the major mode have a similar and mutually helpful effect, our statical analysis shows that the sharp removes do not conveniently associate themselves with modulations to the minor. And while natural feeling suggests that we may readily associate the sadness of the minor with the gloomy flat removes, our statical analysis shows that the flat removes do not conveniently associate themselves with modulation to the major. It will be seen, however, that while one or two not statically very bad removes are neglected because they contradict the æsthetic feeling, several not statically of great value are employed, chiefly because they are wanted for artistic effect. This is the case with the removes which assist the composer in making successive phrases imitating one another a step higher or a step lower. These sequences moving upward a step may be made by the "first flat remove, major to minor." Sequences going downward a step are made by the "first sharp remove, minor to major," or by the "second flat remove, major to major." In both cases the second remove is bolder, but the first remove is more used because it is more easily made, although it somewhat contradicts or softens by its modulation the effect of the step, upward or downward. If we were to place these transitions, modulations, and transitional modulations in the order of their actual importance in the practice of music, or the usage of musicians, we should find this order to correspond with that in which statics also would place them :—

1st. First sharp remove, major to major.
2nd. Simple modulation, major to minor, or minor to major.
3rd. First flat remove, major to major.
4th. First flat remove, major to minor.
5th. First sharp remove, minor to major.
6th. Second flat remove, major to major.
7th. Second sharp remove, major to major.
8th. Third sharp remove, minor to major.
9th. Third flat remove, major to minor.
10th. First sharp remove, major to minor.
11th. Fourth flat remove, major to minor.

Simple Modulation.—In going from the major mode to its relative minor, we make the least possible change of sound, and the two are so intimately related that the ear passes from one to the other quite easily. The modulation is made chiefly by the insertion of the sharp seventh of the minor (se), and by that modal progression of chords and formation of cadences of which we have spoken before. Thus the first principle is satisfied; and the third principle, clearness of leading-tone, is also satisfied. But the second principle is not so fully obeyed, for it is

l	*l*
	..........*se*
s	
f	*f*
ʍ	*ʍ*
r	*r*
d	*d*
t₁	*t₁*
l₁	*l₁*

not the tonic, or dominant, or subdominant, but the submediant of the Doh mode, which becomes the tonic of the Lah mode. We cannot, therefore, place modulation from major to relative minor in the first rank of acceptability to the ear. Modulation from minor to relative major is somewhat less acceptable than the last, because the leading-tone of the new mode does not stand out clear and fresh. Hence it is that, in taking this modulation, an intermediate chord (L) is commonly employed, which may be imagined to belong to either of the two modes. It should be explained that in passing from the major to its relative minor, r is lowered a komma, and becomes **rah**. It has now become the subdominant, and is therefore frequently required to tune well with **f** and **l**. This and other kommatic changes in the process of transition and modulation will be explained in the chapter on True Intonation.

First Sharp Remove.—*Major to Major.*—This transition satisfies the rules—first, of "least change," for only one tone is altered :* second, of "importance of bond," for it is one of dominant with tonic; and third, of "clearness in leading-tone," for it is new and undisputed. No wonder that this transition stands first of all in acceptability to the ear. Probably 90 per cent. of all existing changes in mode or key are from major to major of the first sharp key.

	s	*d'*
		..........*t*
	f	·
	ʍ	*l*
	r	
	d	*f*
	t₁	*ʍ*
	l₁	*r*
	s₁	*d*

Minor to Minor.—This change is equally good with the last-named as far as the second rule is concerned—the importance of bond. But it is very inferior in respect of the other two rules. Three tones instead of one are *changed*. One of the new tones (d) is the restoration of a changed tone (s from se) by the flattening. This restored tone is awkward in its effect, but it would not come into the dominant of the new key, and would therefore not be heard till the key had been established. But the other two new tones (being struck together in the dominant), dispute with each other, for the moment, the right of leadership. Although there has been a great attempt among musicians to put the minor mode on an equality with the major, and this transition has in consequence been used to some extent, yet the ear will assert its supremacy, and where, in the major mode, the heightening and brightening effect of the first sharp

	ʍ	*l*
		..........*se*
	r	
	d	*f*
	t₁	*ʍ*
	l₁	*r*
	se₁	
		..........*d*
		..........*t₁*
	f₁	
	ʍ₁	*l₁*

* Kommatic changes are neglected throughout this analysis.

key is used, in the minor mode modulation to the relative major is commonly used in its place.

KEY Bb. *Lah is G.*

Major to Minor.—This change has nearly all the weak points of the last-named, with the addition of inferiority of bond. First, two tones are changed, not three; second, the bond is mediant only to tonic; third, there is the contest of major and minor leading-tones, both newly struck in the dominant. Musical practice corresponds with these statical facts, for this transitional modulation is but sparingly used. It is nevertheless somewhat more used than the last, because it can be entered gradually—the major leading-tone being struck first, and the minor leading-tone entering afterwards. This puts it statically on a level with the last-named, and that has for musical effect a good substitute, which this has not.

m	l
....	se
r	
d	f
t,	m
l,	r
s,	d
....	t,
f,	
m,	l,

KEY F. **C.t.** *Lah is A.*

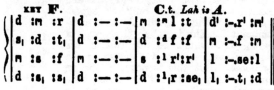

Minor to Major.—First, two changes (fe=t and s from se=d) and one of these (the restoration of altered tone) will not occur in the dominant, by which the new mode is entered; second, no bond to the new tonic; third, the new leading-tone very clear. On account of its weak point, in relation to the second rule, this transitional modulation is scarcely ever used except with the apology of a descending sequence, in which case it is very valuable.

See "Construction Exercises," p. 99, and "How to Observe," pp. 83, 84.

d'	
....	t
f	l
m	l
r	s
d	f
t,	m
l,	r
se,	
....	d

KEY G.

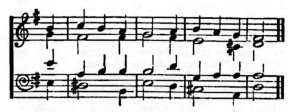

First Flat Remove.—*Major to Major.* —First, there is as little change of tone as in the first sharp remove; second, the bond is slightly inferior, as the new tonic is built upon the old subdominant instead of the old dominant; third, the leading-tone is equally clear and indisputable with that of the first sharp remove. But its inferiority consists in its being a *downward* leading-tone, and its leading to the third of the key, not to the tonic. Its inferiority under the last two rules causes it to be very much less used than the corresponding sharp remove. A peculiarity of transition to the flat removes is that they cannot well be taken on the dominant chord of the new key as the sharp removes are, because the simple dominant (whatever may be said of the dominant seventh) does not contain the distinguishing tone. In the present case there is added the consideration that the dominant chord of the new key would sound only like the reassertion of the tonic of the old key. In sudden or passing transition the change is made on the dominant seventh. In gradual transition the new tonic is emphatically asserted, and the distinguishing tone follows in the subdominant chord, sometimes in that of the new R chord. In the last case the f often ceases to have the effect of a leading-tone, being allowed to go upward. The motion of the bass in these cases of gradual transition assists the assertion of the new key. In this way this first flat remove is frequently used for quiet "returning" transition.

d'	f'
t	m'
l	r'
s	d'
f	t
....	
m	l
r	s
d	f

KEY Bb.

Minor to Minor.—First, three changes (ta = f. de = se, and s from se = r), but the first is not a change in cases where the sharp sixth of the minor (ba) is used in the transition, for that would practically correspond with the old tone (t). The restored tone would not occur in the dominant of the new key, and the disagreeableness of its effect would be greatly lessened through the key being already established. Second, the tonic is built on the old subdominant. In just intonation there is a kommatic difference between the two, the new l really corresponding with **rah**. Third, two new leading-tones, but not disputing each other's influence; rather helping each other in bringing the ear to decision. This transition is not common, and the upward leading-tone often appears before the other new tones are heard, that being sufficient to decide the ear.

l	r^l
se	
	d^l
	t
f	
m	l
	se
r	
d	f
t_l	m
l_l	r

KEY B♭. *Lah is G.*

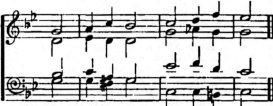

Major to Minor.—First, two changes (ta = f and de = se), which is better than the last in not having to restore the previously altered s. Second, the character of the bond is not high, as the new tonic is built only on the supertonic of the old key, although it bonds dominant and subdominant. Third, two new leading-tones, but not contradictory. These two tones, however, seldom occur together except in 'SE, the se being quite sufficient to define the new key and mode. This transitional modulation is much used, especially in cadences. It is also of service in making sequences a step upward. It is almost as frequently used as transition to the first flat major.

l	r^l
se	
	d^l
	t
f	
m	l
r	s
d	f
t_l	m
l_l	r

KEY G.

Minor to Major.—First, two changes (ta = f and s from se = r). Second, the new tonic is built on the submediant; not a strong bond. Third, one leading-tone. The difficulty of this transition is that you cannot get into the new key by the dominant, dominant seventh, or supertonic chords without using the "restored" tone, which seems to disturb the ear without a meaning. I cannot otherwise account for the disuse of this transitional modulation, which has so little else of difficulty in its statical relations. It might be entered through its subdominant, leaving the restored tone to occur afterwards.

d^l	f^l
t	m^l
l	r^l
s	d^l
	t
f	
m	l
	se
r	
d	f

From a Hymn-tune, by

KEY **D.** *Lah is B.*   t.G.   MONK.

Second Sharp Remove.—*Major to Major.*—First, two changes (de = t and fe = m). Second, tonic built on supertonic. Bonding, dominant and subdominant. Third, the clearness of leading-tone would be doubtful if the two new tones occurred together in the dominant. But this is not so; the m comes in afterwards. This is rare as a principal transition, but is common in subordinate transition, and especially in sequences moving a step higher.

r^l	d^l
	t
d^l	
t	l
	se
l	s
se	
s	f
f	
m	r
r	d

KEY E♭.   F.t.m.   From a Chorale.

Minor to Minor.—First, three changes (le = se, fe = m, de = t). Second, new tonic built on old supertonic, bonding old dominant with new subdominant. Third, the three new sharps all heard together in the new dominant, and each claiming the office of leading-tone. These statical conditions are quite sufficient to explain the disuse of this transition.

Major to Minor.—First, same three changes as in the last case. Second, new tonic built on leading-tone. Third, the same strife in the new dominant as in the last case. That which musical statics thus condemns, the good taste of composers has instinctively avoided.

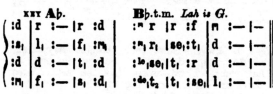

Minor to Major.—First, three changes (de=t, fe=m, s from se=f). Second, new tonic built on the old subdominant. Third, neither the restored tone (f) nor the m need appear in the first chord struck; but the new t is not quite sufficient to declare the new key, because the ear might mistake it for the minor of the first flat key. This transition is but rarely used.

Second Flat Remove.—*Major to Major.*—First, two changes (ma=f and ta=d). Second, no bond for the new tonic, but dominant and subdominant bonded together. Third, doubtfulness of leading-tone, the new f and d, which may occur in the same chord, disputing preeminence for the moment. This transition is often gradual, introducing ta=d (which suggests the *first* flat key) first, and then ma=f in a following chord. When taken suddenly this transition commonly introduces only one new tone (f) at first. It is very rare as a principal transition, but is common in subordinate and "oscillating" transition, especially in sequences moving the music a step downwards.

Minor to Minor.—First, four changes fe=se, ma=f, ta=d, and s from se=l). Second, no bond to the new tonic, but dominant and subdominant bonded. Third, three new tones, any two of which *might* appear together, disputing the leadership. This remove, statically so bad, is practically ignored.

Major to Minor.—First, three changes (fe=se, ma=f, ta=d). Second, the new tonic is built on the old dominant. Third, the three new tones disputing, as in the last case. This "two removes, major to minor" would be as bad as "two removes, minor to minor" if it was not free from the restoration tone, s from se=l, and if it had not so good a bond.

Of the three cases in "Text Book," two introduce it gradually, striking at first only the new **f**; and one takes it suddenly, striking at first only the new **se**.

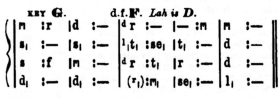

Minor to Major.—First, three changes (**ma=f, ta=d, s** from **se=l**). Second, no bond to new tonic. Submediant becomes dominant, a poor bond. Third, two new tones disputing; but these could be introduced one at a time The difficulty of this transition lies in its restored tone. The **s** from **se=l**, being struck as a new tone, draws attention to the tonic of the minor mode, while the object of the transitional modulation is to produce the bright effect of a major mode. These difficulties, with its bad bond, have condemned this "second remove, minor to major," to disuse.

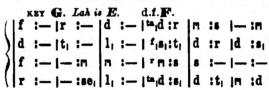

Third Sharp Remove.—*Major to Major.*—First, three changes (**se = t, de = m, fe = l**). Second, the new tonic is built on the submediant, a poor bond. Third, although there are three new tones, only one can appear at a time. This transition is exceedingly rare, especially as a principal one.

Il. 17. KEY **G.**   **E.t.m.l.**

l	dˡ
se	⋯⋯ t
s	
	⋯⋯⋯ l
f	se
n	s
r	f
	⋯⋯⋯ n
d	
t₁	r
l₁	d

Minor to Minor.—Three changes (**my = se, fe = l, de = m**). Second, no bond to new tonic. Third, two tones, both necessarily struck at the same time in the dominant, disputing leadership. This is as rare as the preceding transition.

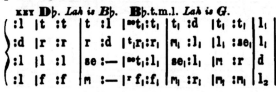

Major to Minor.—First, four changes (**my = se, fe = l, de = m, and se = t**). Second, no bond to the new tonic. Third, worse than the last. Three new tones (**m, se, t**), appearing together in the new dominant, competing for leadership.

Minor to Major.—First, only two changes (**de = m, fe = l**). Second, the new tonic is built on the old tonic. Third, no new leading-tone, no difference between the old dominant and the new. The first change comes when the tonic enters, taking a major instead of a minor third, which is very easy for the piano or any mere instrument to do. The second changed note occurs when the new subdominant, supertonic, or submediant enters. This transitional modulation is the commonest among three sharp removes. Its bond is very good; its two changes come in gradually, but it has no new leading-tone; it shines out with a cold artificial brightness. Some modern composers are very fond of this and the corresponding third flat remove, major to minor. But they do not touch the heart like the changes from the relative minor to its major, and *vice versa*. It is remarkable that this, which is statically the best of the third sharp removes, should also be æsthetically most wanted, for the same instinct—that of brightening the music—which leads the composer to move from the minor mode to a sharp remove would lead him also to the major mode.

Third Flat Remove.—*Major to Major.*—First, three changes (la=f, ta=s, ma=d). Second, no bond for the new tonic. Third, if the key is entered by the subdominant there are two new flat tones, f and d, disputing; if by the dominant seventh two others, f and s. This statically bad transition is not much used.

Minor to Minor.—First, two changes (ma=d, and the peculiar change of se to f). Second, the new tonic is built on the old mediant. Third, the upward leading-tone is not new; the downward leading-tone has an awkward relation to the upward leading-tone of the previous key. This change from the upward to the downward tendency is rather a chromatic than a transitional effect.

Major to Minor.—First, two changes of tone (ma=d, la=f). Second, the new tonic built on the old one. Third, no new leading-tone. The dominant chord the same in both cases. The first change occurs in the tonic chord itself, whose third is flattened. This is the commonest of all the third flat removes. Its effect of shivering woe is much employed by some musicians. It is often called the tonic minor as the other is called the tonic major. Both these changes are difficult to the singer, partly because of the forced and artificial flattening or sharpening of the third, and partly because of the kommatic changes to be referred to in the chapter on True Intonation. The piano, ruled by mechanism, does not feel this difficulty, and persons not accustomed to sing by the ear and mind alone, without accompaniment, seldom appreciate it.

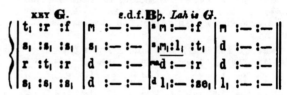

Minor to Major.—First, three changes (ta=s, ma=d, and the peculiar change of se to f). Second, no bond to the new tonic. Third, the new f, s, d competing.

Fourth Sharp Remove. — *Major to Major.* — First, four changes (re = t, fe = r, se = m, de = l). Second, new tonic founded on old mediant. Third, two new tones which must occur simultaneously in the dominant compete for leadership. The transition is on all points statically bad, and is not used, except in declamatory songs and recitatives.

Minor to Minor. — First, four changes (ty = se, de = l, re = t, fe = r). Second, no bond for the new tonic. Third, two new tones, se and t, compete in the same chord. This transition is worse than the last.

Major to Minor. — First, five changes (ty = se, de = l, re = t, fe = r, se = m). Second, no bond for new tonic. Third, three new tones, all in the dominant, competing. So violent a transitional modulation is necessarily neglected.

Minor to Major. — First, three changes (re = t,

fe = r, de = l). Second, new tonic built on old dominant. Third, two new tones—t and r—in the dominant chord compete for leadership. It must be this last statical element which causes the disuse of a transitional modulation with so good a bond.

Fourth Flat Remove. — *Major to Major.* — First, four changes (ra = f, ma = s, la = d, ta = r). Second, no bond for new tonic. Third, if the new key is entered by its subdominant, there are two new flat tones competing for attention; if by the dominant seventh, three new tones. Rarely this transition is used, being entered gradually, and only two of the new tones appearing together.

Minor to Minor. — First, three changes (ra = f, ta = r, with the peculiar change of se to d). Second, new tonic on old submediant. Third, only one of the new tones, t, need be used in the dominant chord, but that is not the leading-tone of the new minor mode. It outshines se, which is not a new tone. Nevertheless a few cases of this transition may be found.

Major to Minor.—First, three changes (ra=f, la=d, ta = r). Second, new tonic on old subdominant. Third, new dominant chord corresponds with the old tonic chord, and only one new tone (a flattened third) is necessary to make the new tonic chord. With so good a bond and so easy a passage-way, it is not surprising that this should be the commonest of all the fourth removes.

KEY **G.**   r.s.d.f.**E♭.** *Lah is C.*

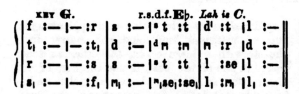

Minor to Major.—First, six changes (ra=f, ma=s, la=d, ta=r, s from se=t, and the peculiar change of se and d). Second, new tonic built on old leading-tone. Third, the new dominant seventh chord is formed entirely of new competing flats. If entered by the subdominant, only one new tone need be used in the first chord. This transitional modulation is scarcely used.

KEY **D.** *Lah is B.*

r.s.d.f.**B♭.**

More distant transitions need not here be analysed. Some modern composers, especially among the French, have done wild things in this way. They seem to feel no necessity of maintaining a sense of unity of key throughout the piece. The German and English feeling seems to require that the principal key of the piece should never be lost sight of; but some of the French composers delight in violent changes and distant removes. Here again we have an illustration of what Mr. Graham called "the fatal facilities of the piano." What need of our keeping the key in mind? The piano can remember! Some reference to the two sorts of "enharmonic modulation" may be properly deferred to the next chapter.

CHAPTER VI.

True Intonation *versus* Temperament.

The student, coming from the examination of other arts and sciences to that of music, is perplexed to find, what he has never found before, a conflict between Art and Nature. In all other arts he has found an earnest seeking for what is true—true to the instincts of human nature, and true to the principles of science. But in music he finds a revolt against all this, and a distinct attempt to set up a tempered, or altered scale, as really better, and to be more closely followed, than that which we have been considering. It is admitted, that when the best musicians play a quartet or septet of stringed instruments, which is the most delicate and perfect instrumental music in existence, they listen for one another and tune with one another naturally and according to the principles of true intonation. But it is required that, when these same instrumentalists play with the piano, the organ, and the harmonium, they shall adapt themselves to the altered, or tempered scale of those instruments. It is admitted, that an un-accompanied trio or quartet when sung by the best singers in the world, is studiously sung by them in perfect tune. The delicious effects of the chords thus heard at our great festivals and concerts is admitted to arise from true intona-tion. But it is required that the same persons shall sing a tempered scale when they have any-thing like a vigorous and independent accompani-ment by the pianoforte or organ. I have observed that when the accompaniment is light, the best singers naturally employ true intonation. Let me give two illustrations:—On hearing the Jubilee Singers of Fisk University, I was much struck by the effect of the opening chords of their piece "Steal away to Jesus." The singers stood close together, and their voices were tuned to one another with marvellous accuracy. I saw that the chords were in their own nature simple and plain, but when afterwards I tried the same chords upon a good and well-tuned piano of rich quality, I found it impossible to attain anything like the same chordal power and sweetness. By chordal power, I mean not loud-ness, but that power over the senses which a chord possesses by virtue of its internal unity. The singers had naturally used true intonation; the piano had been carefully tempered. A friend has just mentioned to me that he knows a dis-tinguished artist who holds two appointments, one as principal tenor and choirmaster in a church with a large organ, the other as tenor singer in one of the best, if not the best of our glee unions, and this gentleman says that he has to study carefully two intonations—the true, which alone he can use in the delicate chords of the glee union, and the tempered intonation which the organist expects from him in his church choir.

The actual difference between true intonation and temperament is shown in the diagram on page 83. The method introduced by Mr. Ellis is adopted of dividing the octave into 1200 equal intervals called cents. Thus on an instru-ment accurately tuned according to equal temperament, there will be 100 cents in the interval between any two adjacent notes; or in other words, a cent is the one-hundredth part of a semitone in equal temperament.

The column on the left hand shows the old organ or mean-tone temperament, and that on the right hand what modern tuners commonly profess to use—the equal temperament. It will be seen from our study on the Definiteness of Intervals, pp. 38 *et seq.*, that next to the octave, *the fifth* is that interval which it is most im-portant to keep pure and true, the slightest flattening changing its consonant partials into dissonance. The old temperament flattens this interval by five cents. The equal temperament flattens it by only two cents. In this it is better than the old temperament. Although this flattens the fifth by such a small amount, it is quite perceptible to the common ear. Anyone who will sound a pure, bright, natural fifth on a violin, or with the voice, and then try the same interval on a piano, will instantly feel how great a difference of effect so little a change can make. Mr. James Barnhill, jun., in an able and original book, entitled "Statics of Harmony" (Metzler & Co.), speaks of those who are striving to realise true intonation on keyed instruments as possessing ears which are "acutely and morbidly sensitive," and describes the error of a komma as too small to be seriously deprecated. My own experience contradicts this implication that only a very fine ear feels the necessity for true intonation. In natural musical endowment I am probably below, certainly not above, the

TUNING OF THE SCALE.

OLD TEMPERAMENT.		TRUE INTONATION.		EQUAL TEMPERAMENT.
1200 1200		**DOH¹**	1200 1200	
		Little Step 112		
1083 1088		**TE**	1088 1100	
		Greater Step 204		
890 884		**LAH**	884 900	
		Smaller Step 182		
697 702		**SOH**	702 700	
		Greater Step 204		
503 498		**FAH**	498 500	
		Little Step 112		
386 386		**ME**	386 400	
		Smaller Step 182		
193 204	182	**RAY** RAH	204 200	
			Greater Step 204	
	Smaller Step 182			
0 0		**DOH**	0 0	

INTERVALS.

Intervals.	Example.	Vibration Ratio.	Cents in Interval.
Octave	d¹ / d	2 : 1	1200
Major Seventh	d¹ / t	15 : 8	1088
Minor Seventh	f¹ / s	16 : 9	996
* Harmonic Seventh		7 : 4	969
Major Sixth	l / d	5 : 3	884
Minor Sixth	d¹ / m	8 : 5	8.4
Fifth	s / d	3 : 2	702
Diminished Fifth	f¹ / t	64 : 45	610
Tritone	t / f	45 : 32	590
Fourth	f / d	4 : 3	498
Major Third	m / d	5 : 4	386
Minor Third	d¹ / l	6 : 5	316
Greater Step	s / f	9 : 8	204
Smaller Step	l / s	10 : 9	182
Little Step	d¹ / t	16 : 15	112
Larger Chromatic	fe / f	135 : 128	92
Smaller Chromatic	se / s	25 : 24	70
Komma	r / r	81 : 80	22
† Skisma			2

*The interval between the IVth and VIIth partials.

† The difference between a Fifth in True Intonation and in Equal Temperament.

It may be seen from the above that

The Greater Step is rather more than 9 kommas.   The Larger Chromatic is rather more than 4 kommas.
 „ Smaller „ „ „ 8 „   „ Smaller „ „ „ 3 „
 „ Little „ „ „ 5 „   „ Komma equals 11 Skismas.

average of men. I cannot consciously and intentionally make the distinction of a komma with my voice, if there is no change of chord in the accompaniment, and yet on the question of being in or out of tune, I can in certain circumstances perceive the difference of even a skisma, which is only one eleventh part of a komma. There is something, as already explained in the definition by partials and differentials of the two tones which form a fifth, which makes that interval more easy to perceive than the third, sixth, or fourth. And very often when, in giving a public lecture, I have asked the audience to sing a fifth after my pattern, I have thought it a trifle too flat, very much like the dull fifth which the tempered piano gives. I have asked them to make it brighter. They have immediately done so, and have thus given satisfaction not only to my ears, but also to those of the musical men who are generally to be found in such an assembly. In several careful experiments which I have made in teaching friends to sing, who were exceedingly dull of musical perception, I have found that when I could not get them to produce the third of the scale with any accuracy, I was able to succeed very well with the fifth; they could hear it better, and so could better imitate it. *The Third of the Scale*, although it is not so keenly defined and so jealously guarded as the octave and the fifth, is one of the most important intervals in music, because every chord depends on it for sweetness. The redeeming feature of the old temperament is its respect for this interval, in the keys which are most used: it retains the third of the scale unaltered. But the equal temperament sharpens this interval by fourteen cents, which is about two-thirds of a komma. Now, it may be allowed that two cents of sharpening or flattening would not produce so serious an effect on the third as it does on the fifth, because the third is not so well defended and defined; but this sharpening to the extent of fourteen cents makes the third very harsh and unpleasant to the ear. The evanescent character of the pianoforte tone helps the ear to endure this temperament; but the continuous tones of the organ make it very unwelcome on that instrument, so that organ-tuners have still a great fondness for the older temperament. *The Sixth of the Scale* is that which first attracted my attention to the subject of mental effect—that peculiar influence of a tone upon the mind which it obtains, not from its absolute pitch, or its quality, or its loudness, but from its mentally perceived relation to the other tones of the scale. See pp. 10, 11. I noticed its peculiar emotional effect when sung slowly. Many of my readers will remember this at a high pitch recurring several times and in different keys on the second syllable of the word "Behold," in Handel's "Behold the Lamb of God." They will also remember it at a low pitch on the words "Like unto His sorrow," in Handel's "Behold and see." It is difficult to find words properly to express the effect of the slowly-moving sixth of the scale; but it has been called " sad," "sorrowful," "weeping." Now I could never get that effect satisfactorily on an equally-tempered piano. The disappointment is explained when we see how sharp the sixth is made by temperament. No wonder that all the touching effect is taken out of it. In the equal temperament it is sharpened by sixteen cents, which is worse than the third of the scale. The old temperament is not so bad; it sharpens the tone by six cents. But this is quite enough to spoil the delicate mental effect of the sixth of the scale. *The Seventh of the Scale* is very important as the leading and distinguishing tone of the key. It stands sufficiently near to the key-tone above, to indicate its upward relation and tendency, and sufficiently distant to show its independence as a tone, and to put it in tune with the major dominant and supertonic. It is remarkable that one of these temperaments makes this tone a little too flat, and the other a great deal too sharp. The old temperament flattens it by five cents. The equal temperament sharpens it by twelve cents, and makes the seventh of the scale nearly as bad as the third. It may be partly from a revulsion against the dulness of the old temperament that, as soon as equal temperament came into fashion, violinists and singers, accustomed to accompany the piano, have most unnaturally striven to make the seventh creep up to the octave, until there often seems to be no difference between them. How entirely

ERRORS OF THE TEMPERAMENTS.

	MEAN TONE. CENTS.		EQUAL. CENTS.	
d'				
t	5	♭	12	♯
l	6	♯	16	♯
s	5	♭	2	♮
f	5	♯	2	♯
m			14	♯
r	11	♭	4	♭
d				

this foolish affectation puts the tone out of tune with its proper chord, and destroys its individuality I need not describe. *The Fourth of the Scale* is less altered by temperament than those just mentioned. The old temperament sharpened it by five cents, the equal temperament sharpens it by only two cents. In so defined an interval as the fifth, this variation is felt, but in the interval of a fourth it is not noticed. Compare pp. 38, 39. *The Second of the Scale* is, as we have seen, a variable tone. See p. 8. The old temperament comes exactly between the grave and the acute form of the second of the scale; it fails to tune with the dominant and leading-tone, being too flat, and it fails to tune with the fourth and sixth, being too sharp. In both cases it is seriously wrong. The equal temperament is much nearer to the acute form of the second (that which is most used), being only flattened by four cents; but it fails egregiously, when it is wanted to tune with the fourth and sixth of the scale, being then too sharp by eighteen cents, and this is the largest variation from the truth we have yet met with in this temperament. The extent of the errors in both temperaments may be seen at a glance by the diagram on p. 85, which shows whether the temperament raises or lowers the tone, and to what extent.

The question naturally arises, how has this state of things come to pass? The answer is not difficult. Musicians preferred true intonation as long as a piece of music was confined to the limits of a single key; and even when transitions and modulations to the closely-related keys became common, the old organ temperament with its sweet thirds was considered to answer fairly for those keys which lie nearest the central key of C. And on this temperament Handel played his music. But when composers like Handel and Bach began to enjoy the effects of more distant transitions and modulations, they naturally desired finger-board instruments which could give better tune in the more distant keys. The mechanical genius of their time was not able to produce an instrument which could do this perfectly without a four or five-fold expense, and therefore the mechanicians asked of the musicians a compromise. The old temperament got worse and worse as one departed from the key of C, and they now proposed to make the nearer keys not so good as before, in order that the more distant ones might be made a little better. The musicians accepted the compromise; and Bach was so delighted with the means it gave him of roaming from key to key at his own good pleasure, that he chose for the first title of his two volumes of preludes and fugues "The Well-tempered Clavier." I cannot doubt for a

moment that if the mechanicians of his day had been able to produce a finger-board instrument which could play in perfect tune in all needful keys, Sebastian Bach would have entitled his work with much greater joy, "The True Intonation Clavier." But he, like the other great men who have followed him, was obliged to be content with the best instruments he could get. It is evident, therefore, that music has gone before its instruments. The development of modern harmony, in connection with transition and modulation, has brought into use a greater number of keys than before, and has employed those keys which are distant from the central key (C) to a much larger extent. The violins, the violas, the violoncellos, and the double basses, which form the foundation on which an orchestra is built, can follow the composer and give him true intonation in any keys he pleases. To a considerable extent the slide trumpets and trombones can do the same, and even the brass instruments which are played with pistons can be humoured to the extent of a komma by the loosening or tightening of the lips. The smaller instruments of the orchestra can be adapted to true intonation without much additional expense, by using a different instrument for every two or three different keys. But the finger-board instruments still lag behind in the race. Since the days of Sebastian Bach they are wonderfully improved in quality and power, but in beauty of intonation they have not gone a step beyond the "well-tempered clavier."

The mechanicians alone are not to blame for this. The mechanical genius of the Anglo-Saxon race has rarely failed, when Art and Science clearly showed the way. Let musicians, and especially those of them who understand the mathematical relations of tones, only agree among themselves, and point out definitely what modern music requires, and I doubt not that mechanical skill will soon master the difficulty. Meantime, discussion is the best means of bringing men to agreement, and I therefore ask those students who are interested in the matter, to consider with me the system of keys as they find it employed in the works of the great masters, in relation to true intonation. Our study of transitions and modulations in the last chapter of this tract shows us that composers are in the habit of taking some one key as the principal key of the piece they are writing, and of moving from it to other keys and modes which are nearly-related, and that the keys nearly-related in the first degree are those which take their new key-tone from the dominant or the subdominant of the original key. This has suggested what musicians call the "Generation of keys, described on page 71. By general consent the key C has been fixed on as the central key for all finger-board instruments, although the keys of B♭, E♭, D, &c., are made the central keys of other instruments. The established staff notation follows the usage of the finger-board instruments, and writes the key C on its open staff, as they give that key on their white digitals. From this acknowledged centre, the system of keys moves by "dominant generation" through key G, key D, key A, &c., and by "subdominant generation" to F, B♭, E♭, &c.; and this forms the system of keys actually used by musicians. In the diagram on p. 88 I have endeavoured to exhibit pictorially the true intonation of the central key of C, with that of the other keys of the great system in the order of their generation. It should be carefully noticed that on this plan (in order to maintain the relation of greater and smaller steps) every sixth of a scale becomes, in passing to the dominant key, a komma higher — every l becomes lay; and that every second of the scale becomes, in passing to the subdominant key, a komma lower — every r becomes rah. It should also be noted that every change to an adjacent key (major) thus involves *two* changes of tone—this kommatic change, and that of the distinguishing-tone, the new flat or the new sharp—so that in the course of *four* such "removes" no one tone will remain the same as any tone of the scale from which the departure was made.

To play in just intonation on a key-board instrument in the major and relative minor of the fifteen keys at the top of the diagram on p. 88, we should require a separate note to correspond to each of the numbers there given. Arranging these numbers in order,

1200	998	816	658	476	296	160
1180	996	794	612	454	294	114
1178	976	792	590	408	274	92
1156	974	772	588	386	272	90
1110	906	770	568	384	204	70
1088	886	702	498	364	184	68
1086	884	682	490	318	182	2
1066	862	680	478			

we have 53 tones to the octave. Or we may obtain more detail by proceeding in this way:— To play in true intonation in C major, we require eight tones to the octave, viz.,

d   r   r   m   f   s   l   t

A transition to G major requires two new tones, t and r, and similarly each successive sharp key demands two new tones. A transition to F major also requires two new tones, f and r, and in the

same manner every successive flat key must have two new tones. Therefore to play in the fifteen major keys enumerated at the top of the diagram we should want $8 + (2 \times 14) = 8 + 28 = 36$ tones to the octave. Again, beginning at the left hand of the diagram, the relative minors of C♭ and G♭ require two new tones each, viz., ba and se, but the relative minors of the other thirteen keys only want one each, viz., se, for the ba of these keys is identical with the se of the keys two removes to the left. Thus to play in true intonation in the relative minors of all these keys we must have $4 + 13 = 17$ additional tones thus making as before, for both major and minor, $17 + 36 = 53$ tones to the octave.

Two or three points now present themselves for discussion. In the FIRST place, a double form for the Fourth of the Scale has been advocated. Mr. H. W. Poole (Sillman's American Journal of Science) says that, in the chord of '8 the f should be tuned in agreement with the VIIth partial of s. This would flatten the f in the diagram 27 cents, making it 471, a greater difference than between r and r'. Mr. Poole provided for this tone in his organ.

It is said that the Swiss, in their melodic *jodels*, employ this harmonic seventh. I do not wonder at their doing so, for they prefer consonance to dissonance in these ornamental melodies; and no one who has heard in a lecture room, acoustic experiments, which show the difference between the two sevenths, can doubt for a moment that the harmonic seventh is more consonant. I should not be surprised even if in harmony, where the tones are long-drawn, if a singer, holding the seventh of the dominant, should instinctively flatten it so as to get into consonance, not caring for the harmonic intentions of the composer. My chief objection to the adoption of this grave f is that the seventh of the dominant chord is meant to be a dissonating tone, and fails of its proper effect if it is not so. The beauty of the resolution is gone if it has not been preceded by the seventh *beating* against the root. Some of the greatest effects of modern music arise from the contrast of dissonance with *consonance*. This is a good reason for making the consonances as sweet and true as possible, but it is no excuse for altering a dissonance into a semi-consonance. Taken, therefore, as a piece of melody alone, or as a chord of harmony standing alone, I could not object to it; but when introduced instead of a dissonance where dissonance was wanted, it can only weaken and spoil the effect. Another difficulty is, that the melodic change from grave f' to acute f', or from f' to f', when different chords required the different forms of the tone

THE SYSTEM OF KEYS AND JUST INTONATION.

DOH is C2 Gb Db Ab Eb Bb F C G D A E B f# c#

Lah is ab eb bb f c g d a e b f# c# g# d# a#

1,200   r ...... s ... DOH¹..f

+1,156 .... ba   t .... m .... l (1,178)   se .... ba (1,180)

°1086 ..d¹ .... f   se .... ba (1,066)   TE ...m.....l (1088)   r ...... s .... d ...... f (1,110)

t .... m .... l (974)   r .... s .... d .... f (996)   le .... se .... ba (976)   t| ..... m .... l (998°)

se .... ba (862)   t| ...m... LAH (884)   r ..... s .... d ....f (905)   se (888°)

°570 ..l   r .... s .... d ...... f (792)   se .. .. ba (772)   t| ..... m .... l| (794)   r .... s... (816)

se .... ba (658)   t| ...... m .... l| (680)   r ... SOH .. d .....f (702)   se| .... ba (682°)

588 ..s ....d ....f   se| .... ba (568)   fe .. t| .... m .... l| (590)   r .... s| ..... d .... f (612)

496   r .... s| .... d ... FAH   +454 ..ba   t| .... m .... l| (476)   se| .... ba| (478)   t| .... m... (500°)

°384 ..f   se| ....ba| (364)   t| ... ME ..... l| (386)   r .... s| ..... d .... f| (408)

°272 ..m .... l| r .... s| ..... d ...... f| .... ma (294)   se| .... ba| (274)   t| ..... m| .... l| (296)   r (319+)

se| .... ba| (160)   t| ...... m| ..... l| (182)   RAY ... s| ..... d ...... f| (204)   se| .... (184°)

63 = s   r .... s| .... d .... f| (90)   se| .... ba| (70)   t| ..... m| ..... l| (92)   r| .... s| ...... d (114)

r| ..... s| ... DOH ... f| (0)   r°   t| ...

successively, would be seriously greater than that of r' to r', or r' to r', which some persons object to. Besides, the common melodic approach to the seventh on the dominant from the tone above (|s :f') would be by the unpleasant interval of a greater greater step; that is, a greater step *plus* twenty-seven cents, or more than a komma.

SECOND.—The sharp sixth of the relative minor (ba). Is it the same tone as the sharp fourth of the major (fe), or a komma lower? Mr. Poole makes it the same. I think it should be a komma lower, as in the diagram, for these reasons:—The sharp seventh and sharp sixth of the minor mode I take to be alterations intended to make the upper part of the minor scale to correspond with the major (so that m ba se l shall have the same interval as s l t d'), and in the change to the tonic minor this is actually and necessarily the case. But if this is true, the four higher tones of the minor scale are separated like those of the major by the successive intervals of a smaller step, a greater step, and a little step. Hence this analogy requires the sharp sixth of the relative minor to stand a komma lower than the sharp fourth of the major. Happily, in providing for it the mechanician will not have to make a new tone, as the sharp seventh of the second flat minor stands at the same pitch.

THIRD.—Will it be sufficient if the constructor of an instrument aiming at perfect tune provides for a relative minor to every major key, or is it also necessary that he should have a tonic

1178	l	1200	d' l	1200
1066	se	1088	t .... se	1088
996	s		(s)	(1018)
862	ba	884	l ... ba	884
792	f		f	814
680	m	702	s ... m	702
			r	520
498	r	498	f .... r'	498
476	r'			
		386	m	
294	d		d	316
182	t,	204	r .... t,	204
(1)		0	d .... l,	0

t,
thnor? By "relative minor," I mean the minor mode which commences a minor third below, or a major sixth above, the key-tone of any given major mode; by "tonic minor," I mean a minor

mode which starts from the same sound in absolute pitch with any given major mode. This is sometimes called the synonymous, and sometimes the identical, minor, but these terms are also used in a different sense, for which reason I avoid them. This is a very important question. For if tonic minors are required, the adjacent diagram shows that we shall require at least three new tones for each key; viz., d 316, f 814, and r 520 (in chord of *SE*), as these numbers do not occur in the list, p. 87. Therefore, for all fifteen keys, we should want forty-five new tones! Now the tones of the relative minor of the third flat key (taken from the diagram on p. 88) are placed for comparison on the left of the diagram above. On examination it will be found that each of these tones is twenty-two cents, or one komma, lower than the corresponding tones of the tonic minor on the right. The question naturally suggests itself therefore: Will not this relative minor of the third flat key serve as the tonic minor to our principal key. Most will agree that unless the ear very strongly objects, it is desirable to make one of these minors to answer the purpose of the other; and it seems unreasonable to have to provide for two minor keys only a komma apart while the incomparably more used major mode requires no such double apparatus. Let us therefore consider the question as between the tonic minor and the relative minor. It is obvious that we cannot decide it without knowing very definitely and certainly which of the two minors is, in practical music, the more important or the more used. All musicians know that it is a far commoner thing for music to pass from the major into the relative minor, or from the minor into the relative major, than for it to pass from major to tonic minor, or from minor to tonic major. For curiosity's sake, however, the choruses of two modern works—Mendelssohn's *Elijah* and Macfarren's *John the Baptist*—have been analysed. These composers were chosen, as being likely to use the tonic change more than any others, except Schubert. From this analysis it is found that the music of these works passes

From Major to Tonic Minor, 2 Times
From Minor to Tonic Major, 12 Times
= 14 Tonic Changes.

From Major to Relative Minor, 38 Times
From Minor to Relative Major, 14 Times
= 52 Relative Changes.

The disparity is so great, that, if one has to be sacrificed, there cannot be a doubt which. But I doubt whether any sacrifice whatever need be made, as will presently appear. In studying transitions and modulations the student must have noticed that by far the greater number of flat removes are removes to the minor, and by far the greater number of sharp removes are removes to the major, and that there is a connection between the sad effect of the flat removes and the corresponding sadness of the minor mode, and between the brightening effect of the sharp removes and the corresponding brightness of the major mode. I think also that the fall of a komma is congenial in its effect with a passing to the minor mode; and that the rise of a komma is congenial in its effect with a passing to the major mode. Now, by making the l_1 of the relative minor of the third flat key serve as the d of the tonic major to the principal key, this congenial effect will be secured. I know the objection which will be raised, that transition and modulation are rendered acceptable by the carrying on of one or more tones from the one key into the other, and that this kommatic change breaks the bond. My own experience, however, of the kommatic change in harmony convinces me that, to the ear, it has not this effect.

We should necessarily have the same fall of a komma, in making a transition of four removes to the left on such a key-board instrument as we are discussing; and, of course, a corresponding rise of a komma in transitions to the fourth sharp key. Singers in true intonation would not make this rise if the transition were sudden, but they would if it were gradual; hence vocalists, although singing in perfectly true intonation, would sharpen a komma on their original pitch, in making a gradual transition to the fourth sharp key through the intervening ones, and then returning suddenly. On the other hand, in making a sudden transition to the fourth sharp key, and returning gradually, they would flatten a komma on the original pitch. The sudden and gradual transitions to the fourth flat key are attended with corresponding results. The student will notice that the sudden ascent or descent of all the tones of the scale by a komma, on a key-board instrument, would produce no false intonation, and in fact would be, for the most part, unnoticed.

Closely connected with the matter of Relative and Tonic Minors, which we have just been discussing, is the following:—Some musicians very strongly assert as an essential principle of music itself, that what is called the key of C major and what is called the key of C minor are *the same* key, and they point to the fact, that Beethoven, Mozart, and others not unfrequently commence a tune in a minor key, and close it in the major of the same tonic, in proof of this

assertion. I think that this last-named fact proves, that the composers referred to, regarded the tonics as the same, but it does not prove that they regarded the keys as the same. For the key of C major has a major third and an immovable sixth and seventh, while the key of C minor has a minor third and a changeable sixth and seventh, so that the two keys may often differ in three out of their seven tones. Besides, the character and mental effect of the two keys are quite diverse. Of course it would be quite possible for them to use the word "same" for things which differ in nearly half their features and their whole expression; but it would not be a good use of language. In the year 1870 this question came strongly before me in connection with the names for tones which we have adopted in the Tonic Sol-fa method, and I wrote as follows in *The Tonic Sol-fa Reporter*, July 15th, 1870:—

"There is another great question of nomenclature which links itself so closely with the question, 'What is the truth of the science itself?' that I have not shrunk from a full and anxious discussion of it. It has been a private discussion constantly renewed with one whose opinions on musical art I hold in sincere reverence. This gentleman has said to me:—

'Your Tonic Sol-fa notation would be quite correct if you represented the minor scale in ascending thus— d r ma f s l t d', and in descending thus— d' ta la s f ma r d; for it is a truth in music that C major and C minor are the same keys. This truth you ought to indicate by giving them, as far as possible, the same syllabic names. As long as you fail to do this you represent music untruly, and you forsake your own principle of key-relationship. I say they are the same keys because they have the same pitch-tone as tonic, the same dominant, the same subdominant, the same supertonic; and, in modern harmony, these are the relations which govern a key. In the introduction and formation of a tonic, dominant, or subdominant cadence in C minor you use the same pitch-tones as roots of chords which you would use in C major. It is true that the chords are not exactly alike; they are modified by the constant introduction of ma for m, and of ta and la for t and l. But the movements of the bass flow in the same channel. Beethoven treated these keys as the same, for he often commenced a piece in the major and closed it in the minor of the same tonic, and *vice versâ*.'

"This at first startles the Tonic Sol-faist. He knows at once that such a change in his notation would entirely spoil the association of syllable and interval which he and his pupils have so long been accustomed to; that to try and give d the mental effect of l, and ta the mental effect of s, would be a far more serious difficulty than that which he has hitherto experienced in giving l something of the mental effect of d. He sees, therefore, that practically he will be obliged to continue the old plan of regarding the l as the proper key-tone of the minor mode; for, however much he might wish it himself, his pupils would never allow him to change a plan of sol-faing which they found to be easy, for one which they feel to insurmountably difficult. He, nevertheless, may the uneasy fear, with all this authority against him, that perhaps his favourite method of sol-faing may not fit the truth of music itself so closely as it should; that it may make the thing easy to the learner in his first steps at the expense of unnecessary misunderstandings and difficulties afterwards. But closer study will soon reassure him.

"The fact of the case is, that the LAH mode has never thoroughly and perfectly established for itself the right to be called a key in the clear sense in which the DOH mode has done so. While modern harmony was being slowly developed, there were, of course, many attempts to harmonise the old church modes. But musicians soon decided that a full cadence, to be satisfactory to the ear, must have two major chords—the last and the last but one. After a time, the ear came to endure a minor chord for the last, but it never endured a minor chord for the last but one. Even down to the time of Sebastian Bach, we find the tendency to make the last chord major in spite of unpleasant melodic progressions; and Handel and Bach often omit the third rather than hear its minor effect. All this arises from the fact that minor chords are in their own nature somewhat dissonant, as modern discoveries in acoustics clearly show. The question then came, which of the modes then in common use (of which the DOH mode, the RAY mode, and the LAH mode were the principal) would bear this modern thing, harmony, best. It was found that the DOH mode met these requirements of harmony perfectly without alteration, but that the other modes required some change of note directly harmony was introduced, and among these the LAH mode, with the sharpening of the seventh of its scale in cadences, and the occasional sharpening of its sixth, was the least displeasing to the ear. Professor Helmholtz says :—'The minor tone-system has not the same simple, clear, and intelligible consistency as the major.' He speaks of it as suitable for the expression of weird, desolate, mystical feeling, because of its 'veiled chords, changeable scale, easily departing modulations, and less clear relationships of structure.'

"Thus far the testimony of musical history, which shows the modern minor key to have arisen from the old LAH mode, which was under the necessity of alteration to suit modern harmony.

"Now let us take the facts as we find them at the present time. The minor mode does not hold its own so well as the major. It does not dominate in a tune as the major does, but passes continually into its relative major. It seems as though it could not stand alone. In every few measures it takes, it needs the relative major to support its steps. The very characteristic notes (the *sharpened* sixth and seventh) which distinguish it from its relative major are often not nearly so much used in minor *tunes* as the *flat* sixth and seventh which belong to its relative major. In twelve minor psalm tunes taken at random I find the sharp seventh (se) occurring 106 times, while the flat seventh (s) occurs 142 times. The sharp sixth (ba) occurred only once, while the flat sixth (f) occurred 86 times. This is because the minor tunes so naturally run into the major mode. An analysis of purely minor *passages* would give a different result. It is true that the motion of the bass in cadences is the same as that in the major mode, but the altered nature of the chords themselves makes those cadences sound, not as satisfactory resting-places, but rather as dreamy, dissatisfied recollections of rest. Thus the minor mode, from the changeableness of its own composition, its

readiness to fall back into the relative major, and its infirmity of cadence, is unable to establish the clear, firm character of a key which belongs to the major mode. It is only the imitation and shadow of a key. It is better called a mode than a key. For the various chordal habits in which it is unable to follow the model of the major keys, see 'How to Observe Harmony,' and 'Construction Exercises.'

"But even when the highest importance possible is given to the minor mode, the question of 'How shall we name it?—by what syllables shall it be called?' need not be long undecided. The minor mode, as we know it, bears two relationships; one to the major *of the same tonic*, from which it differs permanently in its third, and more commonly than otherwise in its sixth and seventh, but which has its cadence basses at the same pitch—the other to what is commonly called its *relative* major, whose very tones are the same as its own with only occasional change of the seventh and a rare change of the sixth, and into which, in actual music, it is continually relapsing, as into the arms of its parent. Which of the two relations is the more important? Which shall we denote, and which shall we *connote*? The transitions of good music, and the natural tendencies of the human ear and voice, combine in casting the vote for the relative major. There are more than a hundred transitions into the relative major to one into the major of the same tonic; and the affinity of these two is yet further declared by the fact that the mental effects of the tones in a major key, though seriously modified by the sharpening of the sixth and seventh, and by the peculiar motion of the bass (which makes **l** into an imitation tonic), are far from being obliterated. They still claim their old characters, though struggling through a cloud. The major of the same tonic is felt by the ear to be a key three removes off, and its tonic is really a komma different from the one from which we start. With a tempered-keyed instrument to guide, the transition is not difficult to sing, but *without* an instrument it is always felt to be awkward and unnatural to the voice. The major of the same tonic is then, in practice, a key only distantly related to the minor, while the relative major is part of its own flesh and blood. The system of nomenclature must undoubtedly follow the stronger relationship. If we adopted the plan proposed, our notation would have to make distinct transition marks for the *hundred* changes between the minor and its relative in order to save transition marks in the *one* change between the minor and its major of the same tonic. Both practically and theoretically, therefore, we may well be satisfied with the old English method of making **l** the key-tone of the minor mode.

"One thing, however, should be noted as a fruit of this discussion, that in the study of harmony we shall find it important to distinguish between the chord of L when it is the sixth of the DOH mode and the same chord when it is the tonic of the LAH mode; and so, also, with all the chords when they are treated in relation to **l** instead of **d** as their tonic. All the habits which have been considered peculiar to F, S, and D, are now handed over to R, M, and L. We propose to write the chord L when it is invested with the importance of a tonic, the chord M when it is altered so as to represent the dominant, the chord R when it stands for the subdominant, and so on, by italic capitals—*L, M, R, &c.*; and in speaking of them we call them the *minor* L, the *minor* M, and the *minor* R.

"This discussion gives a remarkable illustration of the power of names over thought and art. It may be that Tonic Sol-faists, following the old historic idea (supported indeed by the unaltered signatures of the old notation) of the origin and relationships of the minor mode, have erred in neglecting the practice of transition to the minor of the same tonic; but certainly, modern musicians, following the mechanical facilities of the pianoforte, have used this artificial and untunable transition, even for vocal writing, far more frequently than they would have done if they had not been misled by theory to suppose that they were moving into a closely-related (or, as my friend says, 'the same') key. A false theory, and want of practice with unaided voices, have misled them. It has been a great misfortune to popular music that modern musicians have, from Arnold and Crotch's time, begun to call C major and C minor the same keys."

I therefore conclude that all the minors should, in accordance with the historical development of the mode, and also, let it be noticed, with the established staff notation of music, be treated as relative minors by the maker of a perfect instrument. But I trust that musicians will put questions of this kind to so thorough a test as will satisfy all, and bring about a speedy agreement.

FOURTH.—Is the musical instrument maker, in providing for transition and modulation, to arrange the keys in groups of four or five, or to consider them all as parts of one great system? In the diagram above, p. 88, the keys named on the top of the diagram are given as the system of keys which music requires — the major keys being named in small capitals, and the relative minors in smaller letters below. The extreme keys on either hand will certainly be seldom, if ever, wanted. Note that the mark ⟋ means a komma higher, and ⟍ a komma lower, than the corresponding tone in the central key. This is very important for the student to notice, as representing the kommatic alterations which are essential in change of key. These kommatic changes are shown as they would really and necessarily occur if a quartet of stringed instruments, or of well-tuned voices, commenced in the key of C, or its relative minor (A minor), and moved by "gradual" transition through all the sharp keys, and then, commencing as before, moved by "gradual" transition through all the flat keys. General Thompson groups his keys on three finger-boards. Mr. Poole follows the same system of major keys with their relative minors which is commonly understood, and on which the staff notation is built. Mr. Ellis proposes yet another system of keys. Musicians wishing true intonation on finger-board instruments must give themselves the trouble of deciding this question. For

myself, I cannot help preferring Mr. Poole's arrangement of keys, and for this reason: It is *necessary* for the composer that he should be able to place himself at any point he chooses in the whole range of keys, and always find himself surrounded by *the same* relationship to neighbouring keys; and this is only possible when the same system of relative tuning is carried on through the whole system of relative keys.

FIFTH.—Which is the more important to be considered, Gradual or Sudden Transition? By "Gradual Transition," I mean the passing from a given key to one which is nearly related to it —differing only by a single sharp or flat, and then on in the same way to the next, and the next, &c.; by "Sudden Transition," I mean the passing to a distant key without these intermediate steps. Thus, we should go from the key of C to that of A♭ *gradually* if we made a cadence in the key of F, then in the key of B♭, then in the key of E♭, and last in the key of A♭; we should make this transition *suddenly* if we omitted the intermediate keys, and at once made a cadence in A♭. The question is an important one, because if we took, for example, this transition (from C to A♭) gradually, we should find the pitch of all our tones which correspond in pitch with those of the original or new key to be (as a little study of the diagram, p. 88, will show), a komma lower; but if we took it suddenly, we should naturally make the tones that are common to the two keys precisely at the same pitch. The questions suggested by this observation are—Which is better? Which shall we do? Or, shall we do both? In making an instrument of fixed tones it is important, for economy's sake, not to multiply the tones more than is necessary, but we must not sacrifice truth to convenience. Our difficulty in ascertaining the truth would be much less if composers were in the habit of returning to the original key exactly in the same way in which they left it; but this is not at all the case; they commonly leave the original key by sudden transition, and return to it gradually. In such cases, they leave the key for some striking effect, and then get back to it in a manner that will be as little noticed as possible. Sometimes, also, in order to *prepare* an effect, they leave the key gradually, and return to it suddenly. They seldom (except in the case of a change to tonic major or tonic minor) go out from the key and return to it in the same way. If, then, we move from C to A♭ suddenly *without altering the pitch*, and return gradually through the keys E♭, B♭, and F, the time we get back we shall have raised pitch of the original key by a komma; and if we took our transition gradually, and then, *without altering the pitch*, return suddenly, we should have lowered the pitch of the original key by a komma. This difficulty will always occur whenever the keys are four removes apart. Now return to us the question—If one of these modes of transitions is to be sacrificed to the other, which must suffer? Or is it *better* to adopt a uniform system, and if so, which?—that of absolute sameness, or that of kommatic change? I have never had the opportunity of comparing the two effects on an instrument, and can therefore give no decisive testimony; but if we had to set one key a komma wrong, I think it would be better to disturb the *subordinate* key —that into which we move for a temporary effect - -than to set the original key of the piece wrong. I have shown that the plan of absolute sameness alters the original key for the sake of the sub-ordinate key. Moreover, if that is to be most considered in the instrument which will be most frequently wanted, undoubtedly the gradual transitions are at least 90 per cent. more used than the sudden, and will therefore claim the recognition of kommatic changes. But is the fall of a komma in a distant flat remove, or the rise of a komma in a distant sharp remove, really a bad thing, even when the transition is sudden? I do not know, but I *expect* that it will *not* be found so, because such changes fall in with the spirit of the transitions. Only ample and careful experiments, however, can settle these questions.

SIXTH.—Can the interval of a skisma (two cents.) be disregarded in preparing an instrument which aims at true intonation? and if so, which tones can be allowed to go wrong by a skisma? It may be noticed, on the diagram, p. 88, that every f is a skisma lower than the t *six* removes to the right, and that every 1 is by the same interval lower than the se *seven* removes to the right. If, under certain circumstances, this interval can be disregarded, it will greatly simplify the work of the maker; but it must be remembered that this would be temperament— temperament like that to which we objected on the fifth of the scale. It has, however, been observed above that the skisma, though very noticeable when it takes away the bright character from so important a tone as the fifth of the scale, is not so observable when it only disturbs the third or sixth. Professor Helmholtz uses a harmonium tuned on this principle of " Skismatic substitution." When there are two tones differing only by a skisma, he makes one serve for both. Mr. Ellis has proposed a similar arrangement in his exhaustive Royal Society paper on " Temperament," June 16th,

1864. If the error is allowed only in the extreme keys, such as B, F♯, and C♯, and A♭, D♭, G♭, and C♭, it will be of small importance. At p. 88, I have marked with an asterisk those numbers which would probably best suffer skis-matic substitution, still leaving four skismas untouched; I have also marked thus (†) three notes which may be *omitted*, one of which is the acute second (ray) of a very extreme sharp key —scarcely ever used—and the other two, the little-used sharp sixth of the minor of very distant flat keys. With these fairly allowable substitutions and omissions, there will remain only three tones in the more perfect, or, as Mr. Ellis would call it, the Teleon instrument, for every one on a tempered instrument; that is, supposing that the tonic minors are not wanted.

SEVENTH.—In a Teleon instrument, what form of finger-board would be most convenient for the practical musician? The answer to this question depends much upon the answer to another— Which is the more important for a player to have before him, absolute pitch, or the relationship of tones in a key and the relationship of key to key? The present finger-board symbolises the relations of tones in one key—the key of C— and every other key is a variation from it by means of the black digitals. Those who think that absolute pitch is the more important thing to keep in mind will naturally lean to General Thompson's finger-boards, which are very in-genious, although they appear very complex. The white digital below the group of two black digitals is the pitch-tone C in all three finger-boards, while the principal key-note of the particular board is shown by colour. Mr. Poole seeks to accomplish the same end by means of the same finger-board precisely which we now use, so that a tune in key G, for instance, would be played by touching the same digitals as are commonly employed. He has a number of pedals arranged in the same order as the keys at the top of the diagram on p. 88. When he presses a certain pedal, it brings the valves of the pipes belonging to its own particular key (and some of its related tones) into connection with the proper digitals, and all others are detached. Those who think that relationship in keys and of keys ought to be more vividly kept in mind than absolute pitch will naturally incline either to a movable finger-board, which makes the digital commonly called C to be always the key-tone (a plan much adopted in France, especially for church music), or to a modification of Mr. Poole's plan. At present, Mr. Poole couples any pipe with any digital he pleases. It would therefore be quite easy for him to couple the key-tone always with the digital commonly called C, which would then be reckoned the tonic for all major keys. This would answer the same purpose as the movable finger-board, and would make the fingering of all keys as easy as that of key C.

The settlement of this point will require careful testing, not by persons accustomed all their life to one plan, but by various *learners* who shall come fresh to the use of a finger-board. For myself, I think that both key-relationship and the relationship of keys will be even better shown to the ear by true intonation than they are at present, and that the finger-board should therefore symbolise these relations, but there might be some contrivance at the back of the finger-board which would show, by means of letters, the absolute pitch of the tones played. The same pedal which brought the proper key into connection might also turn the barrel, or other contrivance, which would show the absolute pitch. I do not find that the plan of a movable finger-board would answer for true intonation, simply because the valves cannot be arranged under the digitals to express the same intervals from each one to the next, as is the case with an equally-tempered instrument. I should prefer Mr. Poole's plan of pedals to change key, but I think that his desire to retain the present finger-board, without the slightest alteration, has led him to use his pedals too frequently for even moderately rapid execution. To get even the chord of the supertonic, he at first proposed to put down the pedal of the first flat key, and he would still put down the pedal of the first sharp key in order to get the sharp fourth, which is so much used in cadences. This constant alteration of the whole instrument for single chords must necessarily be a cumbrous movement. I agree with General Thompson, that players like, as much as possible, to have all the notes beneath their fingers, and therefore recommend additional digitals on the finger-board for the related keys which are in commonest use. [In the first edition, I suggested in this page a Tonic finger-board. But my friend, Mr. Colin Brown, Euing Lecturer at the Andersonian University, Glasgow, has since invented and patented so simple and beautiful a combination of the absolute pitch principle with that of key relation, that I abandon my own plan, and, with slight modification, recommend his. The finger-board of his "Voice Harmonium" will be best understood if the reader takes p. 88 above, and looks at it sideways, placing the right-hand side (the "sharp" side) in front of him. He will then notice that certain tones standing at the same pitch are united by dotted lines. Omitting for the present ba and se, all the rest fall into two groups.

They are all either "f..d..s..r" or "l..m..t." It occurred to Mr. Brown that the first group might be represented on the finger-board by a long digital, and the second group by a shorter one. It also occurred to him that these digitals might be placed one behind the other without preserving the exact level on which they stand on p. 88. Thus, if we commence in the middle where f..d..s..r stands nearest to us, this group would be played by a long digital. Then straight behind it would be a short digital playing the group l..m..t a *komma* lower, and straight behind that a long digital again playing f..d..s..r, a *chromatic semitone* lower, and yet again another short digital playing l..m..t, a komma lower. There is thus always a difference between the digitals on the same line (front to back) of either a komma or a chroma. The tones se and ba are represented by buttons. I have adopted this method of describing Mr. Brown's "Natural Finger-board," because it seemed the easiest way of reaching the reader's apprehension, and it is, indeed, an exact description of my own modifications as shown on page 95. But Mr. Brown preferred to keep the sharp keys farthest from the player, and the flat keys nearest to him, and to make the digitals rise at each semitone. We should, therefore, have to hold up p. 88 to the light, sideways, with the top to the right-hand, and look through it from the back, in order to realise Mr. Brown's finger-board. I propose a perfectly *level* finger-board, and a more exact imitation of the Extended Modulator. The scale fingering would then be exactly the same in all the keys—that fingering which is now used for key F, R.H. × 1 2 3 × 1 2 ×, &c.; L.H. 4 3 2 1 × 2 1 ×, &c. Note that se is represented by a button to the left-hand of 1. The tone ba is produced by the se button of two flat removes. The phrase m ba se 1 would commonly be fingered × 1 × 1 for both hands. These suggested improvements do not invalidate Mr. Brown's patent.]

The cost of a Teleon instrument must, it would appear, exceed that of a Tempered one—first, by the increased expense of the finger-board; second, by the introduction of a pedal movement; third, by the, at least, three-fold number of vibrators, or pipes, or strings, which must be used. Let us see whether there are likely to be discovered any plans which will lessen this cost. First, as musical statics, till Helmholtz, have been but little understood, either by musicians or mechanists, it is reasonable to suppose that some means of altering the tones of strings and pipes by small degrees, without much additional expense, may be discovered by

MODIFICATION OF MR. COLIN BROWN'S FINGER-BOARD.

E♭	B♭	F	C	G	D	A
t	m	l	B♭	s	d	f
l	r	s	DOH'	f	t	r
s	d	f	TE	m	l	r
f	t₁	m	LAH	r	s	d
m	l₁	r	SOH	d	f	t₁
r	s₁	d	FAH	t₁	m	l₁
d	f₁	t₁	ME	l₁	r	s₁
t₁	m	l₁	RAY	s₁	d	f₁
l₁	r₁	s₁	DOH	f₁	t₁	m

some one of the crowd of new students. Erard's harps show us one way of dealing with strings, and I think that even piano strings might be "stopped" at one end or the other, or at both ends, by an "action" which would neither press them down nor loosen them. As for the pipes, although Mr. Liston's plan of "shading" did not answer, I do not despair of making one pipe answer for three tones. I have noticed that a tuning-fork or a strong harmonium vibrator will *govern* the tone of a pipe within a komma or two. It is true that *one* of the three vibrators will obtain from the pipe what Mr. Sedley Taylor calls its tone of greatest resonance, but I suppose (although I have not yet tried the experiment) that a little more wind—or, in other words, a larger mouthpiece to the vibrator—will make the other two equally loud. Such vibrators would act in a very different way from those in a clarinet or hautbois, or the reed-stop of an organ; they would *govern*. Perhaps some simple application of the Jacquard-loom principle will suffice to open the proper valves for the different keys; the electrical plan would be too expensive in the working. I feel confident, also, that Helmholtz's great discovery of the true cause of *quality* in tones will, before long, save us—in part, at least—the expense of that great number of "stops" which are at present required in harmoniums and organs. When different "qualities" of tone can be produced *without* a new set of pipes, by carrying the wind in *regulated proportions* to the harmonics of each of the tones, we are tempted to ask, Why should we any more require, except for greater loudness, the Principal, the Twelfth, and the Fifteenth? On the other hand, it may be found that, for increased loudness, pipes of different qualities are absolutely necessary, for it is a curious fact that pipes of the same quality do not increase the loudness in the proportion that might be expected. Moreover, the wind-channels, which every pipe would require to make five or six other pipes sound softly with it, might be found so complicated and expensive as to make additional pipes cheaper.

Among other instruments practically realising just intonation, Mr. R. H. M. Bosanquet's harmonium may be mentioned. In this instrument, which is exhibited at the Scientific Collection in the South Kensington Museum, and a full account of which will be found in Bosanquet's "Elementary Treatise on Musical Intervals and Temperament," the octave is divided into 53 equal parts, and the finger-board is so constructed that the fingering is the same for all keys. The fifth is out of tune only by $\frac{1}{14}$ of the interval that it is out of tune in equal temperament: a quite imperceptible error; while the third is $\frac{1}{4}$ of

a skisma, or rather less than one-and-a-half cents, flat.

The following extracts will show the liveliness of the discussion which this subject has awakened, and will on many points give illustrations and explanations much better than my own. I will only venture to express surprise at one line of argument adopted by the friends of temperament. They claim that the fact of great musicians having written for the organ and pianoforte, such as those instruments were in their days, and enjoyed their music on them, proves that these musicians desired no further improvement, and that it is presumption in us to be dissatisfied with what pleased them. It is like saying that the early masters of painting who neglected perspective, would not have followed its rules, and welcomed its effects, if they had lived in a more intelligent age. It is like saying that because the great dames who led the fashion a century ago, the very models of fine taste in dress and ornament, never wore dresses resplendent in mauve or magenta, therefore it is quite presumptuous in the belles of the present day to think of such colours.

OPPOSITION TO TRUE INTONATION.

" Now there are two different and opposite opinions respecting the *minimum cogitabile* or rather *sensible* in musical altitude; according, as it is maintained on the one hand, or denied on the other, that the ear is conscious of intervals smaller than five, four, or three kommas, not only to such an extent as to recognise the last mentioned as a distinct interval, but even so as to feel the difference of a whole komma upon any of the ordinary intervals as a serious, according to one writer, an 'intolerable' error; and that the difference of a fraction of a komma occasions a proportionable inconvenience. . . . It is not denied that the interval of a komma may be recognised as a slight deviation from absolute unison; it is only maintained that the deviation in question is too slight to effect any important change, or, indeed, any change at all in the harmony, for the passages called enharmonic would lose little of their musical value were the ♯ Fs changed into ♭ Gs, and *vice versa*, &c.; their musical importance being dependent not on absolute accuracy of enharmonic intonation; or, at least, not nearly so much on that as on the surprise attending the unlooked-for sequence. This is proved by the fact that two-thirds of their original effect can be rendered on keyed instruments tuned on the Equal Temperament. . . . The question, therefore, is one of matter of fact, which every musician must decide for himself. ' Are my ears so acutely, so morbidly sensitive, that the exquisite beauty which other men see in Beethoven and Mozart appears only deformity to me?' Here it becomes a matter of historical interest to ascertain how far musicians have decided it for themselves, virtually or expressly. . . . Both Mozart and Beethoven were ardently attached to the pianoforte and organ, in spite, if not partly in consequence of the imperfect intonation of these instruments. The latter was, if we mistake not, professional organist in his youth; and the former signified his respect for the last-named instrument in the memorable words, 'The organ is still, in my eyes and ears, the king of instruments.' Surely, if it was king of instruments, he was king of the organ; yet how could he have had such enthusiasm for this most majestic of all instruments, were he continually annoyed, even to a slight extent, by the want of perfect intonation? At least, is it conceivable that, ever conscious of this disadvantage, he should not make it the subject of frequent regret or complaint, or that, making complaint, no such complaint should be recorded? We have just shown that a piece played on the organ, closing in the major concord of the key, produces an error of ⅔ of a komma in one interval alone of that chord on the Equal Temperament system; had Mozart's ear possessed the acute sensitiveness of Mr. Poole's, could such an error have failed to mar, in some degree, his enjoyment of that instrument? Yet with what eagerness did he embrace every opportunity of organ playing in his travels! The reader will now see how many considerations combine to prove that the error of a komma was not much more obtrusively offensive to Mozart's ears than to those of Professor Pierce, and indeed the majority, we might almost say the universality, of amateurs. Handel's interest in the harpsichord and organ is attested in the works he has left for those instruments; and yet more impressively in the keys of his own instrument, hollowed out like spoons by his incessant practice. The author of the 'Forty-eight Preludes and Fugues' was an organist almost all his life, and though expressing dissatisfaction with the Unequal Temperament, we are not aware that he uttered any complaint of the Equal. But what need is there to multiply examples? . . . Even conceding that a few ears are sensible of the komma *as a distinct musical interval*, the interests of the great majority of amateurs who are not insensible to the charms of a Haydn, a Mendelssohn, or a Beethoven, though strangers to the existence of the minute interval of a komma, are not to be sacrificed to those of an almost inconceivably small minority, of whom many probably are insensible to these charms. . . . Admitting that absolute purity of intonation were not only possible, but easy of attainment, it would be, when attained, all but thrown away upon every one except the few, perhaps intensely trained and habituated ears, which are, it may be, to be reckoned in the category of imaginary rather than of real existences. The supposed improvement being, to all else, whether performers or audience, almost literally imperceptible. . . . Lastly, if the error of a komma be so extremely offensive as it has been represented, and if large fractions of it are proportionately disagreeable, the necessary inference is that, as 'a common piano is never in tune,' those must be very dull and unrefined ears which can enjoy, or even tolerate, its music. Yet such were those of Beethoven and Mozart. The question is one of matter of fact, as we have already said, and to be decided for himself by every amateur from the experience of his own ear. On all hands it is, or at least ought to be, implicitly if not explicitly acknowledged, that the idea of constructing a scale divided into intervals so minute as to elude the apprehension of most musical ears, and be only by an exercise of the mind intellectually conceivable, is as preposterous as would be the attempt to extend the scale beyond, whether above or below, the limits of musical sonority in extension. If there be a science of such intervals, it is far from our purpose to

attempt its exposition; the science of the great German and Italian masters and our own Handel is the only one, if any, worth expounding. . . . Should the foregoing arguments, and the test of personal experiment have failed to convince or satisfy any of our readers, we must entreat them to regard themselves as the exceptions and not the rule; and to reflect that if they are sensible to a slight refinement of expression in a few harmonies, hundreds, if not thousands, may have been debarred from ever proceeding with, or (it may be) entering on the study of the science at all, owing to the prominence assigned to distinctions either purely nominal, or if real, so minute as to elude their detection."—"*The Statics of Harmony*," by *James Barnhill, jun., M.A.*, pp. 15 to 26.

"Modern music owes much of its beauty to the use of 'doubtful chords;' that is, chords which belong equally to more than one key. Now, if an enharmonic scale were feasible, such chords could not exist, because mathematical correctness of ratio would make every chord strictly in tune in one key, instead of allowing it to be somewhat out of tune in several keys. The whole of our musical literature, from the works of Bach to those of Wagner, would therefore be unavailable for instruments with an enharmonic scale. It is said voices and instruments of the violin class, not only can, but do make use of an enharmonic scale. This is tantamount to saying that singers and violinists, when reading from a separate part, know whether a note they are sounding is used by the composer according to its apparent notation, or as part of a chord of a different nature, or as both interchangeably; and not only this, but are also aware in each case what the fundamental sound is, from which the ratios of vibrations are calculated, and what is the exact ratio of the note they are sounding, and in defiance of notation are altering the pitch of the sound, or in other words are making two or more notes out of the one before them, so as to adapt it to its various combinations. Such a statement may be taken for what it is worth, although it should be said that many practised musicians who believe themselves endowed with an instinct leading to such marvellous results, will be found on examination to have formed for themselves this so-called instinct from the harmonic laws of the tempered scale. Musicians, therefore, have evidently this dilemma before them, either they must adopt an enharmonic scale and sacrifice the existing musical literature, or, if they wish to retain the literature, they must give up the theory of an enharmonic scale. Those who accept the former of these alternatives, are only consistent when they say, 'Is it credible the composer intended the gibberish resulting from making one sound serve for what he has so painfully distinguished?'[*] This kind of music, consisting largely of doubtful chords, which the clever musical mathematician has termed, not very elegantly, 'gibberish,' is the music of Bach, Haydn, Mozart, Beethoven, Spohr, Mendelssohn, and their followers. No apology is needed for saying that the second alternative has been chosen as the basis of this work, though not without very careful consideration. . . . It must surely be right in looking around for a foundation for a theory of harmony, to avoid a compromise such as has been described, which can never succeed in amalgamating two opposing systems. The tempered scale is certainly out of tune, and will not

[*] Perronet Thompson ('Principles of Just Intonation') speaking of Spohr's music. Notes, § 114.

H

bear to have its proportions exhibited to an audience with better eyes than ears, on a white screen ; but its sounds have, nevertheless, been a source of as real pleasure to all great composers, as of imaginary pain to certain theorists. When musical mathematicians shall have agreed amongst themselves upon the exact number of divisions necessary in the octave, when mechanists shall have invented instruments upon which the new scale can be played, when practical musicians shall have framed a new system of notation which shall point out to the performer the ratio of the note he is to sound to its generator, when genius shall have used all this new material to the glory of Art—then it will be time enough to found a Theory of Harmony on a mathematical basis."—" *A Theory of Harmony*," by Dr. Stainer, first ed. *From the Preface, omitted in third ed.*

DEFENCE OF TRUE INTONATION.

"The manner in which the subject of the musical scale and musical intervals is disposed of in our elementary treatises, is discreditable to music, as claiming to be a *science*. It is evident that the fundamental basis of music is not understood by those who attempt to teach the science. If it were necessary to corroborate this statement, we could refer to the blind and mysterious manner in which 'temperament' is treated by modern theoretical writers. In this, which is simply an arbitrary substitution of a false note for two or more true notes, some writers have seen an 'inexhaustible fountain of variety,' 'awful grandeur,' and 'exquisite beauty,' while an English writer calls it an 'inexplicable difficulty which no one has attempted to solve; the Deity seems to have left music in an unfinished state, to show his inscrutable power.'* Temperament is an arrangement of economy by which a small number of sounds (usually twelve to the octave) are made to answer (imperfectly, of course) for the much larger number which would be required to give music in tune in the usual number of keys. This arrangement was originally submitted to, merely for the accommodation of the *instrument-maker* and the *player*. So long as no mechanism had been invented by which more than twelve sounds could be managed by the organist, temperament was necessary in instruments of this class, but this reason no longer exists, as we shall show further on in this paper. Temperament has always been considered by the great masters as an evil attendant upon the 'present imperfect state of instrumentation,'† and hence they preferred that their instrumental music should be performed by skilful artists on violins and other instruments which admit of perfect intonation : and these have held, to the present day, their rank as the leading and most important instruments in the orchestra. It would have instructed a composer like Beethoven, or an artist like Paganini, to have heard of the scale of a modern German theorist, Kollman, which he calls the 'scale of nature,' consisting 'of twelve sounds in the octave placed at equal distances,' on which 'wonderful compound of twelve diatonic, chromatic, enharmonic scales in one,' he declares 'all modern music depends.' The somewhat voluminous treatise of Gottfried Weber, on 'Musical Composition,' has recently been translated in this country, and has been praised as a *scientific* work. The basis from which Weber attempts to explain musical instruments is the *key-board of a pianoforte !* An interval is

* Gardiner's "Music of Nature," p. 433. Boston edition, 1837.
† Beethoven.

the distance of one piano key from another. He defines a fifth thus : 'A fifth is an interval of five places.' When we consider that a common piano, with twelve notes in the octave, is *never in tune*, and cannot by any possibility be put in tune, the value of such explanations is obvious. If he had defined his intervals by reference to the *horn* or *trumpet*, as thus— that the interval between the lowest and the second notes given by the horn is an octave; that the interval between the second and third notes is a perfect fifth, and so on—his definitions could have been depended on, as the horn will *always* (if properly blown) give its intervals *exactly* thus. But so far from attempting to establish his theory on any scientific or mathematical basis, he distinctly declares, 'That it is not susceptible of such an establishment, or at least, has thus far failed of proving itself to be so.' . . In whatever manner the temperament is set, the best chords are given imperfect, and this imperfection is so obvious that the common ear, entirely unskilled in music, can most readily distinguish between chords that are tempered and those that are *tuned perfectly*. We are so constituted, however, that we can get accustomed, in time, to almost any amount of discord, so that it will not be disagreeable. It is said that men whose whole lives are spent in riveting the plates of steamboat boilers, perceive no discord in the harsh clangour of their business. Such artists would probably *prefer* a tempered organ. It is for the natural and uncontaminated, as well as for the cultivated, ear to appreciate fully the beauty and perfection of pure harmony. The best tuners in our large manufactories are free to confess that there is but little satisfaction in leaving an instrument which has been constructed carefully in all its parts, *out of tune*. Notwithstanding the evidence of our senses, that the perfect scale is most pleasing to the ear—notwithstanding the sure deductions from the mathematics, there are those who speak and write against perfect intonation. 'Why,' it is asked, 'if it was intended in nature that music should be in *perfect tune*, has a tempered scale been used for so many centuries?' Admit such an objection, and there is an end of all invention and discovery in this and every other science. Against the greatest invention of the age — the electric telegraph—the same objection has equal force. So long as no mechanism had been invented by which more than twelve sounds could be conveniently managed by the performer, we should naturally suppose that organ builders would manufacture such instruments as we have, and give to them the best tune they could, even if it was somewhat imperfect ; but we might *not* have expected that learned and professedly scientific writers should have attempted to prove from this fact, that *nature of music* does not permit its chords to be in *perfect tune*. It has not been customary, so far as our information extends, for those who profess to treat the *natural sciences*, to charge *nature* with *imperfections*, but, rather, if possible, to discover order and system, where only apparent imperfections were visible. Perhaps scientific writers on music are the only exception to this rule. These imperfections, however, belong entirely to their theories, and have no existence in the nature of music. No science—not even mathematics—can be more perfect and harmonious than music, in the department which relates to intonation. But melody and harmony do not produce all the effect of music, for much depends on the quality of tone, rhythm, expression, &c. It is therefore possible that tempered music may be pleasing, if good in these last particulars, although its melody and harmony be imperfect. But it is certain that, *cæteris paribus*, the more perfect the intonation, the more pleasing will be the music. The importance of absolutely perfect harmony is not equally felt in all kinds of music. In dance music, for example, the *rhythm* stands prominent, and although, even here, the music would be best if performed in *tune*, still, in quick movements, and in the rapid flight of notes, the attention is diverted from the imperfection of the interval. Church music, perhaps more than any other, depends for its excellence almost entirely upon its *harmony*. From church music are necessarily excluded many qualities which add much interest and character to other kinds of music. As its movement is slow and regular, any excellence or defect in its harmony is most apparent. The instrument which has long been used, and is best adapted as a guide and accompaniment to voices in church music is *the organ*. For this purpose it is *the instrument* of all instruments, as its derivation also signifies. It is superior to all others, in the volume of sound and number of parts which can be brought under the control of a single player—it excels in keeping in tune, and can steadily sustain its sounds for any length of time—it will give its sounds, also, with a certainty which even violins cannot always attain. For although these stringed instruments admit of perfect intonation, yet it requires a skill, which very few artists possess, of always striking at once the desired note. The exact relative pitch of every pipe in the organ can be adjusted by the tuner at his leisure, so that (with proper precautions) he may be sure of its sound whenever it is used. If the tuner leaves an interval false, it is beyond the power of the organist to improve it; in this respect the violin has an advantage over the organ, for if a string of a violin fall from its true pitch, skill of the artist, in execution, can overcome the difficulty. *Perfect tune* has been for centuries the great desideratum in the organ and instruments of this class. In the tempered organ, the tuner leaves no chord, except the octave, in perfect tune, and hence, whatever the best organist attempts must be imperfectly done. So long as the organ is used only as a solo instrument, as for a voluntary, a skilful performer is able in some degree to cover up the great imperfection in its tune. By great rapidity of movement, and incessant and startling transitions from key to key, he may divert the ear from criticising the imperfection of the chords. Temperament has doubtless done much to form a style, so prevalent at present among organ-players and composers for that instrument—a style neither dignified nor scientific. Organists and composers are not to be blamed for this faulty style (or a style which would be faulty, if their instruments could play in tune), for, being unable to obtain legitimate harmony, and satisfy themselves or their hearers, with dignified compositions — which show most conspicuously the defects of a tempered instrument—they resort to other expedients to please, and they astonish their hearers with remote and wonderful modulations, and feats of execution."—"*Perfect Musical Intonation*," by *Henry Ward Poole*.

"Among the signs of progress in the times, is a growing discontent with the thing called temperament. Instead of being considered as the crowning exertion of musical skill, it begins to be viewed as a lazy attempt to save trouble, like nailing a telescope to one length for all eyes and distances, or of making the fingers of a statue of one medium size. The know-ledge also gains ground, that all who are able, as for example the singers and violists, do without it, or more properly, perform in tune in spite of it; though the whole course of their education is one effort to tie them down to the convenience of those who can only grind music on twelve sounds. The Tonic Sol-fa Associations have settled this point; for nobody pretends that they sing the tempered sounds. The temptation to the old systematically teaching to play out of tune, was that performers might play 'with perfect freedom in all keys' by playing in none. Hence rivalry in magnitude of organs, and sleight of hand and foot, to conceal being out of tune. But a re-action is setting in; and the world is finding out that music is not in noise, but in concord of sweet sounds. . . . It is amusing to see how the defence would look, if transferred to the kindred subject of Optics. 'Eyes have been left unfinished by the Deity, to show His inscrutable power. Wise men encourage a bad eye, because it enables them to relish bad glasses as well as good. People have only to get used to them, and they will like them better. The eye knows what is meant, and will make allowances. No eye could endure untempered visions. It is only a telescope fixed to one length that can be used with perfect freedom for all eyes and distances. Glasses of that kind have the advantage, that one shows better at one distance and another at another, which makes a treasure of variety. There would be no end of telescopes for all distances; we must therefore "simplify the scale." An adjusting telescope is—(1) A chimæra, and cannot possibly exist. (2) If it was practicable, it would be of no use. (3) It would destroy all existing observations.' Those who will examine, will be surprised to find to what an extent the comparison is literally true. Professional persons will some day discover that playing out of tune is not music, and will lead to neither fame nor profit. . . . The object in view is to obtain the power of just intonation (in other words, of playing in tune), first in a single key, and then in a multiplicity of keys, by making the just intervals over again, beginning from sounds previously established. In which the thing to be impressed on the learner is that of the sounds established for one key, some will be found right for another key, and some will not; and what the *temperers* do, is to mince up the whole into twelve, and say they may serve very well for all. Singers and violists resist this, because it is easier for them to do the right than the wrong. . . . Nobody who has attended to the daily criticisms on musical performances, can fail to have remarked the outcries against one singer or violist for not being in tune, and the praises of some other for what is denominated correct intonation. If the critics are asked what correct intonation is, they reply that the best intonation they know of, is that of a quartet of singers or performers on instruments of the viol family, who, by practising together, have rubbed down their asperities against each other; and they at the same time admit without disguise that this is *not* the intonation of tempered instruments. But an optician does not content himself with shaking pieces of glass together until they take a shape which suits his purpose; he applies himself to investigate principles, and so goes down upon the truth with a precision which tentative processes would never arrive at. All his conclusions must meet the final approval of the eye; but he has a better way than groping for them under direction of the eye. In like manner the ear knows what it approves; and the difficulty, as in the other case, is how to come at it. Shall we proceed to try one thing after another till we get something we like, or shall we go to the root of things, and try principles? . . . But no absurdity can surpass the making an outcry for the presence of a quality, and systematically teaching to do the contrary. That this is what is practically done, is proved by the admissions of musical authorities when the dread of disturbing existing practice does not intervene, and by the magnitude of the errors demonstrable in the common course. . . . 'Few persons are aware how great is the difference between the true intonation of a fine voice, or a violin, &c., and the false intonations of such instruments of fixed sounds as the organ, pianoforte, &c. Many singers, trained to the intonation of a pianoforte, have their ear and voice so misled that they can never afterwards learn to sing in tune. The famous Madame Mara condemns the use of the pianoforte in learning to sing. She said every singer ought to learn to play on the violin, in order to know what true intonation is. In France a number of experiments were tried with Viotti's performance, and it was ascertained that he employed a vast number of very minute intervals, in order to play perfectly in tune in all keys.' * 'There are many degrees of false intonation: some singers are false to a degree that admits of no mistake in their case; but others have it so slight as to be scarcely perceptible to the generality of auditors; but still, even to those auditors who could not tell that the voice was out of tune, the general effect does not please. Those kind of singers will execute passages with the greatest skill, but they have little or no effect. Why? Because in all their embellishments one or more notes are not in perfect tune. In fact, my readers may draw one certain conclusion, that wherever they hear a singer who appears to have a good voice, executes well, and seems to have every requisite to be a good singer, but who, with every exertion, cannot arrive to be a decided favourite with the public, they may be certain that, in nine cases out of ten, such singers labour under a slight error of intonation, which, though not sufficient to be quite apparent, still always prevents the singing from giving a perfectly agreeable sensation to the auditor.'† The author of the article 'Temperament' in Rees' Encyclopædia, writes: 'No experience has yet been brought to show that the human voice sings tempered notes; not even when accompanied by tempered instruments. It seems to us, on the contrary, that an exercised voice, guided by a good ear, sings true, even though accompanied by a mis-tuned instrument, as harpsichords most frequently are, especially in transposed keys.' Scheibler, a modern author, says: 'It is impossible to conceive the effect of a really mathematically true chord when it has not been heard. I keep one to compare with the others. Every one that hears it expresses his joy and surprise at this delightful purity.' . . . Tuners profess to be conscious of the difference between sounds at the eleventh of a komma; and the errors of the vulgar division of the octave, from which practitioners only depart in spite of their instructors, are six, seven, eight, and nine times that quantity in each direction in sounds in the same key, and from ten to twenty-six times in sounds likely to be called for in the course of changes of key. This is what musicians practise and teach; yet they talk

* "Essay on the Theory and Practice of Musical Composition," by G. F. Graham, Esq.
† Costa's "Analytical Considerations on the Art of Singing."

with gravity of the importance of correct intonation. That what the moderns have dimly seen, was familiar to antiquity, though finally abandoned in consequence of mistakes at the outset, is a circumstance so remarkable as to authorise the addition of an Appendix directed to collecting the evidence of the facts. . . . 'Temperament' means 'tempering,' and to 'temper' is to 'form by mixture.' It means taking three or four sounds which ought to be used in different keys, and making one serve for them all. Lest the differences in question should be thought microscopic and fanciful, a visual representation of the principle of the Circle here follows, of the forty sounds in the Table, and of the sounds of what is called the Equal Division into twelve, which, with slight variations, are those of all instruments with twelve sounds in the octave. The

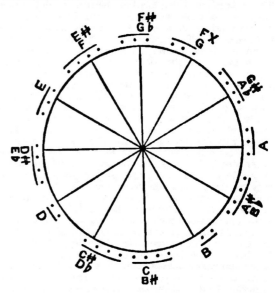

dots on the outside of the circumference serve as counters for the just sounds required to make all the keys in common use, the whole circumference representing an octave. The twelve equidistant radii represent the Equal Division into twelve, the letters opposite being the names given them; and the broken arcs show how the just sounds must be kneaded together by twos, threes, and fours, to make the twelve. From this will be seen how many of the just sounds must be clubbed into one, and what is the extent of the errors thus submitted to; the distance between two neighbouring dots, representing in round terms eleven times what the ear in favourable situations is conscious of. This barbarous contrivance of making one sound do duty for many is what is announced under the title of Temperament. If a sculptor, instead of making fingers of the various lengths nature has made them, should determine to make one medium length serve for all, this would be a Temperament. And if he were to add the declaration that fingers were left imperfect by the Creator, and express thankfulness for the obtuseness of our senses which prevented our being deeply conscious of the difference, he would do something like what has been put on record by the moderns on the subject of musical sounds. Two questions whereon arise. Is there any reason why singers should debase their performance by trying to submit to the recommended clubbing? Is there any reason why violists should do so either? The time cannot be far off, when the two most important classes in music's art will rebel against the obligation to try to perform out of tune, to please the players on instruments with only twelve sounds in the octave. It is as if sailors and astronomers were invited to employ telescopes fixed to one medium length, like those sold for children in the toy-shops, or statuaries to make the joints of their fingers and toes alike. There may be states of the arts where anything to the contrary would be considered ' an unattainable and not very necessary perfection.' It is matter of taste. The following is the definition of Temperament found given in all seriousness :—' Temperament. Operation by which, through the means of a slight alteration in the intervals, causing the difference between the two neighbouring sounds to vanish, we confound them in one, which, without shocking the ear, form (*sic*) the respective intervals of both one and the other. Through this operation we simplify the scale, by diminishing the number of sounds necessary. Without the *temperament*, instead of twelve sounds only which the octave contains, it would require more than sixty to modulate into all the keys.' * What is this but saying, that by making the fingers and toes of the statue alike, *we simplify the scale?* Without this, it would be necessary to copy sixty different articulations, which no sculptor could think of. Make every fifth articulation serve for five, and they will be reduced to twelve, which is a reasonable number. Would any art but the musician's submit to such a process? Destroy people's ears by laborious practice, and you will have no more trouble with playing out of tune. If it is asked, ' Who is to learn to make all these sounds?' the answer is, that for a singer or violist it is easier to make them in their places than not to make them. The performer is guided by the relation to what accompanies or has gone before, and not by the attempt to remember naked sounds. And if he is to make only the twelve, it must be by doing violence to his ear, as the sculptor would to his eye; and the truth is, the art of man cannot make him do it. The singers and violists rebel. They refuse to be sacrificed for other people's convenience. And the difficulty, after all, is none. There is to be no difficulty in making eighty or a hundred stops, which are, in fact, eighty or a hundred organs, for the sake of different qualities of tone; but there is to be difficulty in making an organ with the pipes of three stops for the sake of hearing two notes in tune. When musical writers say, ' No ear could endure untempered music,' they mean that no ear could endure to take an instrument correctly tuned for one key, and make those sounds serve for all keys. They mean that if it is determined to make one set of sounds serve for all, it is better to spoil all the keys alike, than to have one good and the rest intolerably bad. But they do not mean that it would not be better to have all the keys good if they knew how, or that it is possible to make better intonation in any particular key, than is made by applying the just division to it. Again, when they speak of ' the imperfection of the musical scale,' they ought to say ' of their own scale,' for there is no imperfection in the work of Nature, except such as a sculptor might complain of, who thought himself ill-used by Nature's not having made the fingers all of the same length to save him trouble. If twelve of what pass for fifths on the pianoforte are taken in succession (as, for instance, from the lowest C to the G next above it,

* "Dictionnaire de Musique." par Jean-Jacques Rousseau. Article "Temperament."

from the G to the D, and so on), each step being made by counting seven of the manuals, while from C to another C there are always twelve, the manual reached must be the C seven octaves off, because twelve times seven and seven times twelve are both of them eighty-four. But it turns out on enquiry, that if a string is shortened by a third part of itself (which is what makes the interval of a fifth), and the remainder by a third part of itself again, and so on to twelve times ; and if the same string is halved seven times successively (which is what makes seven octaves) —the places reached are not the same. For if the string was thirty-two feet to begin with, the first operation would reduce the length to 2·963 inches nearly, and the other to three inches, making between them the interval which has got the name of ' komma of Pythagoras,' and equal in round terms to an ordinary komma and one eleventh. In all of which there is no more that is wonderful, than that twice three is not five ; all that results from it being, that twelve just fifths are not equal to seven octaves, but are a little more, and consequently if twelve equal intervals are to be packed into the compass of seven octaves they cannot be correct fifths, but must be something less, or *flat*. In arithmetical language the complaint is,

$$\sqrt[12]{\tfrac{3}{2}} \quad \text{is not equal to} \quad \sqrt[7]{\tfrac{1}{2}}\,;$$

which is just as reasonable as complaining that twice three is not five. Yet this is what is held out as mysterious and strange, and one musical writer of the day is found saying, ' This inexplicable difficulty no one has attempted to solve; the Deity seems to have left it in an unfinished state, to show His inscrutable power.' But the wonder, such as it is, is not confined to a fifth; for it is equally plain that twelve just fourths are not equal to five octaves, but are less, by the same quantity that twelve just fifths are more than seven octaves. And three just major thirds are not equal to one octave, but are less, by a greater quantity than the last, as anybody possessed of the use of arithmetic can tell; and three just minor sixths are not equal to two octaves, but are more, by the same quantity that three just major thirds are less than one octave. And four just minor thirds are not equal to one octave, but are more, by a greater quantity still; and four just major sixths are not equal to three octaves, but are less, by the same quantity that four just minor thirds are greater than one octave. Why *should* they be equal? Who *wants* them to be equal? Why should not the statuary as well complain that the joints of toes and fingers were not made equal to please him? From all this the inference is simply that the intervals on instruments with twelve sounds in the octave are not the just intervals whose names they assume ; being a consequence as far from demanding any preternatural interference to cause or to permit, as that when thirteen divisions are crowded into a foot, or eleven made to fill it up, the results should not be inches. *Temperament*, then, is a device for saving the trouble of playing in tune, by playing out of it ; for playing in a variety of keys, by playing in no key at all ; for trying how much untunableness the ear can be educated to bear, instead of how much harmony it can be accustomed to demand; music depends on being in tune, only it is of no consequence whether it is in tune or not, and one thing is as good as another ; make noise enough and there will be plenty to applaud. They set up a mystery they call *wolf*, and declare it to be inscrutable ; being nothing but the grumbling of sounds they always knew to be out of tune. A faint resistance is made by the performers on instruments capable of just intonation like the voice and viol kind; but even on them an effect is produced by assiduous training to the bad, as people born to brackish water learn to think fresh insipid. Singers sing to the pianoforte because they have bad ears, and they have bad ears because they sing to the pianoforte. It is time there should be a division between the classes of performers that can execute in tune, and the classes that cannot. If some have not instruments which will play in tune in a variety of keys, they should be content to play in one, or else improve their instruments. But they ought not to play out of tune and call it music. What they say is, 'It is very difficult to play in tune in a variety of keys; hear how *we* flourish away in them all—*out* of tune.' The childish notion must be got rid of, that tune may be dispensed with to any extent which anybody may find convenient. It would be interesting to know what ingenious person was inventor of the idea, that sounds out of tune might be cured by dividing with the others. There is something like irreligion, in thus mutilating the works of the Creator It is as if an edict had gone forth, that all fingers should be cut to one size, to suit the convenience of sculptors. But they have a refuge. They say their hearers shall get used to it, and like it better. Which is saying that sailors shall drink salt water till they like it. Meantime they insist upon the ease there is in having everything equally bad; which is the sculptor descanting on the comfort of making all the joints alike. The end is to destroy the faculty of judging. A girl of thirteen will tell with precision whether two notes on the organ are best in tune with the swell open or shut. But by the time she is twenty, any nice sense of tune will have been laboriously extirpated, unless she has been fortunate enough to fall in with the Tonic Sol-faists. Another school there is, who stand upon the treasure they possess in the different characters of keys. Do they profess to make the intervals in all keys the same, or do they not? If the first, then it is childishness to claim any effect from their difference of keys, beyond what would arise from a difference in general pitch. If the other, then the matter solves itself into one key being in tune in the parts most prominently required in one piece of music, and another in another. Being the mistake of the man who having knives sharp some at the point and some at the heel, fancied he had an advantage over the man whose knife was sharp all over. If it is urged that the differences are small, the first answer is that it is by small differences all goodness comes. The tenth of an inch may in some senses be called small; but it is a mountain in the edge of a pen-knife, or the nose of a profile. If an artist were to take the mean of the profiles in his studio, and offer it to all comers on the ground that the differences were small, he would do what is done by the temperers. But the next answer is that they are *not* small; for in any single key they are many times over what the ear is conscious of, as making the difference between being in tune and not. The feeling of the difference is no more dependent on science, than of the difference between a blunt edge and a sharp. So that, instead of just intonation being 'an unattainable and not very necessary perfection,' the absence of it can only have been tolerated in consequence of the sense of tune being dulled. As it is, the singers and violists live in a constant struggle with the tempera-

ment; and get rid of it as far as they are able, though a portion sticks by them in the shape of accustoming their ears to what is out of tune. Instead of being 'attended with much cost and inconvenience,' to two of the most important branches of the musical profession—the singers and the violists—it is easier to do right than wrong; while everywhere, the evil might be cured for a tenth part of what is expended upon noise. Instead of being 'a slight imperfection,' it is ruinous to all approaches to perfection; a man might as well try to shave himself with a hand-saw and persuade himself he liked it. Pity it is that some eminent professional will not take the thing in hand. Could we but lay hold of the young Mozart, who *cried* when he heard the music of the temperers! If it is urged that 'the ear knows what is meant, and will make allowances,' as well might be urged in the case of a dish too much or too little salted, that the palate knows what is meant and will make allowances; or that a man may 'hold a fire in his hand, by thinking on the frosty Caucasus.' The question is of what is felt, and not of what would be desired to be felt. Imagine somebody professing to enjoy bad cookery, by dint of a lively consciousness of what it ought to be. A man of mark in the scientific world, said he encouraged a bad ear, because it enabled him to relish bad music as well as good. It is to be hoped he cultivated the same philosophic relish for bad eggs. If it is urged that 'our instruments do so well as they are,' the answer is, that they *do not* do well; and that so universally is this felt, that hardly two schoolgirls will sing a duet without requesting that instruments with twelve sounds in the octave may be kept away. They know the consequence of having them would be, that nothing they did would have any *edge*. The resistance is beginning in the right place; young ladies are refusing to sing out of tune to please their music-masters. And a great comfort it is to a young lady to know that it is neither her voice nor her ear that is in fault, but the instrument. A student of this description was asked to take home a well-known piece of religious music, beginning in F minor, and sing it to the pianoforte. She brought it back after a week's trial and said, 'There is neither A♭ nor D♭ on the instrument I have at home, so how am I to sing it?' This was the first result of emancipation from drilling to sing out of tune; and it is certain that she had never been told the minor third and minor sixth of the key were places where the degradation by temperament was most flagrant. The sense of tune is not dependent on musical skill, nor any extraordinary delicacy of ear, as sometimes intimated; though it is undeniably capable of improvement by practice. But it no more requires any extraordinary science to feel the difference between what is in tune and not, than between a sharp knife and a blunt. If it is urged that 'singers and performers on stringed instruments prefer making their major third not a perfect third to its root, but *sharp*,' the answer is, that finding the note made by tempered instruments too sharp, they prefer doing the same to making a palpable want of unison, and so end by giving in to the general habit. But there is no more evidence that anybody of his own mere notion ever said, 'Make me that third too sharp,' than that he prayed his unisons or octaves to be put out of tune. On the contrary, what everybody remarks on hearing the just instrument is, 'How beautiful are its thirds and sixths!' It is this which to a great extent constitutes the beauty of the sounds of the trumpet and horn, and no temperer was ever heard proposing to have them mended. In Germany a zeal has been displayed for an attunement in which all keys 'should be of an equal degree of purity;' where for 'purity' should manifestly be read 'impurity.' And the reason given is that 'on such an instrument only, can one modulate and improvise with perfect freedom.' What is this but saying, a telescope nailed to one medium length is the only one which can be used for all eyes and distances with perfect freedom? The boasted '*Wohltemperirite Clavier*' aspires to the wretched intonation of the guitar. Professor de Morgan (Professor of Mathematics in University College, London) has launched a declaration very likely to make an epoch in musical practice. 'The system of equal temperament is, to my ear, the worst I know of. I believe that tuners obtain something like it. A newly-tuned pianoforte is to me insipid and uninteresting, compared with the same instrument when some way in its progress towards being out of tune.'[*] This is to the purpose; for the question is not whether a dull man shall thank heaven he cannot distinguish a komma when he hears it, but whether there is not a potency in 'real notes' as a whole, which people acknowledge without asking why. And a strange testimony it is to what the temperers call being in tune, that every departure from it is an improvement. The explanation must be, that every departure makes some keys or others less bad, and these the ear picks out and takes pleasure in. A subsequent allusion to the Corn Laws is a happy one. As there the difficulties arise from interests opposed to those of the public. As Lord King said of the Corn Laws, it is 'the job of jobs.' If any are anxious to possess the 'equal temperament,' it is ready to their hands in the common guitar. A professional organist, speaking of tempered instruments, said, 'I like an instrument to be out of tune. It's pathetic and like a voice. I like to have my fifths too sharp, and my thirds too flat.' By which he meant that he liked to have them different from what they were on the tempered instrument before him. His wish, like the Professor's, was to be rid of what the temperers call being in tune. It is notorious that the way the tuners accomplish what they call 'putting in tune' is by tuning to concords first, and then putting out again by the quantity thought fitting for the 'temperament.' Distribute as they please, there is no bringing a sound thing out of an unsound. In other quarters, the refusal to tolerate the tempered sounds is breaking out. The windows of the military musical-instrument makers at Charing Cross will show wind instruments of complicated constructions, in comparison of which the enharmonic organ, with its one double dissonance at a time, is simplicity. It is amusing to find musicians pleasing themselves with the idea that they do something by tempering. Thus the beginning of Palestrina's *Stabat Mater*, instanced by Dr. Burney ("Hist. of Mus.," I, 65, Note) as 'tempered by the perfect manner in which it is sung,' is only a passage which begins in D major, in the third chord changes to F major, and in the eighth to D again, with entire regularity, and wants nothing but to be let alone. The objections noticed during the present agitation of the subject have been: 1. That 'what is called just intonation is a chimæra, and cannot possibly exist.' 2. That if it was practicable, 'it would be of no use.' 3. That it would

'destroy all existing music.' To which the answers are:—1. That if the quartet-players can produce sounds better than the tempered, there is nothing chimærical in trying to make pipes do the same. 2. That what everybody is glad of when met, must be of use to somebody. 3. That it destroys or alters nothing, except the habit of playing existing music out of tune. . . . The mistake of the moderns on the subject of the enharmonic has been the confounding of intervals between sounds in *different* keys with those between sounds in the *same*. Thus, when what is called an *enharmonic diesis* takes place between two contiguous notes, it is not that some novel interval is to be made for the sake of variety, or as has been somewhere said, 'to express some particular passion,' but that sounds in different keys and differing by this quantity are commanded by the necessity of making concords with other sounds which are successively on the scene in consequence of a change of key. So that instead of presenting any difficulty (as apprehended by those who ask, '*Who is to undertake to sing enharmonic dieses, diaschismas, and the rest ?*'), the difficulty is not in doing them, but in *not* doing. And the fact is, that a singer performs them in spite of efforts to hinder, and a violist the same; though both singers and violists do their best to cause their performance to be ground down and deprived of the edge of its natural proportions, to accommodate the performers on instruments with only twelve sounds for all keys. In the exercises of the circus, the foot-marks of the horse, the first time round, make what may be called *simple* intervals; but in the second and following rounds, if the new foot-marks do not start from the same point as the old, there will be intervals between the old marks and the new, often of curious minuteness and regularity, which may be called *compound*. And if any should say, 'How difficult it must be to teach a horse to make these compound intervals,' they would be answered that there was no difficulty at all, what was wanted being only that the horse should make his regular paces in both rounds, and then these intervals came of themselves. . . . Though the immediate operation of just intonation is on the executive department of music, light must be thrown by it on points which come within the province of the composer. One imminent result may be held to be, that anything which cannot be referred to some key or change of key, will be considered as jargon, or at the best like the sounds a child makes on an instrument and asks if they are not pretty. They may be pretty or not; but science is the road to what is better. And another result will be, that certain combinations of sounds will finally be avoided as harsh. For it never was intended to maintain that under a system of just intonation no combinations could be hit on which were harsh. But the grand benefit will be the getting rid of the necessity composers now are under of endeavouring by noise and movement to conceal the fact that their instruments are not in tune. A clatter of sounds out of tune will no longer be taken for music; and the Tonic Sol-fa Associations are the rebellion of the public ear. There will be witnessed new styles of music, or the revival of old, where the ear will be invited to take its pleasure in the consciousness of harmony, and as it were, taste and relish each particular chord, instead of shuffling everything away as fast as possible, to conceal its being out of tune. At present, everything is done too fast; the natural consequence of being afraid to give time for its being heard. In the

[*] "On the Beats of Imperfect Consonances." p. 16.

executive branch, substantial improvements may be expected from singers and violists being educated to consider themselves as always in some key or other, and consequently engaged, not in a game of hitting twelve holes, but in making sounds having always the same just proportions to whatever may be the key-note, and to each other. And as the road to this, they will be trained in directly the opposite course to what is followed now. Instead of rambling through a wilderness of semitones under the guidance of instruments in which no two sounds within the octave are permitted to be in tune, and with little or no effort on the part of either teacher or pupil to know what key they are in, or whether they are in any key at all—they will be grounded with jealous accuracy in performing in one key at a time, and then be conducted by degrees to all the varieties of change of key, caution being used that the pupil shall never be performing at hazard, the way to prevent which is to demand a declaration of what key every new sound is in, and what station it holds in the key. A learner in this way will make more progress in a week than in the other will ever be compassed at all. And serious must be the accumulated difference between professional persons passing their lives in sharpening their consciousness of the right, and in trying to accustom themselves to insensibility to the wrong. It is difficult to overstate the case; for even when performers attempt departure from the tempered sounds, they are as often taught to make the alterations the wrong way as the right, and to that they labour to accustom their ears. The author of a very able practical treatise was asked if he had not made a mis-print in describing C♯ as *higher* than D♭. To which he replied, 'I know it is wrong, but performers are taught so, and it is not my interest to contradict.' . . . The writer, though inferior in cultivation of ear to what may be expected from every professional musician, can almost always detect an error of a komma in a chord, or a mistake of a komma in a change of key, not so much by the beats, as by a kind of *leaden* effect, as if the sounds, or some of them, had lost their quality of tone. And the learners do the same. If a passage (particularly if connected with an incidental) is bald, meagre, or disappointing, they feel sure there is a komma wrong somewhere. The temperers assure us, it is nothing when you are used to it."—"*Just Intonation*," by T. *Perronet Thompson.*

"The intervals of the tempered scale are so nearly equal to those of the perfect scale, that, when the notes of the former are sounded *successively*, it requires a delicate ear to recognise the defective character of the tuning. When, however, more than one note is heard *at a time*, the case becomes quite different. We saw in Chapter VIII how rigorously accurate the tuning of a consonant interval must be, to secure the greatest smoothness of which it is capable. Such intervals were also shown to be generally very closely bounded by harsh discords. Now since, in the system of equal temperament, no interval except that of the octave is accurately in tune, it follows that every representative of a concord must be less smooth than it would be were the tuning perfect. One of the greatest charms of music, and especially of modern music, lies in the vivid contrast presented by consonant and dissonant chords in close juxtaposition. Temperament, by impairing, even though but slightly, the perfection of the concords, necessarily somewhat weakens this contrast, and takes the edge off the musical pleasure which, in the hands of a great composer, it is capable of giving us. . . . One of the readiest ways of recognising the defective character of equal temperament tuning is, first to allow a few accurate voices to sing a series of sustained chords in three or four parts, without accompaniment, and then, after noticing the effect, to let them repeat the phrase while the parts are at the same time played on the pianoforte. The sour character of the concords of the accompanying instrument will be at once decisively manifested. Voices are able to sing perfect intervals, and their clear transparent concords contrast with the duller substitutes provided by the pianoforte in a way obvious to every moderately sensitive ear. Since the voice is endowed with the power of producing all possible shades of pitch within its compass, and thus of singing absolutely pure intervals, it is clear that we ought to make the most of this great gift, and especially in the case of those persons who are to be public singers, allow during the season of preparation, contact with the purest examples of intonation only. Unfortunately the practice of most singing-masters is the very reverse of this. The pupil is systematically accompanied, during vocal practice, on the pianoforte, and thus accustomed to habitual familiarity with intervals which are never strictly in tune. No one can doubt the tendency of such constant association to impair the sensitiveness to minute differences of pitch on which delicacy of musical perception depends. Evil communications are not less corrupting to good ears than to good manners. I am convinced that we have here the reason why so comparatively few of our trained vocalists, whether amateurs or professionals, are able to sing perfectly in tune. The untutored singing of a child who has never undergone the ear-spoiling process, often gives more pleasure by the natural purity of its intonation, than the vocalization of an opera singer who cannot keep in tune. The remedy is to practise without accompaniment, or with that of an instrument like the violin, which is not tied down to a few fixed sounds. That a violinist can play *pure* intervals has been established by Professor Helmholtz by the following decisive experiment, performed with the aid of Herr Joachim. A harmonium was employed which had been tuned so as to give pure intervals with certain stops and keys; and tempered intervals with others. A string having been tuned in unison with a common tonic of both systems, it was found that the intervals played by the eminent violinist agreed with those of the *natural*, not with those of the *tempered* scale. Even with the pianoforte something might be done, by having it, when intended to be used only in assisting vocal practice, put into perfect tune in one single key, and using that key only. The services of such an instrument would, no doubt, be comparatively very restricted, but this might not be without a corresponding advantage, if the vocalist were thereby compelled to rely a little more on his own unaided ear, lay aside his corks, and swim out boldly into the ocean of Sound."—"*On Sound and Music*," by *Sedley Taylor*, pp. 205, 206, 207, 208.

HISTORY OF THE SUBJECT.

"Various attempts have been made during the last three centuries to remedy the above difficulty, and to reduce the apparent imperfections of the musical scale to a scientific and mathematical basis. Salinas wrote on the subject as early as 1577, and the folio volume of Father Mercenne was published in French and Latin in 1648. These plans were to be effected by multiplying finger-keys, which of course would augment fearfully the difficulty of correct performance. In 1811, two patents were taken out in England ' for improvements in instruments with fixed scales,' an account of which, with drawings, will be found in the ' Lond. Phil. Mag.' vols. 37, 38, and 39. These were improvements in temperament only, without aiming at perfect intonation. Mr. Hawkes's system had seventeen sounds in the octave; Mr. Loeschman's had twenty-four sounds. There were mechanical as well as theoretical difficulties necessarily connected with these instruments, which were fatal to their ever coming into practical use. Mr. Henry Liston, the learned author of the article ' Music ' in the Edinburgh Encyclopædia, has done more in this department than any other writer. His ' Essay on Perfect Intonation,' in one volume, quarto, was published in London in 1812. He also invented an organ designed to give the diatonic scales in perfect tune, which was built by the eminent organ builders, Flight and Robson, of London. This was an instrument of great ingenuity; but as the inventor was a theorist rather than a mechanician, there were mechanical difficulties which alone would have been fatal to it as a practical instrument. To enable one pipe to give different sounds, Mr. Liston employed ' shaders,' which, arranged in classes and worked by pedals, were brought over the tops of the open, and mouths of the stopped pipes to alter their pitch. It is hardly necessary to remark that such mechanism was impracticable, as its correct performance required an accuracy of motion which was incompatible with the material and the nature of the instrument. There were also other mechanical difficulties in his instrument, as well as errors and omissions in his theory (of which we shall speak hereafter), that interfere with its claim of being an instrument of *perfect intonation*. Its harmony, however, was superior to that of the tempered organs, and is thus spoken of by John Farey, sen., in the ' London Phil. Mag.,' vol. 37, p. 273 : ' Sir,—In your twenty-seventh volume, 206th page, I endeavoured to call the attention of Lord Stanhope and other patrons of musical improvements to the perfecting of an organ capable of performing in perfect tune. . . It gives me great pleasure, therefore, to be able to state that the above is no longer a matter of doubtful speculation; but that myself and several others have heard an organ thus perfected by the Rev. Henry Liston; the exquisite effects of which, particularly in accompanying vocal music, far exceed all that Maxwell and myself had written or perhaps conceived of the harmony of such an instrument. Mr. Liston deserves great credit for what he *did* accomplish, and we feel much more inclined to praise him for this, than to speak of what he did *not* do. He himself frankly acknowledges the imperfections of his efforts, and concludes his essay as follows:—"After all, the subject is but just begun. I have been led to travel in some beautiful regions, unknown to such as had confined themselves to the highway. But larger discoveries remain yet to be made by those who shall, with more zeal and better qualifications, follow out the track in which it has fallen to my lot to go a little way before them." ' "—" *On Perfect Musical Intonation*," by *Henry Ward Poole*.

"For more recognitions to the same effect, see Rousseau's ' Dictionnaire de Musique,' article ' Diacommatique;' Callcott's ' Musical Grammar,' § 258, on ' Supertonic;' and with more extensive development in ' An Essay upon Time' (Edinburgh, 1781, in the Catalogue of the King's Library, British Museum under the head of ' Tune '), and in the construction of the Rev. H. Liston's enharmonic organ, where changes in the sounds were made by means of shades connected with pedals (See Rees' Encyclopædia, art. ' Organ;' and ' Philosophical Magazine,' Vol. xxxvii., pp. 273, 328). The work of Père Mersenne ('Harmonie Universelle,' par F. Martin Mersenne, de l'ordre des Minimes. Paris, 1636; an edition in French and another in Latin in the library of the British Museum), enters extensively into the subject; and his drawings of finger-boards were greatly assistant in the construction of the present instrument. A representation is among them of a fingerboard with thirty-two sounds in the octave: but no attempt to divide the sounds among more fingerboards than one.—"*Just Intonation*," by *T. Perronet Thompson*.

"I have consulted the following works and memoirs :—*Huyghens*, Cosmotheoreos, lib. i.; Cyclus Harmonicus. *Sauveur*, Mémoires de l'Académie, 1701, 1702, 1707, 1717. *Henfling*, Miscellanea Berolinensia, 1710, vol. i. pp. 265-294. *Smith*, Harmonics, 2nd ed. 1759. *Marpurg*, Anfangsgruende, der theoretischen Musik, 1757. *Estève*, Mem. de Math. présentés à l'Acad. par divers Savans, 1755, vol. ii. pp. 113-136. *Cavallo*, Phil. Trans. vol. lxxviii. *Romieu*, Mém. de l'Acad., 1758. *Lambert*, Nouveaux Mém. de l'Acad. de Berlin, 1774, pp. 55-73. *Dr. T. Young*, Phil. Trans. 1800, p. 143; Lectures, xxxiii. *Robison*, Mechanics, vol. iv., p. 412. *Farey*, Philosophical Magazine, 1810, vol. xxxvi., pp. 39 and 374. *Delezenne*, Recueil des Travaux de la Société des Sciences, &c. de Lille, 1826-27. *Woolhouse*, Essay on Musical Intervals, 1835. *De Morgan*, On the Beats of Imperfect Consonances, Cam. Phil. Trans., vol. x., p. 129. *Drobisch*, Ueber musikalische Tonbestimmung und Temperatur, Abhandlungen der k. Sächsischen Gesellschaft der Wissenschaften, vol. iv. Nachträge zur Theorie der musikalischen Tonverhältnisse, ibid. vol. v. Ueber die wissenschaftliche Bestimmung der musikalischen Temperatur, Poggendorff's Annalen, vol. xc., p. 353. *Naumann*, Ueber die verschiedene Bestimmung der Tonverhältnisse und die Bedeutung des Pythagoreischen oder reinen Quinten-Systems für unsere heutige Musik, 1858. *Helmholtz*, Die Lehre von den Tonempfindungen, 1863. I am most indebted to Smith, Drobisch, and Helmholtz."—" *The Temperament of Musical Instruments with Fixed Tones*," by *Alexander J. Ellis*. [To these should be added the learned and complete analysis of the subject which may be found in Mr. A. J. Ellis's papers read before the Royal Society. " On a Perfect Musical Scale," January 21st, 1864. " On Musical Chords," and " On the Temperament of Musical Instruments with Fixed Tones," June 16th, 1864; and an article on " Musical Scales," by Sir J. T. Herschell, in the *Quarterly Journal of Science*, July, 1868.—J. O.]

"The writer's earliest publication on the present subject, was ' Instructions to my Daughter for playing on the Enharmonic Guitar,' with Plates, published by Goulding and D'Almaine, 20, Soho Square, 1829; in which was a Table of Sounds for an Organ on the present principle, but in only three keys. Of this there is believed to be a copy in the Library of the British Museum; and it was the subject of an article with extensive extracts in the *Westminster Review* for April, 1832, under the head of ' Enharmonic of the Ancients,' which was republished in the shape of a pamphlet. The first instrument was constructed by Messrs. Robson in 1834, in thirteen keys; another in twenty keys, for the Exhibition in Hyde Park in 1851; and subsequently the instrument of 1856, which is what with some additions and alterations is presented here. The subject has been pursued by the Messrs. Robson for above a quarter of a century, in the hands of four generations; and Mr. Heath, their leading machinist, was engaged sixty years ago in the construction of the Rev. H. Liston's organ. For later observations, see a variety of articles on musical subjects in the *Westminster Review*, between the years 1832 and 1835, and republished in 'Exercises, &c.' by the author of the present work, at Effingham Wilson's, 11, Royal Exchange. . . . When progress had been made thus far, opportunity occurred for an experiment, the result of which was evidence of general success. A young relative (since known as Mrs. Tom Taylor) was introduced to the instrument, who from childhood had been remarkable for an accurate ear, and the power of playing written music at sight and transposing at the same time; to which was added the advantage of possessing considerable mastery on the violin, sufficient to have led to her playing in the presence of Paganini, De Beriot, and other eminent professors. She had assuredly no prejudice in favour of the present innovation, and perhaps a little in the opposite direction. In a week, however, in spite of numerous avocations, she had perfectly comprehended the general principles and design; and in three weeks was able to play Beethoven's Sonatas from memory, without further assistance than occasionally asking for the board on which a key she named was to be found. Of a direct error of a komma, it is no exaggeration to say her sense was as distinct as that of performers in general of an error of what they call a semitone. As an instance, she was playing in the key of G', and on the music changing to the key of one sharp more, she declared herself, after repeated trials, unable to tolerate the results. On examination it was found she had gone to the key of D' on the uppermost board, instead of D' on the middle board. But on other occasions the determination of what was to be chosen was less easy. She has been heard to say, ' This chord can be taken in three ways: I dislike the first, and of the others I prefer the last.' And occurrences of this kind led to comparison and classification, ending in the rules which have been developed in the preceding sections. The chord formed by the major sixth, fourth, and black major second of the key, she called 'her favourite black chord.' She attached particular value to the purity of the *note sensible*; took great pleasure in the difference between G♯ and A♭: and avowed a sensible satisfaction in playing on an instrument where, as on the violin, she could make tunable sounds by seeking for them. Her style of playing was flowing and free, and evidently, after the first rudiments were passed, depended on the ear rather than on a mechanical observation of laws: though the result always was, that the laws were observed. At this period she had no more necessity for marks on the book, than a proficient in an Oriental language has for the written vowels; with exception, as there, of an occasional memorandum in a difficult passage. This experiment has since been abundantly confirmed. An advertisement headed ' Enharmonic Organ' was inserted in the *Times* of 23rd June, 1856, in which, after a description of the instrument, were the words, ' A pupil wanted; if blind, preferred; pupil should be able to play psalm-tunes, and tell the existing key; in which case six lessons deemed sufficient.' A young lady of nineteen, blind from birth, Miss E. S. Northcote, since organist of St. Anne and St. Agnes, in St. Martin's-le-Grand, whose portrait is at the head of this work, presented herself the next day, and after brief instructions sat down to the instrument. She was familiar with the current ecclesiastical music, and being an accomplished pianist, had accustomed herself to take the subject in any key that was desired. Being free from the terrors impressed by sight, she played in the keys which have been called *Principal* on their boards, with nearly the same ease as on an ordinary instrument; the difficulties being limited to an occasional demand to be shown where to find the second form of the dissonance, which she readily connected with the consonances to which it owed its rise. Doubts were felt whether it would be agreeable to her to be asked to classify the sounds under the denominations of white and black; but on the enquiry being made through her attendant, wonder was expressed that there should have been any hesitation, and she was soon able to correct the teacher if a mistake was made on the *colour* of a note. Advancing from one key to another with exemplary energy and patience, after literally only six lessons, and without the advantage of having the instrument to practise on between, she gave two public performances of sacred music as by advertisement in the *Times* of the 17th of July following. It was plain that after an acquaintance with leading principles, she went mainly by the ear, changing from one manual to another, or from one board to another when wrong, as a performer on the violin would amend a faulty fingering. She showed a delight in difficulties, nothing pleasing her so much as playing on two boards at once with two hands; which, as the boards were not alike, was something like playing two games at chess. On being asked why she took a passage on a particular board, she replied, ' Because it was hardest '—an unusual line of argument. From the inability of the teacher to attend, ten months passed without access to the instrument, and not a particle of former knowledge had been forgotten. Though the colours of the manuals were made distinguishable by the touch, no recourse to it was ever observed; so that there must have been a continual reference in the mind, to a plan of some kind so vividly present as to need no illustration from sensible objects. In all this there was much psychological curiosity, as well as evidence that there was something to understand and worth understanding. Her power of repeating anything that had been heard was almost unlimited, and it was reproduced on the just instrument with accuracy and ease. She said she learned opera airs from the hand-organs—an argument, among others, against the persecutors of street music. Another young lady who had practised on the pianoforte, but never sat down to an organ before, worked diligently for three hours, and then exclaimed, ' It *is* so pleasant to play *real notes* !' It was the expression of a great fact; human nature has an attachment to 'real notes,' which may be expelled, as the ancients phrased it, with a pitchfork, but will continually come back. And those three hours produced a substantial acquaintance with principles requiring nothing but practice to carry out. What in all cases was remarkable, was the quickness with which the learners got beyond dependance upon marks, and either made the right sounds or changed to them, by the same sense as would guide a violinist or singer. Being all (except the first) practised Tonic Sol-faers, they had great advantages in their habits of viewing everything with reference to the key-note. In this manner upwards of thirty young ladies rapidly obtained a comprehension of what it is that makes the difference between their voices and the pianoforte; and any of them, with reasonable access to the instrument, would have been competent to discharge the duties of a congregational organist. For imperturbable patience, quiet perseverance, and non-irritability under teasing difficulties, their equals were never seen. It held in some degree of the characteristic noted by theologians, —undoubting belief. They had a conviction there was something to learn, and the consequence was they learned. Not one of them ever said 'I can't,' or 'How is anybody to do this?' To those familiar with the interior of a college lecture-room, the contrast was irresistible."—"*On Just Intonation*," by *T. Perronet Thompson.*

METHODS OF TEMPERAMENT.

"Although temperament may be adjusted in many different ways, yet every possible adjustment can be classified under one, or both, of two general systems, called the MEAN-TONE SYSTEM, AND EQUAL TEMPERAMENT. The first aims to preserve the perfection of the thirds; while the latter sacrifices the thirds and gives preference to the fifths. The first is called the MEAN-TONE system, for the reason that, instead of preserving the distinction between the major tone of *nine kommas*, and minor tone of *eight kommas*, it averages the two, and makes a mean-tone of *eight-and-a-half* kommas. Consequently the sum of two *mean-tones* equals the sum of a major and minor tone, or a perfect major third. In tuning the E in this temperament, it is tuned a perfect major third from C, or E³, as we express it in the table. This E not being high enough by a komma for the E in the series of fifths, the error is divided equally among the four fifths, viz., C to G, G to D, D to A, and A to E, and each is left flat by a *quarter of a komma*. The tuning is continued until *eight* notes have perfect major thirds, and fifths that are a quarter of a komma flat. These are all the chords that can be used in an instrument of *twelve* notes in the octave. In this system a *sharp* cannot be used as a *flat*, as it will be false by the *enharmonic diësis*, or about two kommas. This is the interval by which three major thirds fall short of the octave, and it is obtained in this manner. Commencing with C, we tune E a perfect major third; from this E, tune G♯, a major third; and from C, an octave above the first, tune downward a major third to A♭. This A♭ is not as low as G♯ by the diësis, and G♯ will not answer at all for A♭. When common organs which

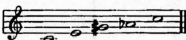

have but one sound for G♯ and A♭, are tempered on this system, one of these notes, usually A♭, is left so false that it cannot be used. Some organs have an A♭ supplied by a different pipe. The Temple organ in London has two notes thus supplied, A♭ and D♯, by the aid of which that instrument is enabled to play in two scales more than those tuned in this temperament, which have but twelve sounds in the octave. The mean-tone system bears, in many respects, more resemblance than any other temperament to the perfect scale. It recognises a distinction between sharps and flats, diatonic and chromatic semitones, has perfect major thirds, and has its minor thirds nearer to perfection than in any other temperament. With these advantages, however, it is justly censured for its discordant fifths, and its 'wolfishness' when the modulation is carried into keys where it is not prepared to play. The EQUAL TEMPERAMENT preserves the fifths nearer to perfection than the mean-tone system, and consequently throws the discord or 'wolf' (as it is termed by tuners), into the thirds. The fifths, however, although they are favoured are yet not given in perfect tune. It is found in perfect tuning that a series of twelve fifths will end a komma higher than the note commenced with. In equal temperament it is designed to make the series meet, and consequently this komma is equally divided among the twelve fifths, leaving each a *twelfth of a komma* flat. If this be accurately done, the octave will be divided into twelve equal parts, and one fifth will be equally as good (or bad) as another. To set this temperament, it is only necessary to temper the fifths carefully, as has been stated, without regarding the thirds at all. The major thirds will be found sharp by an interval eight times as large as the error in the fifths—that is, *two-thirds* of a komma. The minor thirds will be flat *three-fourths* of a komma, or the sum of the temperament of the fifth and the major third. As it is designed in the equal temperament to have every chord of the same name equally tempered, the necessity of leaving the thirds in this condition will be further made obvious. The third part of the octave must be used as the major third, and as three *perfect* major thirds do not equal the octave by the *diësis*, each third must be sharped by one third of the *diësis* or two-thirds of a komma. Again, the minor thirds must be each one-fourth of an octave; but four *perfect* minor thirds overrun the octave by *three* kommas; this excess, therefore, is equally divided among the four minor thirds, and each is left flat by *three-fourths* of a komma. The equal temperament has this great advantage over all others — its twelve keys can all be used, they are all tempered alike. The ear, too, is better satisfied when all the chords are *equally out of tune*, than when it listens to a constant transition from a better to a worse chord. It can also be demonstrated that in equal temperament, the *sum* of the temperament of all the chords—if the instrument be used in the twelve keys—will be less than in any other. Any other than the equal system is simply an attempt to improve part of the thirds by sacrificing not only the fifths but the remaining thirds."—"*Perfect Musical Intonation, by Henry Ward Poole.*

"HEMITONIC TEMPERAMENT—the usual tuning, or the so-called equal temperament. Each key is exactly alike. The characteristic of the tuning is, that in all keys the tones are too sharp or flat by the fraction of a komma. . . . This is the only temperament by which it is possible to play in *all* keys, with only twelve tones to the octave. The fifths and fourths are passable; the thirds and sixths, very bad. The general method of tuning is always in fault. MESOTONIC TEMPERAMENT.—This is the oldest system of temperament, universally employed till about a century ago, and was hence the tuning used by Handel and all the old writers, and it is still used on many country organs. Its principle is to keep the *major thirds perfect*. To do which, it is necessary to make the fifths a quarter of a komma too flat. The name *Mesotonic* (mean-tone) is derived from the fact that the mesotonic interval,

C to D, is precisely a mean between the just intervals, C to ♯D [D'] and C to D. . . . No other keys than B♭, F. A, C, G, D, A major and D, A minor, should be attempted, as the substitutions required produce 'wolves.' . . . The only chords that can be played properly are :—

Major.	Relative Minor.	Synonymous Major.
E♭ G B♭		
B♭ D F	G B♭ D	G B D
F A C	D F A	D F♯ A
C E G	A C E	A C♯ E
G B D	E G B	E G♯ B
D F♯ A	B D F♯	
A C♯ E	F♯ A C♯	
E G♯ B	C♯ E G♯	

This is by far the best system of temperament, so far as it goes, but as sharps and flats are different, and it does not possess D♭, D♯, G♭, A♭, A♯, it has fallen into disuse, except on the English concertina, which possesses D♯, A♭."—"Notes on Music," by A. J. Ellis, F.R.S.

"The contest lies, therefore, between the Mesotonic and the Hemitonic systems. The Mesotonic is that known as 'the old organ-tuning,' or, since it was generally used as a defective twelve-toned system, as the 'unequal temperament.' Within the limits of the nine scales already named, the superiority of the Mesotonic to the Hemitonic system has long been practically acknowledged. But the extremely disagreeable effect of the wolves (more especially to the performer himself) has finally expelled the system from Germany altogether, and from England in great measure. On the pianoforte the Hemitonic system is universally adopted in intention. It is, however, so difficult to realise by the ordinary methods of tuning, that 'equal temperament,' as the Hemitonic system is usually called, has probably never been attained in this country, with any approach to mathematical precision."—"On the Temperament of Instruments with Fixed Tones," by A. J. Ellis, F.R.S.

ORGAN AND CHOIR.

"When played with the choir, the defects of the organ are most perceptible. As the organ usually plays the same parts which the choir sing, the singers must temper exactly like the organ—which probably no choir was ever trained to do accurately—or there will be a continued want of agreement between them. A perfect major third, a child, who has had no musical instruction, will strike most readily and almost unconsciously, for it is in the simple ratio of 4 : 5, and the ear instantly detects the coincidence of the vibrations; but a tempered major third, two thirds of a komma sharp, he knows nothing about; it requires the skill of a scientific and well-drilled musician to give it correctly. If the singers could learn to temper with the organ it would be at the sacrifice of that pure harmony which they would make if they sung in tune without a tempered accompaniment. The ordinary agreement (or rather disagreement) between a choir and organ accompaniment, can be illustrated to the eye by the following example.

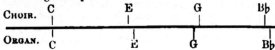

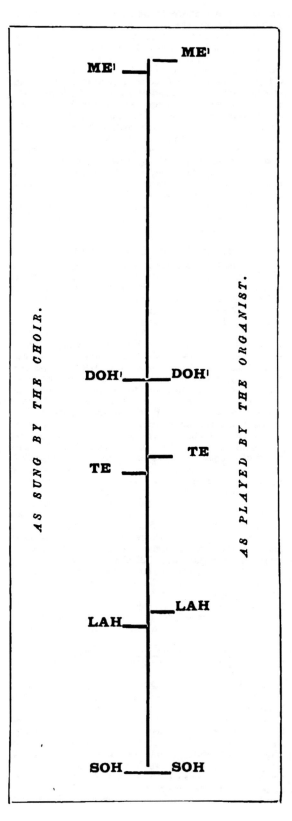

AS SUNG BY THE CHOIR.

AS PLAYED BY THE ORGANIST.

We will suppose that an organ, tuned in the equal temperament, is accompanying the choir, when it is singing the common chord of C. The key-note of C will, of course, be the same in the organ and the choir. The fifth (G) of the organ will be slightly, but perceptibly, flat—viz., one twelfth of a komma. The third (E) of the organ will be very discordant with the choir, being two-thirds of a komma sharp. If B♭, in the chord of the seventh, be added, the discord will be much greater than in either the fifth or the third, the organ being a komma and a quarter too sharp. Any one who will notice the singing of a good quartet with a tempered organ, may perceive the variation and discord of the organ upon these thirds and sevenths, particularly the last. For this reason these notes are sometimes omitted, as in chants, to the great improvement in the general effect. Good natural singers, who give their thirds and sevenths correctly, on first singing with an organ, have been accused by organists and conductors ignorant of the matter, of singing *flat*, because by temperament these notes on the organ were *too sharp*. [On the other hand, in reference to the seventh, it should be noted that Mr. Poole's harmonic theory leads him to make this tone twelve or thirteen times as much too low as the temperers make it too high—too low, I mean, for tuning with the third and fifth above it, or the third and fourth below it *in the same scale*. Melody requires scale-relation, and even harmony is not improved by altering what moves as a dissonance into a consonance. Mr. Poole's illustration of the organ and choir is shown more fully by the perpendicular diagram at the side, and I suppose the organ and choir to be giving the notes s ! t d! m!. No wonder that some organists, whose ears have been spoiled by temperament, are tempted to think that their choirs give the fifths too sharp, and the sixths, sevenths, and thirds too flat !] The discord is more conspicuous when the organ plays the vocal parts, as above, than when it plays a separate accompaniment, as is sometimes done. A tempered instrument, as a pianoforte, may be properly used in this manner, as an accompaniment only, without impairing materially the perfection of a melody which is sung by a voice."—"*On perfect Musical Intonation*," by Henry Ward Poole.

THE MINOR MODE.

"We find it stated in certain theoretical treatises 'That the major and minor keys of the same letter' (as C major and C minor) 'are nearly related, inasmuch as the two tonic chords are alike, with the exception of the third, and both have the same dominant chord.' We will write the tonic and dominant chords of C major (in the natural scale) and of C minor (in three flats) and from the table, ascertain the notes of each. We find the notes of the two keys entirely different, and consequently C major is not related to C minor, except in the *fourth* degree, through the following keys, viz., F, B♭, E♭, and C minor.

	C MAJOR.			C MINOR.	
	E²	D²		E♭¹	D¹
	C²	B²		C¹	B¹
	G²	G²		G¹	G¹

As upon the keyed instruments, it has been necessary to use the same sounds in C major and C minor, the writers referred to were led to make the statement we

have quoted "—"*On Perfect Musical Intonation*," by Henry Ward Poole.

THE COMPLEXION OF KEYS.

"We have before us a musical work, of no small reputation, from which we copy the characters, or 'complexions,' of several of the keys. 'C, bold, vigorous, commanding. D, ample, grand, noble. D♭, awfully dark (!). E, bright, pellucid, feminine. F, rich, mild, sober. G, gay and sprightly. A, golden, warm, sunny. A♭, the most lovely of the tribe; unassuming, gentle, soft, delicate, and tender, having none of the pertness of A in sharps. B (in sharps), keen and piercing. B♭, the least interesting of any,' &c. &c. These ideas have been formed and perpetuated by a sort of musical creed, and is said to have for its authority 'the common consent of musicians.' It is not so much our purpose to oppose this beautiful theory, as to show that no argument can be drawn from it to sustain temperament. If temperament be assigned as the cause why the key of A differs in character from the key of A♭, the difference must be found in the fact that one is tempered differently from the other. If temperament was adjusted in any uniform manner, through the different classes of instruments, and by different tuners, there would be a show of argument, in the fact, for temperament. But we find no such uniformity; different instruments are tempered in a widely different manner, and on one instrument the key of A is tempered like the key of A♭ on another. If an instrument be tuned in the *equal temperament*—which is more common and popular —every key is tempered *precisely alike*, and consequently all peculiarities from the cause assigned will disappear. If an alteration of *pitch* either be the cause, as some have supposed, of this peculiarity in the different keys, as instruments often vary from one another in pitch a semitone, it will often be difficult to decide which is the 'soft and tender' key of A♭, and the 'pert' key of A. If an organ be tuned correctly in the key of A♭, (or four flats), and the temperature of the room rise a few degrees, the relative pitch of the whole organ will rise a komma, and the music played in *four flats* will have the character (if this theory be correct) of the key of *eight sharps*. NOTE.—There is something so very imaginative in this theory of the different keys having different characters, that one might reasonably doubt whether such a theory had any supporters. Such, however, we are compelled to say is the fact—it is found in the books, and is taught at the present day by many teachers of reputation. If any one still doubts the fact, we would refer him to a recent number of the *London Quarterly Review*, vol. 83, p. 274, Am. ed., where, in an elegantly written article on 'Music,' the characters and complexions of the different keys afford the writer a theme for many sublime remarks, as if the theory had never been questioned. 'A whole Bridgewater Treatise,' this writer says, might have been not unworthily devoted to the wonderful varieties of keys alone. He (the composer) knows whether he requires the character of triumphant praise given by two sharps, as in the "Hallelujah Chorus" of Handel, or the Sanctus and Hosannah of Mozart's *Requiem;* or the wild demoniac defiance (!) of C minor, as in the *Allegro* of the *Frieschutz* Overture; or the enthusiastic gladness of four sharps, as in the song *Di Piacer;* or the heart-chilling horror (!) of G minor, as in Schubert's *Erl King*, and all the Erl Kings that we have known.' A very proper reply to this writer in the *Quarterly*, can be found in an article on 'Greek and Modern

Notation of Music,' in the volume of the *Westminster*, to which we have already referred in a previous note. Undoubtedly in perfect intonation, a certain key is frequently more appropriate for a given composition than any other key; but that a certain key gives to music performed in it any such peculiarity as we have quoted, is (in our opinion) as fanciful as to suppose that the size of the canvas determines the character of the painting. We will suppose a composer has an idea which he would express in a soft and gentle air, thinking that the character of A♭ renders it the most appropriate key for the expression of his idea; he writes his music in that key and arranges it for a quartette. He executes the music, thus arranged, on his pianoforte, and the soft and gentle effect desired is produced. He then gives it to a quartette to perform without any accompaniment. They take their pitch a semitone higher than his A♭—that is, exactly in his 'pert' key of A. Would the composer himself perceive any difference in the effect of his music? We think not: and say, moreover, with confidence, that no one in listening to an instrument, to the pitch of which he is not accustomed, can, with any degree of certainty, decide in what key the music is played. A flute player may judge correctly as to the key, when listening to an air performed on his own flute—perhaps a flute to which he is not accustomed—for different tones on the flute have different qualities; the high E, for instance, has a different quality from the E♭; but this is admitted to be an imperfection in that instrument which art has endeavoured to obviate. The character of music depends on other things than the key in which it is written. Many 'soft and tender' compositions have been written in A♭, and many of an opposite character. One key is more appropriate for a composition than another, for the reason that there will be employed in that key a range of sounds which are best adapted to the quality and compass of the voices or instruments for which the music was composed. Thus, if a melody of this compass (an octave and a fifth) were written for a soprano or tenor voice, it would not probably be placed in the key of C, as in that key the highest notes would be too high, and the lowest notes too low for convenient execution. Such a melody would more appropriately be placed in a key in the vicinity of F. Assuming F to be the *best* key for it, we believe that the nearer the key is brought to F, the better will be its effect; that is, the key of D, will be better than C, E♭ better than D, and E better than E♭. Melodies of small compass may be adapted to several keys. In different collections of music before us, the 100th Psalm—whose melody is contained in the compass of an octave—is written in four different keys, viz., F, G, A♭, and A."—"*On Perfect Musical Intonation,*" *by Henry Ward Poole.*

EXPERIENCES WITH TRUE INTONATION.

General Thompson for many years interested himself in watching the practice of young people with his organ, which was then established, by permission of the Tonic Sol-fa Association, in the Schoolroom at Jewin Street. During this period he noticed many points of practical interest to those who wish to pursue the study of true intonation. It will save the student much hesitation and experiment to know at once what, in difficult cases, commended itself to General Thompson's ears and to those of his pupils. I have, therefore, summarised those of his observations of this kind which I think will be useful to students on the tonic principle. I have also turned to the examples which he refers to, and print the most important of them here in the Tonic Sol-fa notation.

1st. It is well understood that **rah** is to be sounded with **f** and **l**, and **r** with **s** and **t**.

2nd. In the chord of **'S**, the dominant seventh, the ear prefers **ray**. General Thompson says this is because **soh** makes a "worthier," or a more perfect, "consonance" with it than **fah** can do. Another reason is, that the **fah** enters that chord as an intruder, and its dissonance is best shown by making the chord into which it enters as perfect as possible. He says, "The case may be taken as that on which the universal principle shall be tried, which directs that in all cases of rivalry the *worthiest* concord shall be made. It is interesting to observe how soon, on a true instrument, the ear acquires the power of judging in all these cases, and how constantly its decisions agree with the rule. If it is asked why the fourth should not be altered to make it form a concord with the major second, it is because the consonances, as being of the simplest proportions, are the groundwork of musical construction, and to alter them would throw the whole fabric into disorder. Besides which, altering the other sounds to suit the dissonance, would necessitate doubling twice as many sounds. It would therefore be like altering the room to fit the carpet, instead of the carpet to fit the room." See "Just Intonation," Ninth Edition, pp. 23, 59.

3rd. He suggests that in some cases, where it is not desirable to change from **ray** to **rah**, or *vice versa*, in holding or repeated tones, **soh** may be inserted in the music, so as to decide the ear for **ray**. He calls this a "supporting fifth." Such insertions, however, appears to me of doubtful propriety, and in the following example, to which he refers, I think that the continuance of the **soh** through the second measure would spoil the beauty of the **rah** chord, which is evidently intended in that place. See "Just Intonation," p. 24.

KEY **D**.   From HANDEL's "Water Music."

$$\left\{ \begin{array}{l} r^1 \quad : \quad |r^1{}_{,}m^1{}:r^1{}_{,}m^1| \; f^1{}_{,}s^1{}:f^1{}_{,}s^1|m^1{}_{,}f^1{}:m^1{}_{,}f^1| \; s^1 \\ t \quad : \quad |t_{,}d^1{}:t_{,}d^1| \; r^1{}_{,}m^1{}:r^1{}_{,}m^1|d^1{}_{,}r^1{}:d^1{}_{,}r^1| \; m^1 \\ s \quad : \\ s_1 \quad : \quad |s_1{}_{,}s{}:f_{,}m| \; r_{,}m{}:f_{,}r|l_{,}l_{,}{}:s_{,}f|m \end{array} \right.$$

4th. When both **s** and **l** occur in the same chord with **r**, he thinks that **rah** should be used if it is *under* them: the **s** and **l** and **ray**, if it is over them. In the following case of **rah** (from King's anthem, "O pray for the peace of Jerusalem"), to which he refers, there is another, and I think, a better reason why **l** should rule instead of **s**; it is because **s** enters and passes out of the chord as a dissonance, and the rest of the chord should be as perfect as possible, in order to set off the dissonance. The first **r** in the following example from Shield's "Streamlet," he thinks sounds better as **ray**, because the **s** is *under*. He says it is a solitary instance, and Shield was fond of part-pulse dissonances. The **m** is a passing

KEY **G.**.

$$\left\{ \begin{array}{l} :s \quad | \; s \quad :f \quad :- \\ :t_1 \quad | \; l_1 \quad :d \quad :- \\ \qquad \qquad |\quad \quad :l_1 \\ :r \quad | \; r \quad :r \quad :- \\ :t_1{}_{,}d| \; r_1 \quad :r_1{}_{,}m|{}:f_1{}_{,}s| \end{array} \right.$$

KEY **C.**

$$\left\{ \begin{array}{l} :l \; .r^1|f^1{}_{,}r^1{}:d^1{}_{,}t \; | \; d^1 \\ :l \qquad | \; - \quad :s \quad | \; s \\ :d \; .s|f \qquad :m_{,}r| \; m \\ :f \; .m|r \qquad :s \quad | \; d \end{array} \right.$$

tone, and the **s** a very intrusive guiding tone. The harmony is that of F moving to RAH, and I think that this harmony would be better felt if **r** obeyed the **l** and not the **s**. Melodically, too, the **rah** is demanded. He says that where the **r** stands between **s** and **l**, it may be doubtful whether it is to be grave or acute. He gives the following example from Himmel's " Inclina ad me," which he thinks will be better with **rah** than with **ray**.

:m	f	:r	|m	:d	r	:t₁	|d
:d¹	l	:t	|s	:l	f	:s	|m
:s		:f	|t₁	:m	l₁	:r	|d
:d	d	:					
:m	f	:r	|m	:d	r	:t₁	|s
:s₁	—	:—	|—	:—	—	:—	|—

I quite agree with the conclusion, but for another reason ; the **s₁** is an intentionally dissonating pedal tone, the special effect of which is, that the other parts are making perfect harmony *against* it, and its opponents, **f** and **l**, need all the support they can get from the just intonation of **rah**. General Thompson looks for mathematical reasons for things where I, for one, should recognise musical and æsthetical reasons as of more importance.

5th. In the following case, from the tune " University," he thinks the **r** should be **rah**. He notices, however, a strong melodic tendency, when harmony does not overrule, to make **ray** in ascending, and **rah** in descending. In the following case, from " Missionary hymn," he thinks that the second of the scale should be **rah** ; and I think so too, because **t** moves like a rising part-pulse fore-stroke, and the dissonating tone does not require just intonation like the tones of a chord. But if this were on a strong pulse, with **t** at the bottom and **l** at the top, we should feel the

KEY D.

d	:r .m	f
d	:d	r
l	.t :l .s	l
l	.s :f .m	r

KEY E♭.

l	:t .d¹|r¹ :d¹	t
d	:r .m |f :m	r
f	:l .s |f :s .l	t
f	:f .m |r :m .f	s

chord to be that of ¹T, and **l** being the dissonance, and **f** (the imperfect fifth) being the semi-dissonance in that chord, would not be regarded so much as the root and third, so that **ray** would, I think, be preferred by the ear to **rah**.

6th. In treating the minor mode, General Thompson regards its fourth, **rah**, as a fixed tone, and alters its seventh, **soh**, into **sah**, to agree with it. His plan of tonic minors led him even to this ; if he had looked on all minors as relative minors, he would have been satisfied without introducing another variable tone into the common scale. If he had allowed the **r** to change in the minor as in the major, there would have been no need to change his **s**, for **ray** to **s** is quite as good a fourth as **rah** to **sah**. If it is replied, " but then you make the very subdominant of the minor mode a changeable tone," our answer would be, " The minor mode, as adopted by modern harmony, is subjected to far more serious makeshifts than this—witness its changeable sixths and sevenths, and it is a great pity to make more variable tones than the human ear really requires."

7th. In cases like the following, in which the chord of RAH proceeds to that of S, he would use **rah** in the first chord, and **ray** in the second. Describing the attempt to do otherwise, he says, " The effect of leaving the faulty interval was very perceptible, and its correction noted by the blind young lady as at improvement ; and the probability is that with the voice or viol kind, the change would take place by a sliding or gradual alteration, which, if sensible at all, would have the effect of a grace. Where there is change of key, the dissonance always changes where required to preserve agreement with the sounds it accompanies.'

KEY A.

.m	f	:r	m
.d	l₁	:t₁	d
.s	f	:s	s
.m	r₁	:s₁	d

8th. Where melody stands alone, he thinks that **r** should take the same form which it would take if its preceding and following tones were sounded with it together in a chord. Thus the following from the " Red Cross Knight," would be correct \|f : r \|s, \|, and the following, in " Angels ever bright and fair," would sound well, without the accompaniment, \|s :l \|r¹ \|, while this, \|s :l \|r¹ \| would sound better with it. I question whether, in melody alone, the more accented tone (whether **f** or **s**), and the tone which comes before rather than after the **r**, should not have upon it the greater influence.

9th. I do not follow General Thompson in his examples of transition and modulation, because that subject has been much more fully analysed above, as well as in " How to Observe Harmony," and " Construction Exercises."

TONIC SOL-FAISTS AND TRUE INTONATION.

" The musical notation in ordinary use evidently takes for granted a scale consisting of a limited number of fixed sounds. Moreover, it indicates, directly, *absolute pitch*, and only indirectly, *relative pitch*. In order to ascertain the interval between any two notes on the stave, we must go through a little calculation, involving the clef, the key-signature, and, perhaps additional ' accidental ' sharps or flats. Now these are complications, which, if necessary for pianoforte music, are perfectly gratuitous in the case of vocal music. The vocalist wants only to be told on what note to begin, and what *intervals* to sing afterwards, i.e., is partially concerned with absolute pitch *only at the start*, and needs be troubled with it no further. The established notations encumber thus the vocalist with information which he does not want, and yet fails to communicate the one special piece of information which he *does* want, viz., the relation which the note to be sung bears to its tonic or key-note. There is nothing in the established notation to mark clearly and directly what this relation is in each case intended to be. Unless the vocalist, besides his own ' part,' is provided with that of the accompaniment, and possesses some knowledge of harmony, he cannot ascertain how the notes set down for him are related to the key-note and to each other. The extreme inconvenience of this must have become painfully evident to any one who has frequently sung concerted music from a single part. A bass, we will suppose, after leaving off on F♯, is directed to rest thirteen bars, and then come in *fortissimo* on his high E♭. It is impossible for him to keep the absolute pitch of F♯ in his head during this long interval, which is perhaps occupied by the other voices in modulating into some remote key ; and his part vouchsafes no indication in what relation the E♭

stands to the notes, or chords, immediately preceding it. There remains, then, nothing for him to do but to sing, at a venture, *some* note at the top of his voice, in the hope that it may prove to be E♭, though with considerable dread, in the opposite event, of the conspicuous ignominy of a *fortissimo* blunder. The essential requisite for a system of vocal notation therefore, is that, whenever it specifies any sound, it shall indicate, in a direct and simple manner, the relation in which that sound stands to its tonic for the time being. A method by which this criterion is very completely satisfied shall now be briefly described. . . . I have enjoyed some opportunities of watching the progress of beginners taught on the old system, and on that of the Tonic Sol-fa, and I assert, without the slightest hesitation, that, as an instrument for imparting the power of sight-singing, the new system is enormously, overwhelmingly, superior to the old. In fact, I am prepared to maintain that the complicated repulsiveness of the pitch-notation, in the old system, must be held responsible for the humiliating fact that, of the large number of the musically well-endowed persons of the opulent classes who have undergone an elaborate vocal training, comparatively few are able to sing even the very simplest music at *sight*. Set a young lady thus instructed to sing a psalm-tune she has never seen before, and we all know what the result is likely to be. Now, there is no more inherent difficulty in teaching a child with a fairly good ear to *sing* at sight, than there is in making him *read* ordinary print at sight. A vocalist who can only sing a few elaborately prepared songs ought to be regarded as on a level with a school-boy who should be unable to read except out of his own book. If evidence be wanted to make good this assertion, it is at once to hand in the fact that the youngest children, when well trained on the Tonic Sol-fa system, soon obtain a power of steady and accurate sight-singing, and will even tell you whether a new tune pleases them or not, after merely looking it over, without uttering a sound. The reader is requested to observe that the above remarks are strictly limited to the achievements of the Tonic Sol-fa system in *vocal* music. I express no opinion as to the applicability of its notation to *instrumental* music, nor do I wish to maintain that even in the vocal branch it has arrived at perfection. On the contrary, I am doubtful whether its time-notation, when applied to very complicated rhythmic divisions, does not become more difficult than the system in ordinary use, and I consider the notation adopted for the minor mode to be unquestionably defective. On the main point, however, viz., the decisive superiority of its pitch-notation over that of the established system, and the vitally important consequences as to purity of intonation which necessarily follow from this superiority, I desire to express the most confident and uncompromising opinion." — '*Sound and Music*,' *by Sedley Taylor.* pp. 209, 210, 214, 215.

"The ancients had clearer notions of changes of key than the moderns. A *change of key* consists, or ought to do, in beginning on a new portion of the string for key-note, and thence calculating the divisions of the octave afresh, by the just proportions over again. Which is no great mystery; requiring nothing but the Rule of Three. This is what the ancients aimed at, by what they called the *Enharmonic*, and is practically done by the Tonic Sol-faers. The change is most frequently to one of the consonances of the original string; but sometimes it is to a dissonance, and sometimes, though rarely, to a sound which was not among

the previous divisions at all. . . . An effective way of representing a change of key, is to divide a string in the just proportions for a single key, by frets in the manner of a guitar, and after bringing it to the pitch chosen to represent the first key-note, screw it up till it produces the sound previously made at one of the frets; whereupon the frets will produce the just sounds in the new key. . . . At a later period, it was discovered that the children who could read the Tonic Sol-fa notation played instinctively on the organ with 40 sounds in the octave, which would frighten the *Conservatoire*, requiring only to be shown the place of Do. They were made to begin by running up and down the sounds of the major in easy keys, taking the *white* major second in ascending, and the *black* in descending, which familiarizes them with its presence; and when they proceeded to perform their tunes, they had only to make a pencil-mark under the black when wanted in company with other black notes. The colours, which perplex general performers, seemed made for their special use and benefit. Nor was this effect limited to the young. The generality of grown persons have learned their music through a process, of which, like teething and other juvenile sufferings, they have forgotten the difficulties. But it is easily credible, that to a beginner the ordinary finger-board may present an unpromising wilderness, compared with one where the intervals shall be distinctly marked. It must be like playing on a chess-board where all the squares should be of one colour. The learners all declare the coloured manuals are easiest. . . . In all these processes, the advance was in proportion to the previous habits of performance; and it is surprising how rapid will be the progress when every step is presented as a discovery and not as a difficulty, and how soon a kind of instinct is displayed, founded on cultivation of the ear, by which what is out of tune is continually exchanged for what is better. Under such circumstances it is impossible not to sing. Learners have their likes and dislikes; and one will take to the performance of one of the additional keys, and another another. But they always end by mastering all, as they find they want them for changes occurring in practice. They should be taught the use of the second form of the dissonance first in the key they find easiest; and they will speedily read off the fourth, fifth, &c., for this purpose upon the book, without referring to the colours of the manuals. In which the Tonic Sol-faers have the advantage, as having been accustomed to distinguish these sounds by positive names. In the contest between tuning and untuning, it is no wonder the Tonic Sol-faers beat. It is only to let them loose upon the instrument, and their own taste and judgment will make them play. Their progress will at first be mechanical and slow; but they will soon find their feet in a large room, and wonder how they ever could do wrong. It is simple mockery to talk of being 'conscientious,' when the first of all rules is to be that everything is to be out of tune. It is wonderful how soon a young lady performer takes delight in finding the sound she produces from the instrument agree with what she would like to sing. . . . In England triumphant progress has been made in popularising just intonation, by the Association under the direction of the Rev. John Curwen, of Plaistow, London, E., whose 'Tonic Sol-fa system' (meaning Sol-fa upon the key-note) is a restoration of the principles of Guido and the ancients. Beginning by discarding the tempered sounds, they practise the performance of the just concords in one key first; which they find easy through the recognition of the double dissonance. And then they proceed to perform the same intervals in other keys; in which the great engine of their success is their notation, by which the key-note, second, third, &c., is always represented by the same symbol. Nothing is easier than to read the old notation with constant reference to the places in the key, *when the habit is acquired*. But the question was how to acquire the habit, and this is what the Tonic Sol-fa notation teaches. The Tonic Sol-faers have the root of the matter in them; and the consequence is that their young men and maidens know more and can perform more than the *grosses perruques* of former generations. Through their exertions, it is breaking upon the public, that singers and violists will perform in tune if tempered instruments can be kept away—and temperament is a grave jugglery, a combination to make us drink salt water and call it fresh. The ambition of the just instrument is to embody what it is they do. And *they* say in turn 'Our voices and this instrument are friends; the others are enemies.' Scarcely a thing could be shown to them on the instrument without their saying, '*That* is exactly what we should have done in Sol-faing.' And one special use they found in it was that in any dubious passage they could embody the rival sounds and judge between them at their ease. If it is asked what is the use of an instrument to Sol-faers if they can sing by themselves; it is because more progress is made by all aiming at a model, than by setting everybody to find out for themselves what the sounds agreed in should be. It is for the same reason they use a modulator. The Tonic Sol-faers wisely attach themselves to youth. When people have passed long lives in trying to sing out of tune, it is not likely they will reform. Harvey never knew a physician above forty years of age, who accepted the circulation of the blood. In like manner the performers of the present day will go on endeavouring to arrive at tunableness by untuning, till the Tonic Sol-faers raise up a new generation to supersede them. Meantime Tonic Sol-faers see with pleasure the testimony borne to the soundness of their views by Professor Helmholtz. . . . Singers with good ears invariably exclaim in these places, '*That* is not like the tempered instrument.' And with tempered instruments the singers will always be found to hesitate at these passages, and perform them distressfully, like things they are glad to get over. . . . Singers to the just instrument often exclaim, 'How finely our voices *come out!*' The simple reason being, that they are in tune, and the instrument also. . . . There is no difficulty in making an orchestra of instruments of the viol family practise with the just instrument: for this purpose nothing being required from the violists, but to follow the old rule of avoiding open strings. . . . Without this, in every key there would be one pair of strings (either on the violin, or on the viola and violoncello, or on all three) which must be tuned to a komma less than a fifth. This therefore is an obstacle to using the open strings, where there is to be anything like a variety of changes of key in the same piece of music. The point of importance for the violists, is that they should know distinctly where the strength of the Sol-fa system lies—that it lies in scouting the temperament as the invention of a rude age, which popular good sense in the present day is rising to resist. They should have a clear vision of the fact, that the sounds which are in tune in one key are not in tune if introduced in another key; that is to say, some of them are in tune, and some are not. And the modest

request of the temperers is, that the violists will swallow the bad, by dividing their defects among the good. When almost every kind of instrument is breaking out into attempts to get rid of the temperament, it will be passing strange if the violists, to whom by the nature of their instrument it is easier to play in tune than not, should be found submitting to the dictation of the incapables."—"*On Just Intonation*," by *T. Perronet Thompson.*

"Since the publication of the first edition of this work, I have had an opportunity of seeing General Perronet Thompson's Enharmonic Organ [the General's work on 'Just Intonation' is cited in a foot note], which allows of the performance of related harmonies in twenty-one different major and minor keys with just intonation. This instrument is much more complicated than my harmonium.* It has forty different pipes to the octave, and three different key-boards, with sixty-five finger-keys to the octave ; some notes occurring on two or even on all three finger-boards. This instrument admits of the performance of far more extended modulations than the harmonium I have described, without requiring any enharmonic substitutions—[that is, without requiring a chord or a key to be played a komma higher or lower than the succession of harmonies indicates]. Tolerably rapid passages and ornamentations can be executed upon it, notwithstanding its apparently very complicated finger-board. The organ is erected in the Sunday School Chapel, 10, Jewin Street, Aldersgate, London. It has only one stop, the usual principal, has Venetian blinds as a swell, and is provided with a peculiar mechanism to correct the influence of temperature upon its intonation. Sequences of chords upon this instrument are extraordinarily harmonious. On account of the softer quality of tone, they are more strikingly harmonious than on my harmonium. For the same reason, however, the difference between chords rightly and wrongly struck, is not so sharp and distinct on this organ as on the harmonium. I had, at the same time, an opportunity of hearing a lady sing, who was accustomed to the accompaniment of the enharmonic organ, and can certify that her singing produced a peculiarly satisfactory feeling of perfect certainty in intonation, which is usually absent when the voice is accompanied by a pianoforte. There was also a [blind] violinist present, who had not been much used to play with the organ, and accompanied known airs by ear. He adapted himself perfectly to the intonation of the organ as long as the key remained unchanged, and it was only in isolated, rapid modulations, that he was not able to follow it exactly. I had also an opportunity in London of comparing the intonation of this instrument with the natural intonation of singers, who had learned to sing without any instrumental accompaniment at all, and only follow their ear. These are the members of the Tonic Sol-fa Association, who are numerously spread over all the larger towns in England (there were 150,000 of them in 1862), and whose great progress is very noteworthy for the theory of music. This Association represents the notes of the Major Scale by the syllables *Doh, Ray, Me, Fah, Soh, Lah, Te, Doh*¹; so that *Doh* is always the tonic. Their songs are not written in the usual musical notation, but with ordinary letters, representing the pitch by the initials of the syllables above-named. When the tonic is changed in the course of a modulation, the notation is also changed ; so that

* An instrument with two finger-boards, of the ordinary construction, in which the notes are so tuned as to play just intervals in all the major and many minor keys.—A. J. E.

I

the new tonic is still termed *Doh*, and this change is indicated in writing by giving the note on which the change takes place *two* letters—one belonging to the old and one to the new tonic. By this notation, therefore, the relation of each note to the tonic is rendered especially prominent; while the absolute pitch of the whole piece is only marked at the beginning. Since the intervals of the natural Major Scale are transferred to every new tonic, as it occurs in the course of modulation, all keys are performed without any tempering of the intervals. That in a modulation from C Major to G major, the *Me* (or B) of the latter scale is precisely the same in pitch as the *Te* of the former; and the *Ray* (or acute A) of the second is nearly of the same pitch as the *Lah* (or usual A) of the first scale, is not indicated at all in the notation, but left to be pointed out in the course of instruction. Hence the pupil has no motive for confusing the acute with the usual A. [In a foot note are cited the names of the principal works on the Tonic Sol-fa system, and principal pieces of music in its notation, as prepared by Mr. Curwen.] It cannot be denied that this notation has the great advantage of giving prominence in teaching singing, to what is of the greatest importance to the singer in determining the tone, namely, the relation of the tone to the tonic. Only a few persons of extraordinary powers are able to fix and recover an absolute pitch when other tones are sounded near it. Now, the usual musical notation only directly gives the absolute pitch, and that only for a tempered intonation. Any one who has been used to sing at sight, will know how much easier this is to do from a pianoforte score in which he can see the harmonies, than from a single voice-part. In the first case, it is easy to see whether the tone to be sung is the fundamental tone, third, fifth, or dissonance of the chord struck, which is a sufficient guide; in the second case, the singer has only to take the required intervals up or down as well as he can, and trust to the accompanying instruments and other voices for forcing his own voice into the proper pitch. Now, the facilities which a singer, well acquainted with musical theory, derives from the pianoforte score, are immediately presented by the Tonic Sol-fa notation even to the uninstructed. I have convinced myself that the use of this notation enables a person to sing from a single voice-part much more easily than if it were written in the ordinary musical notes; and I had an opportunity of hearing more than forty children, between eight and twelve years of age, in one of the working-class schools of London [Mr. Gardiner's, Tottenham Court Road], go through singing exercises, with a certainty in reading the notes, and a justness of intonation, which astonished me. The London Tonic Sol-fa Schools are in the habit of giving an annual concert, with two to three thousand children's voices, in the Crystal Palace at Sydenham, which, as I am assured by persons who understand music, produce a powerful effect on the audience by the harmoniousness and musical justness of their performance. The Tonic Sol-fa performers then sing by natural, not by tempered, intervals. When their choruses are accompanied by a tempered organ, strongly marked differences and disturbances result; whereas, they are in perfect tune with General Perronet Thompson's enharmonic organ. Many remarks that have been made are very characteristic. A young girl had to sing a solo in F minor, and took the notes home to practise them with the piano. When she returned she declared that the A flat and D flat on her piano were out of tune. These are the third and sixth of the key in which the errors of the tempered system of tuning are really most conspicuous.

Another young lady was so pleased with the enharmonic organ, that she practised on it for three hours in succession, declaring that it was so extremely agreeable to play ' real notes.' In general, it resulted in a great number of cases, that young people who had been taught to sing on the Tonic Sol-fa method, found their way on the complicated finger-board of the enharmonic organ by themselves, and without instruction, and always selected the intervals indicated by theory. Singers find that it is easier to sing to the accompaniment of this organ, and also that they do not hear the instrument while they are singing, because it harmonizes thoroughly with their voices, and gives rise to no beats. I have also myself remarked, that even singers who are accustomed to the accompaniment of the piano, when they are asked to sing simple melodies to the accompaniment of my justly intoned harmonium, sing natural thirds and sixths, and neither the tempered nor the pythagorean intervals [the tempered, as on the piano; the pythagorean, as in the old Greek music, in which third, sixth, and seventh of the major scale are too sharp by a komma.] I accompanied the beginning of the melody, and paused when the singers had to strike the third or sixth of the key. When he had struck it, I sounded on the instrument either the natural, or the pythagorean, or the tempered interval. The first was always in tune with the voice: both the others produced distinct beats. These experiments, I believe, remove the last shade of doubt as to the fact *that those theoretically determined intervals—which I have called natural in this book—are really natural for an unspoiled ear; that the departure of tempered intervals from the natural, are really observable and unpleasant to the unspoiled ear; and thirdly, that notwithstanding the fine distinctions in isolated intervals, it is really more easy to sing correctly by the natural than by any tempered scale.* The complicated calculation of intervals necessary for the natural scale, and which certainly throws difficulties in the way of execution on instruments with fixed tones, has no existence for the singer, and even for the violinist if he allows himself to be guided by his ear. For in the natural progression of a correctly modulated piece of music, they must always proceed by the intervals of the natural diatonic scale. It is only the theoretician that has to perform a complicated calculation, when he finally compares the result of a great number of such progressions with their initial tone. That the natural system is executable by singers, has been proved by the English Tonic Sol-fa singers—that it can be also executed on bowed instruments—and is really executed on them by the best players—I have no longer any doubt, after the above-mentioned experiments of Delezenne, [*] and what I myself heard

* On p. 325 of the text there is the following notice of Delezenne's experiments from the ' Recueil des Travaux de la Société des Sciences, &c., de Lille,' 1826-7 :—' Delezenne determined the values of the several notes of the major scale as they are performed by the best violinists and violoncellists, by means of a very accurately divided string, and found that they played exactly just, not tempered or pythagorean thirds and sixths. But if performers of the first rank, who are thoroughly acquainted with the pieces they play, are able to overcome the deficiencies of their school, and the tempered system performers of inferior powers would find it much easier to obtain perfection in combined pieces, if they were accustomed from the first to play the scales in the natural intervals, and the greater trouble of the first exercises would be amply repaid by the subsequent results. It is also more easy to comprehend the differences between different notes of the same name in just intonation than is usually believed, when the ear has once become accustomed to the sound of the pure harmonies. The interchange of the acute and ordinary A on my harmonium, in a consonant chord, strikes my ear as quickly and distinctly as an interchange of A and A♭ on the piano.' [I can corroborate this statement by my own experience on a justly intoned concertina. —A. J. E.]

from the violinist who accompanied the enharmonic organ. As regards the other orchestral instruments, the brass instruments naturally produce just intonation, and can only be forced with difficulty into the tempered tuning. The tones of the wooden instruments (flutes, &c.) can be slightly altered so as to suit their tuning to that of the rest. I believe, therefore, that the difficulties of the natural system are not insuperable; nay, I believe that many of our best musical performances owe their beauty to the unconscious introduction of the natural system, and that we could more frequently enjoy this beauty if just intonation were systematically taught and made the foundation of musical instruction, in place of the tempered system which prevents the human voice and bowed instruments from developing their full powers of harmony, merely to facilitate the fingering of the organ and pianoforte."
—" *Theory of the Sensations of Tone, as a Physiological Foundation for the Theory of Music,*" by Professor Helmholtz. Translated by A. J. Ellis, F.R.S., for the " Tonic Sol-fa Reporter."

It must seem remarkable to those who are not acquainted with the Tonic Sol-fa Method, that so many musical men, who are not at the same time mathematicians and natural philosophers, should speak favourably of the Tonic Sol-fa Method and Notation. The late Sir John Herschel, without referring directly to this System, wrote strongly in favour of the principle on which it is founded —that of the movable Do. Mr. A. J. Ellis, F.R.S., was a member of the Tonic Sol-fa College; and the testimonies of General Thompson, Mr. Sedley Taylor, and Professor Helmholtz, are given above. It is not merely that Tonic Sol-faists have studied this question of True Intonation and shown a personal interest in it, which draws these two parties—the philosophers and the singers—towards one another; but they both seek for truth, and both have faith that whatever is true will finally prove itself cheapest and best. Of all who have laboured for the promotion of True Intonation, General Thompson has done most. It was in 1857 that I took a company of the best Tonic Sol-fa teachers, male and female, to Messrs. Robson's to hear the enharmonic organ, which had been greatly improved and completed. For thirty years, the author of " The Anti-Corn-Law Catechism," whose insight and keen wit stirred up Cobden, Bright, and others, to obtain cheap bread for the people, had then employed his leisure time in studying this subject and bringing his instrument to perfection, at the cost of several thousand pounds. After singing various pieces with the organ, the remarks of my friends were, " This is quite different from other organs," " It is so pleasant to sing with," " We have nothing to sing *against*," " It feels like our friend." The organ was soon removed to the rooms of our London Association, in Jewin Street, where it remained for many years. Unfortunately for practical purposes, it was not powerful enough to

accompany the singing of a school or congregation, and occupied too much space for its proper place —a drawing-room. But there, on Wednesday afternoons, for many years, General Thompson met his pupils, meanwhile circulating his pamphlet in thousands far and wide. Tonic Sol-faists were permitted to obtain copies for the postage, and availed themselves very extensively of the privilege, so that nine large editions were exhausted. He did not content himself with explaining his views to the learned, but tried to make them plain to the masses of the people. In the *Tonic Sol-fa Reporter*, August, 1857, the points are mentioned on which I then ventured to differ from him. I think that a simpler system of keys, the use of relative instead of tonic minors, and a less complex finger-board on the tonic principle would have made the organ more easily understood, and more generally useful. But everyone who has watched the progress of this subject, believes that General Thompson has given to it the mightiest impulse it has received during the present century. In one of the last letters he wrote, scarcely two days before his death, he committed his organ to my care. Since that time, it has stood in the School-room at Plaistow.* I have been interested in this subject ever since Sir Charles Reed showed me General Thompson's articles in the *Westminster Review* while I was preparing the second edition of the " Grammar of Vocal Music." The increasing use of organs has pressed it more strongly on my attention in later years. Especially I have noticed that choirs and congregations which are trained to sing with the organ and like the organ, are more than any others liable to flatten when deprived of their prop. Of course there are other causes of flattening, such as loud and strained singing, or lazy singing, or the use of wrong registers; but I have had clear proof that this is one of the greatest. I have heard one of the best church choirs in London flatten to the extent of a minor third in the course of three or four verses, when its organ was under repair. I account for this thus:—In the very nature of things it is easier for the singer to strike the right tone, than to strike one which is wrong by an exact interval. Even if it were easier for a learner to strike a wrong tone than a right one, it would still be more difficult for him to strike one which should be wrong in a certain exact proportion, neither more or less; and yet this is what is required when we are told to sing in tune with a tempered instrument. When we try to sing in Just Intonation there is everything to help us. The partials and differ-

---

* The organ is now (1897) in the South Kensington Museum, but not kept in working order.

entials help to put us straight. The harmony almost *forces* us into our right place. But all these helpers are put to confusion when we try to sing tempered tones. It is therefore easier, as well as better, to sing with Just Intonation. I hope that this Tract will stir up many young minds to the study of the subject, and will make the path of invention so much easier and plainer that the world will soon discover the Teleon Finger-board Instrument.

J. CURWEN AND SONS, LTD., MUSIC PRINTERS, PLAISTOW, LONDON, E.

STANDARD WORKS ON MUSIC.

BOY'S VOICE, THE. By J. Spencer Curwen. Price 2/-; post. 1½d. 2nd edition. Practical information for choirmasters.

CANDIDATE IN MUSIC, THE. By H. Fisher, Mus.D. Book I, Elements, paper, 1/6; cloth, 2/-; post. 1½d. Book II, Harmony, paper, 2/-; cloth, 2/6; post. 2½d.

CHORAL and ORCHESTRAL SOCIETIES. By L. C. Venables. Price 2/6; postage 2½d. A book of practical hints and experiences for the use of Conductors, Secretaries, &c.

COMPANION FOR TEACHERS. By J. S. Curwen. Price 1/-; post. 1½d. This work gives the school teacher all necessary information on the Tonic Sol-fa system.

COMPENDIUM OF HARMONY. By Geo. Oakey, Mus.B. Price 2/-; postage, 2d. Comprises the subject matter of the first half of the author's "Text-book of Harmony," the examples in Sol-fa only.

CONSTRUCTION, TUNING, AND CARE OF THE PIANOFORTE. Edited and largely re-written by H. Fisher, Mus.D. Price: limp cloth, 1/-; postage 1½d. How to repair and tune pianos, harmoniums, and American organs.

FIGURED BASS. By Geo. Oakey, Mus. B. Price, limp cloth, 1/-; postage 1d.

FIRST STEPS IN HARMONY and the Harmonising of Melodies. By Ralph Dunstan, Mus.D. Price 2/- cloth; post. 2d. A concise manual for beginners, staff notation.

HANDBELL RINGING. By C. W. Fletcher. Price 2/-; postage 2d. Shows how to organise and train handbell ringers, and gives exercises and tunes arranged for the bells.

HANDBOOK OF ACOUSTICS. By T. F. Harris, B.Sc., F.C.S. Price 3/6; postage 3d. A handbook for the use of musical students.

HISTORY OF ENGLISH MUSIC. By Henry Davey. Traces the history of English music. Contains many new and important facts. Price 6/-; post. 4½d.

HOW TO OBSERVE HARMONY. By John Curwen. Price 2/-; postage 2d. The Text-book of Harmony on the Tonic Sol-fa Method. Illustrations in both notations.

HOW TO READ MUSIC. By John Curwen. Twenty-four chapters, pp. 128. Eighth edition. Price : cloth, 1/6; paper, 1/-, post. 1½d. Teaches sight-singing by the Tonic Sol-fa system, then applies the knowledge to the Old Notation.

HYMN LOVER, THE. By the Rev. W. Garrett Horder. Price 5/-; postage 4½d. The rise and progress of English Hymnody.

MANUAL OF MUSIC, A. By R. Dunstan, Mus.D. Price 2s. 6d.; post. 3d. Fourteenth edition. Both notations. Prepares Pupil Teachers and Training College Students.

MANUAL OF ORCHESTRATION. By Hamilton Clarke, Mus.B. With Appendix. Price 1/6; post. 2d.

MECHANISM of the HUMAN VOICE. By Emil Behnke. Ninth edition, enlarged and revised. Cloth, 2/6; paper, 1/6; post. 2d.

MEMORIALS OF JOHN CURWEN. By his son, J. S. Curwen. Price 2/-; post. 3d.

MUSICAL HAUNTS IN LONDON. By F. G. Edwards. Chapters on Handel, Haydn, Mendelssohn, Weber, and many other musicians. Price 1/-; postage 2d.

MUSICAL INSPECTION, and How to prepare for it, The. By a School Inspector. Price 1/6; post. 2d. A course of lessons and instructions on the Tonic Sol-fa method.

MUSICAL PROFESSION, THE. By H. Fisher, Mus.Doc. Price 5/-; post. 4½d. Contains advice for music teachers in every department of the art.

MUSICAL SELF-INSTRUCTOR. By J. Sneddon, Mus.B. Price 2/6; postage 2d. Both notations. Self-help in musical elements and vocal practice.

MUSICAL THEORY. By John Curwen. Price 3/6; postage 3d. Or in parts—I, 4d.; II, 4d.; III, 1/4; IV, 4d.; V, 1/-. All the musical examples are given in both notations.

MUSICIANS OF ALL TIMES. Compiled by David Baptie. 2nd and cheaper edition, 1/6. A concise biographical handbook.

NEW GRADED HARMONY EXERCISES. By Geo. Oakey, Mus.B. A complete course of exercises in both notations, without instruction. Price 2/-, cloth; postage 1½d.

ORGANS, ORGANISTS, and CHOIRS. By E. Minshall. Price 1/6; postage 1½d. A book of hints and suggestions for all interested in Nonconformist Church Music.

PRIMER OF ELOCUTION in Recitation and Song. By Frederick Harrison, M.A. Price, cloth, 1/6. Systematises the study of Elocution, summarises vocal physiology, gives specimen recitations, pronunciation of Italian in singing, &c.

PRONUNCIATION FOR SINGERS. By A. J. Ellis, F.R.S. Price 3/6; postage 4d.

SCHOOL MUSIC TEACHER, THE. By J. Evans and W. G. McNaught. Price 2/6; post. 3d.

SHORT DICTIONARY of MUSICAL TERMS. By Arnold Kennedy, M.A. Price 1/-, postage 1d.; cloth, 1/6, postage 1½d. Includes about 2,700 terms.

SOLO SINGER, THE. By Sinclair Dunn. Price 1/-; postage 1½d. A handbook giving hints to those who desire to become solo singers.

SPECIMEN LESSONS on the TONIC SOL-FA METHOD. Edited by J. Spencer Curwen. New and enlarged edition. Cloth limp, 1/6; postage 1d. Contains specimen first lessons on Time, Tune, Transition, &c.

STANDARD COURSE, THE. By John Curwen. Price 3/6; post. 3d. Lessons and Exercises on the Tonic Sol-fa Method of teaching music.

STUDENT'S MUSICAL HISTORY. By H. Davey. Price: cloth, 1/6; paper, 1/-; post. 1½d. Second edition. In handy, popular, and modern style.

STUDIES IN WORSHIP MUSIC, First Series. By J. S. Curwen. Second edition, revised and enlarged, 5/-; postage 4½d. **Studies in Worship Music, Second Series.** By J. S. Curwen. Price 2/6; postage 2½d. A continuation of the above work.

TEACHER'S MANUAL, THE. By John Curwen. Fourth Edition. A manual of the Art of Teaching in general, and especially as applied to music. Price 4/-; postage 5d.

TEXT-BOOK OF COUNTERPOINT. Ninth edition. By Geo. Oakey, Mus.B. Price 2/- cloth; post. 1½d. All the examples are given in both notations, and a set of subjects for exercises are given at the end.

TEXT-BOOK OF HARMONY. By Geo. Oakey, Mus.B. Eighth edition, price 3/-; post. 2½d. 17 chapters, with about 150 Graded Exercises. All examples in both notations.

TEXT-BOOK OF MUSICAL ELEMENTS. By Geo. Oakey, Mus.B. Price, in paper, 1/-; cloth, 1/6; postage, 1½d. With an Appendix of questions and exercises.

TRAINING COLLEGE MUSIC COURSE. By E. Mills, Mus.B. Price 3/-; postage 2½d. O.N. Course, Vocal and Theoretical.

UNITED PRAISE. By F. G. Edwards. Price 3/6; postage 3d. A practical handbook of Nonconformist Church Music.

LONDON: J. CURWEN & SONS, Ltd., 8 & 9 WARWICK LANE, E.C. 12/97

J. CURWEN AND SONS'

STAFF NOTATION MANUALS.

THE CONTINUATION COURSE.
            J. S. Curwen   3d.
For Evening Classes (boys and girls)
under the Code.

MUSICAL TRAINING.
            J. Sneddon, Mus. B.   1s.
The latest elementary Staff course.

**TRAINING COLLEGE MUSIC
COURSE.**   E. Mills, Mus. B.   3s.
Vocal and Theoretical Course to
prepare for Christmas and other
Examinations.

GUILD OF MUSIC. J. S. Curwen   6d.

MUSIC AT SIGHT. J. S. Curwen   6d.
The newest elementary Staff Notation Course on Tonic Sol-fa
principles.

CHORAL SINGER. J. S. Curwen   1s.
Contains ninety-three Exercises,
Rounds, Part-songs, Anthems,
Time and Expression Studies,
Illustrative Chants, and Ele-
mentary Rhythms.

PRACTICE FOR SINGERS, Part I.
            J. S. Curwen   6d.
A Course of Graded Exercises,
Part-songs, and Anthems.

PRACTICE FOR SINGERS, Part II.
            J. S. Curwen   6d.
An Advanced Course of Sight-
singing for Mixed Voice Classes.

**THE STAFF NOTATION, with new
Appendix.**   John Curwen   8d.

**THE STAFF NOTATION, Appen-
dix only** ....   3d.
Used in the Postal Courses of the
Tonic Sol-fa College.

PRIMA VISTA ....   6d.
A Collection of Specimen Sight
Tests for the Advanced Certifi-
cate.

STAFF NOTATION PRIMER ....   6d.
An Elementary Course of writing
exercises.

**CROTCHETS AND QUAVERS, Parts
I to III (see separate advt.)** ....   3d.

THE SHORT COURSE ....   2d.

THE TONIC SOL-FA PRIMER
(See separate advertisement)......   1s.

HOW TO READ MUSIC (see separate advertisement) ....   1s.

GRADED ROUNDS, O.N. (see separate advertisement) ....   3d.

**INTERMEDIATE STAFF EXER-
CISES** ....   1d.

ADVANCED STAFF EXERCISES   1d.

BOOKS FOR VOICE CULTURE.

THE VOICE TRAINER. By J. A. BIRCH.
Practical hints and exercises for vocalists, conductors, and members of choral
societies and choirs. Price 1s., *both* notations.

FIFTY VOICE EXERCISES. By J.
CONCONE. Edited by C. L. B. O.N.
with accompaniments, voice part in *both*
notations, 2s.

VOICE TRAINING EXERCISES. With
studies in Musical Ornaments, Phrasing,
and Style. By J. PROUDMAN assisted by
ANNIE I. STAPLETON. O.N., 2s. ; Tonic
Sol-fa, 2s.

THE SOLO SINGER'S VADE MECUM.
By SINCLAIR DUNN. A pocket size collection of Voice Exercises as used by all
the principal Voice Trainers. Exercises
in *both* notations, 1s.

THE SOLO SINGER. By SINCLAIR
DUNN. Price 1s. 6d. Hints to intend-
ing Solo Singers. Companion to "Solo
Singer's Vade Mecum." Second edition.

**STANDARD COURSE VOICE EXER-
CISES.** Consisting of the Voice Exercises from JOHN CURWEN'S "Standard
Course," comprising Chest, Klang, Tuning, and Register Exercises. For use in
classes. Tonic Sol-fa. First and Second
Sets, each ½d.

VOICE REPORT BOOK. For Register-
ing the Examination of Voices, giving
particulars of Compass and Best Region,
with the Quality, Volume, and Blending
of each of the Registers. With Coun-
terfoil, perforated, price 1s.

MECHANISM OF THE HUMAN VOICE.
By EMIL BEHNKE. Paper covers, 1s. 6d. ;
cloth, 2s. 6d.

CHORAL DRILL EXERCISES. A Series
of Voice Exercises by L. C. VENABLES.
New edition, revised and enlarged.
O.N., 6d. ; Sol-fa, 2d.

**VOICE CULTURE FOR CHORAL SO-
CIETIES.** By G. F. ROOT. Exercises
in Breathing, Vowel and Consonant
Practice, Phrasing, Expression. *Both*
notations, 2d.

VOICE DEVELOPMENT. By P
HARTSOUGH. For Classes and Choirs
Register and Breathing Exercises, Expression, Vocalisation, Resonance, Classification, &c. *Both* notations, 9d.

LONDON: J. CURWEN & SONS, 8 & 9 WARWICK LANE, E.C.

MUSICAL INSTRUMENTS AND APPARATUS

Sold by J. CURWEN & SONS.

PIANOFORTES & HARMONIUMS.

Lists post free on application.

BRASS INSTRUMENTS.

	£	s.	d.
Cornets.—soprano, B♭, £1 10s.; £2 5s., £3,	3	10	0
Saxhorns.—Alto, B♭, 3 valves, £2 14s.; C, 3			
valves - - - - -	2	10	0
Tenor, F or E♭, 3 valves - -	3	11	0
Baritone, B♭ or C, 3 valves - -	4	10	0
Euphonium, B♭ or C, 4 valves - -	6	0	0
Contrabass, F, 3 valves, £6 15; E♭, 3			
valves, £7; B♭, 4 valves - -	8	0	0
Bombardon, C, 3 valves, £7 12s.; C, 4 valves	9	0	0
Trombone, tenor slide, C or B♭ £1 12s., £2,	2	5	0
Trombone, bass, G - - -	2	0	0

Besson's Brass Instruments
Particulars on application.

WOOD WIND INSTRUMENTS.

	£	s.	d.
Bassoons.—Sycamore, 10 German silver keys	9	16	0
" " 12 Brass keys-	10	16	0
Oboes.—Stained boxwood, 13 German silver			
keys - - - - -	3	10	0
Ebony or cocoa, 13 German silver keys	4	10	0
Clarionets, cocoa.—A, B♭, C, or E♭, 6 keys,			
German silver tips and keys -	1	10	0
Ditto, 8 keys, £1 15s.; 10 keys, £2; 13			
keys - - - - -	2	5	0
Fifes for Bands—Boxwood, B flat per doz	1	8	0
Cocoa, B flat - - - per doz.	2	0	0
Flutes, B♭, cocoa.—1 key, 4s.; 4 keys and			
tips, 10s.; 5 keys and tips 12s., 6 keys			
and tips - - - -	0	14	0
For Thirds.—1 key 8s., 4 keys 14s., 5 keys			
16s., 6 keys - - - -	0	18	0
Concert Flutes, cocoa.—6 German silver keys	1	8	0
8 G. silver keys, broad tips and lip plate	1	13	0
8 G. silver keys, bushed holes and lip			
plate - - - - -	1	18	0
Piccolos, D, E♭, or F.—1 German silver			
key on pillar slide head - -	0	4	6
Ditto, 4 keys, 8s.; 5 keys, 9s.; 6 keys-	0	10	0
Flageolets.—D, 1 key - - -	0	4	6
With piccolo heads, German silver keys			
and tips, 1 key 8s., 4 keys 12s., 5 keys			
13s., 6 keys - - - -	0	14	0

PERCUSSION INSTRUMENTS.

	£	s.	d.
Side Drums, cords.—12 in. £1 5s., 13 in. £1			
10s., 14 in. - - - -	1	15	0
With screws, 12 in. £1 14s., 14 in. -	2	3	0
Bass Drums.—28 in. £3 16s., 30 in. £4, 32 in.	4	5	0
Tambourines with screws and brackets.—			
3 pair jingles, 5s., 6s.; 6 pair, 7s., 9s.;			
12 pair - - - - -	0	10	6
Cymbals, all fitted with leather straps, 10			
in., 12s.; 11 in., 14s.; 12 in., 16s.; 13 in.	0	18	0
Triangles, with beaters, 9 in., 6s.; 10 in.			
6s. 8d.; 11 in., 7s. 4d.; 12 in. -	0	8	0

ACCORDIONS AND CONCERTINAS.

	£	s.	d.
German Accordions or Melodeons, 1 stop,			
broad reeds, German silver mount-			
ings - - - - 12s. and	1	6	0
Harmoniflutes or Organ Accordions, best			
make only, 3 octaves, 1 stop -	4	10	0
3 octaves, Tremolo and Sourdine stop-	7	10	0
Stands for ditto - - - -	0	16	0
Concertinas.—German, 20 keys, 10s., 12s. 6d.,			
15s., &	1	0	0
Anglo-German, 20 keys, £2; 22 keys,			
£3; 24 keys - - - -	3	4	0
Chromatic Anglo-German, 26 keys,			
£2 10s.; 28 keys, £2 12s.; 30 keys -	2	16	0
English, from G to C, all 48 keys, double			
action and screwed notes, rosewood,			
£4 4s., £5 5s.. &	6	6	0

STRING INSTRUMENTS.

	£	s.	d.
Violins - - - 10s., 12s. 6d., 15s.,	1	0	0
Copy Violins £1, £1 7s., £1 10s., £1 16s., £2,	2	10	0

	£	s.	d.
Genuine old violins - £2, £3 10s., £4,	4	10	0
Tenor violins - - 17s., £1, £1 5s.,	1	10	0
Violoncellos - £1 12s., £2 2s., £2 12s..	3	10	0
Double basses, machine heads £4 10s., £5,	6	0	0
Guitars.—Peg head, varnished 12s. and	0	18	0
Machine head, varnished - £1 1s. and	1	5	0
Mandolines - - - 18s., £1 1s. and	1	5	0
Zithers - - - £1 1s., £1 5s. and	1	12	0
Banjos, 6 strings 5s. 6d., 7s., 9s. 6d., 13s. and	0	15	0
Fairy Bells.—Mahogany, 8 notes, 13s.; 10			
notes - - - - -	0	15	0
Dulcimers.—Small size, handsomely inlaid	3	0	0
Full size, handsomely inlaid -	3	10	0

BATONS.

	£	s.	d.
Sycamore (white) - - - -	0	1	6
Rosewood (red) - - - -	0	2	6
Ebony (black) - - - -	0	3	0
Sycamore or Rosewood, lightly and elegant-			
ly mounted with silver, chased or			
engine-turned, butt, tip, and band			
for inscription - - - -	1	1	0
Ebony, very handsomely mounted in silver,			
beautifully engraved - - -	1	10	0
Ivory, in silver, or plated gold, in various			
styles and sizes - £2 5s. to	5	0	0
Cases, in leather, velvet-lined, spring catch,			
from - - - - -	0	8	0

TUNING FORKS AND PITCH PIPES

	£	s.	d.
The Teacher's Fork - - - -	0	1	0
The Pupil's Fork (smaller size) - -	0	1	0
The Ladies' Fork, silver-plated, 1½ in. in			
length, for the watch-guard, 2s.;			
electro-gilt - - - -	0	2	6
Chromatic Pitch Pipe - - -	0	5	0

METRONOMES.

	£	s.	d.
Mahogany, clockwork - - -	0	16	0
Rosewood " - - -	0	17	0
Best English make " - - -	1	10	0
Mahogany, clockwork, with bell -	1	4	0
Rosewood " " -	1	5	0
Best English make " " -	2	2	0
Silver plates for inscription, - -from	0	10	0
Inscription engraved - -from	0	5	0
New Brass Pocket Metronome - -	0	2	6
"The Tonic Sol-fa Metronome" -	0	1	0
Greaves' Tape Metronome, brass -	0	5	0
Ditto, German silver - - -	0	6	0
Ditto, electro silver - - -	0	8	0
Ditto, electro gilt - - -	0	10	0

MISCELLANEOUS.

	£	s.	d.
American Portable Music Stands.—Iron			
Japanned for Bands, &c., 19s.; double			
desk - - - - -	1	12	0
Brass, single desk, £1 18s.; double desk	2	16	0
Solid Walnut pillars, carved legs, and			
brass telescope pole, single desk £2 2s., &	2	10	0
Ditto, double desk - - £2 12s. and	3	0	0
Band Cards.—Eight or nine staves per 100	0	6	0
Romberg and Haydn's Toy Symphony In-			
struments, superior quality, includ-			
ing music - - - -	2	10	0
Musical Handbells.—Peal of 8 bells, 4½ in.,			
key C - - - - -	10	0	0
Ditto, 5½ in., key G - - -	12	0	0
Violin Bows - 3s., 3s. 6d., 4s., 5s., 7s. 6d.	0	10	0
Tenor Bows - - - 4s., 6s.,	0	8	0
'Cello Bows - - - 4s., 6s.,	0	8	0
Double Bass Bows - - - 7s.,	0	10	0
Violin Strings, 4d., 6d., 8d.; 'Cello strings			
1s., 1s. 6d.	0	2	0
Violin Cases, black wood, with lock -	0	8	0
Table Musical Boxes.—Four airs, rose-			
wood case, inlaid - £3 10s. and	4	10	0
Ditto, 6 airs - - - -	5	0	0
Small size, 3 airs, fancy wood case -	1	8	0
Ditto, 6 airs - - - £2 12s and	3	0	0

LONDON: J. CURWEN & SONS, 8 & 9. WARWICK LANE. E.C.

Lightning Source UK Ltd.
Milton Keynes UK
UKOW022137310113

205682UK00006B/453/P